The Evolution of the Negro College

BY

DWIGHT OLIVER WENDELL HOLMES

AMS PRESS
NEW YORK

Reprinted from the edition of 1934, New York
First AMS EDITION published 1970
Manufactured in the United States of America

International Standard Book Number: 0-404-00172-6

Library of Congress Card Catalog Number: 74-128993

AMS PRESS, INC.
NEW YORK, N.Y. 10003

To
Lucy Messer Holmes
Comrade and Counselor

FOREWORD

THE zeal with which investigators are carrying forward studies
on all phases of education at the present time indicates a realization of the importance of extensive and exact knowledge as a
basis for justifiable practice in directing our educational machinery. It is obvious, therefore, that because of the many peculiar
problems arising from the segregated schools for white and colored
people which exist in certain areas in the United States, the field
of Negro education at the present time calls for an investigation as
careful as and possibly even more extensive than one in the
general field which, because of its favored position, has received
preferential treatment in this regard.

Since established principles and practices are common property,
the Negro school has profited, of course, both directly and
indirectly, by every advance made as the result of the scientific
investigation of education. In another sense, however, the study
of this field has been somewhat neglected because Negroes constitute a disadvantaged group and hence receive tardy attention
in education as in other matters. In spite of this handicap, a
considerable beginning has been made in an effort to collect,
interpret and publish the facts concerning the education of the
Negro at all levels.[1] To date, elementary and secondary schools
have received most attention because they fall largely within the
sphere of public education; hence public officials have studied
them as part of their administrative routine. This is as it should
be since the work at the lower levels is fundamental.

But the study of the higher education of the Negro is more and
more urgently demanding the attention of investigators. There
are several reasons for this. In the first place, the rapid increase
in enrollment in American colleges since the close of the World
War has brought to the Negro college the same problems that the

[1] See such bibliographies as:

Work, Monroe, *Bibliography of the Negro*, chapters on Education (Atlanta University Press,
1905). Caliver, Ambrose, *Bibliography of the Education of the Negro* (U. S. Office of
Education, Bulletin, 1931, No. 17). *The Journal of Negro Education*, bibliography sections
of successive issues. *The Journal of Negro History*, indexes of the several volumes for
studies in education.

other colleges of the country are now studying so seriously. In
the second place, the socio-economic status of the Negro population, as compared with that of the American people as a whole,
creates peculiar problems with reference to the financial support
of this group of schools, and to the policies for their development.
In the third place, the Negro college has a history peculiarly its
own. Its establishment was an emergency measure and its
evolution has been guided by the missionary motive arising from
a sense of the duty of a stronger social group to a weaker. The
other colleges of our country were established and developed by
white Americans for their own children. The Negro college was
established by the zeal of these same Americans and their descend-
ants, but for the children of slaves. Hence it originally was, and
to a considerable extent continues to be, a missionary venture.

As a background for other studies in this field and for the information of the general public and students of education, it is
the opinion of the author that a compact account of the development of the Negro college is needed. This study is an effort to
contribute to that need.

The author is especially indebted to three members of the staff
of Teachers College, Columbia University. They are Professor
E. S. Evenden, who suggested the need of an account of the rise
of the Negro college; Professor Edward H. Reisner, who gave
valuable technical suggestions from the standpoint of historical
method; and Professor Mabel Carney, whose deep and active
interest in the education of the Negro has been a constant inspiration. The Rev. Fred L. Brownlee, Executive Secretary of
the American Missionary Association, and Dr. Frank A. Smith,
Secretary of the American Baptist Home Mission Society, have
generously placed at the author's service the libraries at their
central offices in New York. Dr. Merrill F. Holmes, Secretary
of the Board of Education for Negroes of the Methodist Episcopal
Church, supplied a file of the annual reports of that body. President Arthur D. Wright of the John F. Slater Board and the Anna
T. Jeanes Board not only gave valuable advice, but made available
at his office in Washington, D. C., all the annual reports and other
publications of both boards. To all these, the author is under
obligation, as well as to the numerous persons engaged in the work
of Negro education who have furnished facts and opinions through
correspondence.

CONTENTS

PART I—PRELIMINARY STATEMENTS

PART II—THE FEDERAL GOVERNMENT AND THE FREEDMEN

PART III—THE EMERGENCE OF THE COLLEGE

TABLES

PART I

PRELIMINARY STATEMENTS

CHAPTER I

INTRODUCTION

PURPOSE, SCOPE, AND METHOD

THE purpose of this study is to present, within the limits of a single volume, the circumstances surrounding the establishment and development of the Negro college, in order to furnish an integrated background upon which to project the problems that arise from an inquiry into the present place and function of this group of schools in the scheme of higher education in America. On the basis of the facts presented and in view of the present situation in American education, it is hoped that some guiding principles may be established upon which justifiable modifications in practice relative to this group of schools can be effected. It is not intended to present here in chronological order the events in the life of the Negro college as an institution. The object is rather to interpret the events, the social forces, and the attitudes of individuals and groups which have affected the establishment and development of these schools and thus determined the character of the opportunities for higher education available to Negro youth today in segregated colleges, universities, and professional schools located mainly in the Southern states. For this reason, overlapping and repetition necessarily appear in the narrative. No apology is needed for this common characteristic of historical studies of this character.

The investigation is necessarily limited in scope. In view of the purpose indicated, a study of the individual Negro colleges is neither necessary nor desirable, since historical sketches of the several schools of college grade can usually be found in the successive annual issues of their respective catalogs or elsewhere. All the schools for Negroes, however, which offer courses above the secondary level are listed and a few are considered in some detail at appropriate points in the study for the purpose of illustrating a type of school or a mode of development.

The method followed is primarily historical. The selection of data has been made from such sources as federal and state statutes and other records; reports of surveys and statistical material issued by the United States Office of Education; official records, orders, and correspondence of the Civil War; the several issues of the federal census; records of the several religious denominations and philanthropic bodies engaged in Negro education; and reports of surveys and studies made by educational associations and other reliable authorities. These original sources have been supplemented by biographical material considered reliable, articles and items from contemporary newspapers and magazines, histories written by persons intimately acquainted with the subject treated, and such other data as seem of historical reliability and value.

THE SIGNIFICANCE OF HISTORICAL BACKGROUND

In the Southern part of the United States, where the large majority of the Negro population resides, the dual system of education is at the present time a legal requirement and a generally enforced social policy. The states making up this area are Alabama, Arkansas, Delaware, Florida, Georgia, Kentucky, Louisiana, Maryland, Mississippi, Missouri, North Carolina, Oklahoma, South Carolina, Tennessee, Texas, Virginia, and West Virginia. In addition, there is considerable separation of the races in schools without legal compulsion, in other states bordering this area, especially in their southern counties, as in New Jersey, Pennsylvania, Ohio, Illinois, and Indiana, and even in such important cities as Trenton, Philadelphia, Indianapolis, Columbus, and Cincinnati. This practice gives rise to problems in education peculiar to such a situation, problems which do not appear in those areas where the separation of the two races in schools is neither a legal requirement nor a social policy. As a result, Negro schools are not only confronted with the same problems as schools in general but, in addition, must meet and solve those arising from the policy that demands that they be conducted as units separate from those patronized by the white people of the same communities.

Since the states supporting two systems of schools are, in general, the poorest economically,[1] and hence the least able to afford the extra expense involved, such problems as the distribu-

---

[1] National Education Association, *Research Bulletin*, Vol. IV, Nos. 1 and 2, *passim.*

tion of public school funds between the two races, the enforcement of compulsory education laws, the qualifications of teachers of different races who are required to do the same work on different salary scales, and others of similar nature become acute and are constantly forcing themselves, through painful experience, upon the attention of the Negroes. At the same time, these problems demand the most earnest attention of the general public, of organized philanthropy, of the state and local legislative bodies concerned, and most of all of the school officials operating in the areas of separate schools who bear the heavy responsibility of supervising the education of the whole people in a democracy while preserving at the same time the principle of racial segregation in schools. For purposes of effective action in such a complex situation, the student of education must supply the necessary facts.

The facts needed, however, by students who approach any phase of the education of the Negro are by no means limited to comparative numerical data referring to costs, enrollments, intelligence quotients, and the like or to the results of any manipulation of such figures. Nor will statements relative to the social and economic situation found existing today, however carefully derived, prove sufficient. Quite as important and possibly even more significant are certain historical facts resulting from (1) sociological and economic conditions prevailing in America at several periods since 1860, especially in the Southern area, and (2) the variety of mental attitudes induced by slavery, the Civil War, and reconstruction, characteristic of each of the groups which have been actively interested in the welfare of the Negro. Such historical facts are necessary bases for valid interpretations of statistical material showing the status of Negro education in America at any time, on any level, and in any area.

The future of the Negro college in America depends upon the attitude of the American people in general toward its program. This is so obvious that it needs no elaboration. But whatever is done in this field, if it is to be effective, must be projected and carried forward as the result of conference and coöperation between the races. Those whose opinions on the matter will determine largely the nature of the efforts in this field, in their capacity as molders of public opinion, are the college and university men and women who are intensively engaged in the study of our educational problems.   For purposes of this discussion these students of education may be considered as constituting three groups: the white people of the North and West, the white people of the South, and the Negroes.

There is always danger, however, that remoteness in time and place of historical events may dim the significance of their bearing on present problems.   American students who have been seriously interested in educational problems belong for the most part to a generation born after the stirring events of the anti-slavery movement, the Civil War, and the reconstruction period had ceased to agitate the public mind and to challenge seriously the zealous interest of the American people as a whole.   The majority of these students belong to the first group, those who live in the North and West, and, hence, outside the area where the majority of the Negroes reside and where Negro education is not a problem. In general the members of this group, excepting those individuals who happen to be migrants from the South, are naturally some-what uninformed and consequently indifferent to questions per-taining to the Negro and his education except in a purely academic sense.   This is due partly to their geographical remoteness from those areas where such problems are very much alive, partly to the presence of new questions of greater interest and intimacy, and partly to a vague conviction that all matters concerning the Negro were settled with the passage of the Fifteenth Amendment to the Constitution of the United States.   In short, the Negro and his affairs are not looked upon as the concern of the group and seldom come to its attention.   And what is true of the students of education is also largely true of the general population in the same area.   That this group, constituting a large majority of the people of the United States, should be ignorant of or indifferent to a major problem of such social significance as the education of one-tenth of the total population is regrettable to say the least, certainly from the point of view of this study.   For, from this group must ultimately come much of the financial support and some of the ideas by which the Negro college will be carried on. This generalization of course does not apply to those promoting organized philanthropy either with or without religious affiliation. But even the zeal of churchmen in these areas is gradually sub-siding as 1863 becomes more and more remote.   For during the high tide of economic prosperity in the 1920's, the index of financial support for Negro colleges lagged behind the general economic upturn.

To the white student of education located in the South the problems arising from the education of the Negro are always present and of the most vital interest since they concern not only the immediate welfare of more than one-third of the population of the Southern area but also the ultimate happiness of the other two-thirds. As a result, there is in this area a genuine and sympathetic awakening of interest in matters concerning the education of the Negro. A number of important investigations in this field have been made in recent years and are now being made by Southern white men and women in the colleges and universities of that section in an effort to furnish reliable information as a basis for rational procedures in dealing with the educational problems incident to social situations in the South.[2] But even the Southern student, in attacking some of the most vital problems in this field, must keep clearly in mind the historical factors which form the basis of interpretation of many of his findings.

It goes without saying that the Negro student cannot afford to forget the foundations upon which colleges for his group have been built, the conditions amid which they have been developed, and the reasons for the difficulties which they have encountered at any given time. It is impossible, of course, for the Negro in the South to forget for a moment that he is a problem. The spirit of segregation and discrimination in its myriad forms constantly reminds him of this stubborn fact. The progressive Negro student is justly intolerant of such grave inequalities which he observes in educational facilities at all levels, and naturally demands immediate reform. This attitude is necessary and wholly commendable unless the reformer has fallen into the error of ignoring the long, slow processes of human experiences and psychic evolution that produced the present social attitudes in the South. Negro students, too, must continue to gather facts with persistence and to present them with logic. Their interpretations, at the same time, must be made in view of the history of the relations of the two races, particularly in the United States.

---

[2] For such articles see *The Journal of Negro Education*, April 1933, as follows: Alexander, Will W., "Southern White Schools Study Race Questions," pp. 138 ff.; Weatherford, W. D., "Changing Attitudes of Southern Students," p. 147; Reckless, W. C. and Bringen, H. D., "Racial Attitudes and Information About the Negro," p. 128; Knox, Ellis O., "The Negro as a Subject of University Research," p. 165.

Thus fortified, the earnest students of both races and all sections, if true to their trust, will constantly work toward an ideal democracy, recognizing always from their respective viewpoints the defects in present practice and striving to correct these defects through the mediums of scientific investigation and ethical interpretation.

For these reasons the writer has dwelt at some length upon those historical aspects of the subject under consideration which center around the Civil War and its aftermath, in the midst of which the education of the Negro had its beginning on a large scale and which are responsible for the evolution of the Negro college.

THE EDUCATIONAL STATUS OF THE NEGRO AT THE BEGINNING OF THE CIVIL WAR[3]

It must constantly be borne in mind in any consideration of the Negro college that at the beginning of the Civil War the Negro, generally considered, began his academic education at zero.   The attainment of any institution of learning for Negroes, including the higher institutions, must be measured from that point.   The cultural level of the constituency of Harvard and of William and Mary, when founded, and of the other American colleges which followed them even in colonial times was far different from and in general far above that of the freedmen in 1863.   The colleges for Negroes are unique, therefore, among American institutions of higher learning.

The zero mark referred to, however, must not be taken too literally, for, from the institution of slavery in America in 1619 to the beginning of the nineteenth century, a considerable number of persons of color received academic instruction in varying degrees, ranging from the rudiments of reading and writing to skill in such subjects as foreign languages and mathematics.[4]   Many slaves throughout the South kept accounts for their masters; thousands could read and write;[5] and a few attracted attention for scholarly achievement.   Benjamin Banneker,[6] a Maryland Negro, was a mathematician and an astronomer, publishing a series of

---

[3] For a full and scholarly account of the education of the Negro before the Civil War see *The Education of the Negro Prior to 1861* by Carter G. Woodson, Editor of *The Journal of Negro History* (Putnam, 1915).

[4] *African Repository*, XI, 267, 268.   [5] *Seventh Census of the United States*, Illiteracy.

[6] Benjamin Banneker, *The National Cyclopaedia of American Biography*, V, 35.

almanacs[7] and assisting in the original survey of the District of Columbia,[8] thus winning written commendation for his scholarship from Thomas Jefferson and other prominent men of the time.[9] There was a large number of free Negroes in the South as well as in the North, many of whom acquired considerable learning. Some Negroes held slaves of their own with whom they often shared their knowledge.[10]

Nor was this kindly practice confined to this group. The general attitude of slaveholders toward their slaves was often one of paternalistic benevolence prior to the day when Eli Whitney made his epoch-making invention. This kindliness often extended to the instruction of their slaves in reading and writing, a practice in the case of house servants which became quite general in certain localities.[11] As a matter of ordinary good sense and for purposes of increased efficiency, many plantation owners had their slaves instructed in trades appropriate to plantation life.[12] Indeed, before the invention of the cotton gin and the consequent rise of the importance of the cultivation of cotton, there was evidently no strong and consistent objection anywhere to the pursuit of knowledge on the part of Negroes whenever they felt the urge and could find the opportunity.[13] It must always be kept in mind in this connection that, before the Civil War and for several decades after its close, popular education among the masses of the white people in the South was in a very deplorable state.[14]

After the invention of the cotton gin in 1798, the situation was changed abruptly.[15] Demand for slave labor rose sharply and traffic in slaves was renewed and pursued in more brutal fashion than ever. The plantation system in the great cotton-growing areas of the South created the social situation that exhibited slavery at its worst, and brought in an era of cruelty not known before. In retaliation the Negroes often became sullen and resentful, an attitude which grew serious when such insurrections broke out as those headed by Denmark Vesey in South Carolina in

[7] "A Brief Sketch of the Life of Benjamin Banneker," *Poor Will's Almanack for the Year 1817*, pp. 17, 18; Norris, J. Saurin, *A Sketch of the Life of Benjamin Banneker*.
[8] Tyson, Martha E., *A Sketch of the Life of Benjamin Banneker*, Ch. V, 36–38. (The three works last referred to are available in the 135th Street Branch of the New York Public Library.)
[9] Bergh, Albert E. (Ed.), *The Writings of Thomas Jefferson*, VIII, 241 (Washington, D. C., 1907). Letter to Benjamin Banneker.
[10] Mitchell, Samuel C. (Ed.), *The South in the Building of a Nation*, X, 179–81.
[11] Hart, Albert Bushnell, *Slavery and Abolition*, The American Nation Series, XVI, 94, 95.
[12] Reuter, Edward B., *The American Race Problem*, pp. 244, 245.   [13] Hart, *op. cit.*, Ch. V.
[14] Mitchell, *op. cit.*, pp. 196–208.   [15] Turner, Andrew J., *Rise of the New West*, pp. 49, 50.

1822 [16] and Nat Turner in Virginia in 1831.[17]   Since leadership in these outbreaks was traced to persons who could read and write, harsh laws forbidding the instruction of Negroes in reading, writing, and arithmetic [18] were passed as a defensive measure throughout the South.[19]

As a result of such laws, formal education among people of color in the slave states had been practically eliminated by 1860, although there was naturally widespread evasion of the laws by the lettered members of the race, who eagerly shared their accomplishments with their less fortunate brothers,[20] and there was considerable flouting of the statutes by the slaveholders and their families, who considered such laws unjust and unnecessary.[21] Although in some of the state codes the teaching of all Negroes was prohibited, no such restriction was made relative to free Negroes in Florida, Kentucky, Maryland, Tennessee, and Texas.[22] Making due allowance, however, for all the favorable factors in the situation, it is not surprising to find that the most liberal-minded and sympathetic students of the period in question estimate that probably not more than ten per cent of the Negro population of the United States at the date of the Emancipation Proclamation could read.[23]   While it is impossible to verify such estimates, it is probably fair to state that, although in the South the Negro had few schools at the beginning of the War, there existed, nevertheless, a nucleus of formal education, an acquaintance with the English language and with the arts and usages of civilization that not only removed him far from the level of barbarism so often pictured but prepared him to seek eagerly the opportunities for education that were offered him following his emancipation.   He was, therefore, fertile soil for the rapid germination and development of the seeds of learning that were planted as a result of the missionary zeal to aid the freedmen, so strongly manifested during the Civil War and after its close.

[16] For an account of four slave insurrections consult Brawley, Benj. G., *A Social History of the Negro*, Ch. VII.

[17] *The Confession of Nat Turner*, American Negro Monographs, No. 1 (Washington, D. C., April, 1910).

[18] *Laws of Virginia*, 1830–31, p. 108, Secs. 5 and 6; 1831–32, p. 20; *Laws of Delaware*, 1832, pp. 208–10; 1863, pp. 330 ff.

[19] Cobb, *Digest of Laws of Georgia*, p. 555; Prince, *Digest of Laws of Georgia*, p. 658.

[20] Woodson, Carter G., *The Education of the Negro Prior to 1861*, p. 208.

[21] Rhodes, James F., *History of the United States, 1850–1877*, I, 329–34; Phillips, Ulrich B., *Life and Labor of the Old South*, pp. 198, 199.

[22] Reuter, *op. cit.*, p. 260.   [23] *Seventh Census of the United States*.

CHAPTER II

A PREVIEW OF THE STUDY

WITH the exception of teachers colleges, the colleges for Negroes constitute the youngest group of institutions of higher learning in America. Nine American colleges, beginning with Harvard in 1636, were founded during the colonial period and more than five hundred had come into existence by the end of 1860.[1] The Negro college, on the other hand, is in the main an outcome of the Civil War and emancipation. The first one founded[2] has been in existence, therefore, less than eighty years. This span, for the purposes of this study, may be considered as covering four fairly distinct periods.

The first period extends approximately from 1860 to 1885, thus covering the first twenty-five years following the beginning of the Civil War. During this time the Union army, Northern benevolent societies and denominational bodies, the Negro church, and the Freedmen's Bureau were busily engaged in applying emergency measures in an attempt to bring order out of confusion and to extend to the Negroes not only material aid but the beginnings of educational opportunity. From these initial efforts there emerged a class of schools engaged in providing the rudiments of learning to the Negro and bearing names which were usually the expression of distant hopes rather than actual descriptions. This is particularly true of those institutions which were designated as colleges and universities, but which naturally were compelled for some years to spend their major energies in work at the elementary level.

That many mistakes were made in projecting the education of the Negro during this period cannot be denied. That the correction of these mistakes is a slow and expensive process is equally

[1] See Tewksbury, Donald G., *The Founding of American Colleges and Universities Before the Civil War*, p. 28; also Cubberley, E. P., *An Introduction to the Study of Education*, pp. 357, 358.

[2] The Presbyterians founded a school in Pennsylvania for the education of Negroes which was chartered as Ashmun Institute in 1854 and as Lincoln University in 1866. In 1856 the Methodist Episcopal Church founded Wilberforce University in Ohio, for the same purpose. This institution was sold to the African Methodist Episcopal Church in 1863.

true. However, when the thoughtful student of the times considers the appalling nature of the tasks that faced those who undertook the business of relief in the South during the period of the
Civil War and that immediately following its close, the extensive
territory to be covered, the vast number of freedmen pleading for
relief and enlightenment, the chaotic economic and social conditions prevailing in that region, and the difference in the attitudes
of the white people of the two sections toward the education of
the Negroes, he must realize that there was little opportunity for
the formulation of any comprehensive scheme of relief.

The need was immediate and pressing. As a result, almost
every religious sect and many other philanthropic organizations,
aroused to the highest pitch of missionary zeal by the tremendous
moral forces resulting from the slavery agitation and the War,
rushed to the South to give succor of all kinds to the freedmen
wherever the need seemed greatest and in whatever manner it
could be most speedily administered.[3]

One of the unfavorable results of this situation and the attend-
ant promiscuous emergency measures was the duplication of
effort in some places with the consequent neglect in other less
favored localities. Another was that, with so many agencies
working with frenzied zeal, often spurred on by denominational
motives of conquest, there was little inclination to study the situation carefully and to apply aid in accordance with the findings.
A third is found in the overemphasis of the classical type of
education for a people just emerging from slavery. Under such
conditions, however, it was probably impossible for the work to
be carried on in any other way that would have brought such
speedy results.

The second period begins with 1886 and extends through approximately three decades. After about 1885, although very
inadequately equipped and supported, a number of these schools
were fairly well organized and enrolled a few students in work
above what was considered the secondary level at that time,[4] and
which followed in general the pattern of the classical academies

[3] Seventy-nine societies which at one time or another were engaged in aiding the freedmen are
listed by Thomas Jesse Jones in *Negro Education: A Study of the Private and Higher Schools for
Colored People in the United States*, pp. 299–301 (U. S. Bureau of Education, Bulletin, 1916,
No. 38).

[4] *Annual Report of the United States Commissioner of Education*, 1889–90, II, 1083 (cited hereafter as *U. S. Com. of Ed., An. Rep.*); The John F. Slater Fund, *Proceedings of the Trustees*, 1886,
p. 41 (cited hereafter as Slater Fund, *Proc.*).

and colleges in which had been trained the white teachers from the North who, in the main, constituted the faculties of the Negro schools attempting college work. This group of students, preparing mainly for the Christian ministry and for teaching, furnished the leadership of the next generation. Some of the graduates of these schools supplemented their training by attending Northern colleges, and thereby served as a link between the two fields of educational endeavor. A few Negro students took their entire college course in Northern schools. Since it was the repeatedly expressed plan of the missionary bodies to help the Negroes to help themselves, this period is characterized by the addition of colored persons to the faculties of the group of schools in which they had been educated, thus constituting the feeble beginnings of a Negro-college-teacher class of professional educators. The schools supported by Negro church denominations, of course, maintained Negro faculties from the first.

It was after 1882 that the problem of the place of industrial education in the colleges was definitely raised, largely perhaps, as a result of the inclination of the trustees of the John F. Slater Fund, which was founded in that year, to favor those schools which gave such training as part of their curricula.[5]

Although some of the reconstruction governments established systems of public schools open to both races, the reaction which followed resulted in the establishment of the dual system, by separating the races in schools.[6] It was about 1885 before it could fairly be said that the public school system in the South was a going concern, and even then its progress was very halting.

As the economic situation improved and the animosities resulting from the War became less keen, educational conditions began to grow better and the idea of public education supported by taxation received more general acceptance.[7] One of the results of this attitude is seen in the beginnings of the land-grant colleges which later became recognized as a promising factor in the secondary and higher education of the Negro. For it was during this period that this group of schools for Negroes took on importance, largely as a result of the second Morrill Act in 1890.[8]

[5] Slater Fund, *op. cit.*, 1891, pp. 28 ff.

[6] The reconstruction governments, dominated by Negroes and Northerners known in the South as "carpetbaggers," hoped to establish equality among the races by permitting no legal form of public segregation.   [7] Hart, Albert Bushnell, *The Southern South*, pp. 291–92.

[8] *U. S. Statutes at Large*, Vol. 26, p. 417. See also *U. S. Office of Education Bulletin, 1930,* No. 9, II, 839.

The third stage in the evolution of the Negro college dates from 1917, when an epoch-making survey of Negro education, made by the Phelps-Stokes Fund, was completed and published by the United States Bureau of Education.[9] This survey proved a decided surprise to the country in its revelations, and resulted in an awakening which focussed attention in a comprehensive way upon the condition of the Negro college as well as upon the schools of lower grade. It also produced a critical attitude which led to rapid improvement through more adequate support from the responsible bodies.[10] It was during this period also that several of the great philanthropic foundations, such as the General Education Board [11] and the Julius Rosenwald Fund,[12] began to give serious attention to plans for the systematic and rational improvement of Negro education all along the line. Higher education for the Negro was naturally benefited by this added interest of these wealthy and hence powerful foundations. The state governments of the South were also impressed by the findings of the survey referred to and, following its publication, the curve of state support for Negro education began to increase its upward slope. Since the Negro land-grant colleges, located in seventeen Southern states, were favorably affected thereby, the importance of this attitude toward the higher education of the Negro is obvious.

Prior to the survey of 1926–28 the Negro colleges located in the area of the Middle States Association of Colleges and Secondary Schools and of the North Central Association of Colleges and Secondary Schools were eligible to membership in and accreditation by these regional bodies. The Negro colleges in the area of the Southern Association of Colleges and Secondary Schools were not so fortunate, however, since that body had not been willing, up to that time, to take the responsibility for passing judgment upon them. Thus, whatever the quality of their work, they were deprived of the advantages that are associated with accredited relationships. In 1930, however, as a result of conferences between its representatives and those of the Association of Colleges for Negro Youth, the Association of Colleges and Secondary Schools of the Southern States agreed to accept the

[9] Jones, *op. cit.*
[10] *The Twenty-Year Report of the Phelps-Stokes Fund*, 1911–1931, pp. 13–14.
[11] *The General Education Board, An Account of Its Activities, 1902–1914*, pp. 8–14.
[12] *Julius Rosenwald Fund, A Review to June 30, 1929*, pp. 6 ff.

responsibility for the examination and rating of the Negro colleges in its area.[13]

At the present time, therefore, the Negro colleges are making serious efforts to satisfy the requirements of standardization, with all that such activity implies, and hence have reached that stage of development which has proved so trying and at the same time so stimulating to the American colleges as a whole. Excessive sympathy in their conduct and support has given way to cool, calm judgment. Enthusiastic claims as to accomplishments are checked by scientific methods, and the yardstick of American educational standards is being applied to the work of schools without allowances for color or circumstances.

These movements seem to indicate that America is taking the problem of the higher education of the Negro seriously. In the Southern states it is, at present, the evident social policy to maintain separate schools for the two races. If the nation intends to continue the dual system of education in any area whatever, it cannot afford to apologize for the Negro school or for its product. It would seem, therefore, that as a result of this responsibility, serious attention must be given and large sums must be contributed to the Negro college. The Federal Government, philanthropy, the Negro himself, and, most of all, the several states involved will doubtlessly meet this challenge.

[13] *Minutes of the Association of Colleges for Negro Youth*, 1929, p. 5.
Proceedings of the Association of Colleges and Secondary Schools of the Southern States, 1930.

PART II

THE FEDERAL GOVERNMENT AND THE
FREEDMEN

CHAPTER III

MILITARY GUARDIANSHIP

THE NEGRO BECOMES CONTRABAND OF WAR

THE outbreak of the Civil War in 1861 was the culmination of a long series of conflicts between two groups of the American people who held different views on the question of the extension of slavery. It is true that the declared reason of the Federal Government, on the one hand, for mustering its armies to attack the rebellious states, was the preservation of the Union; and on the other, the Confederacy justified armed resistance to these attacks on the grounds that any state had a right to secede. Many persons, however, believed that the very existence of slavery might depend upon the outcome of the conflict. Wherever niceties of political phraseology were used to explain either position by those engaged at first in the discussions and later in the fighting, there is considerable evidence that there was little doubt in the minds of those slaves who thought about it at all that they themselves were the cause of the war and their freedom the issue at stake.[1] Every advance of the Northern armies into Southern territory, therefore, meant to many of them a physical manifestation of their deliverance and the answer to their age-long prayer.[2] A bishop of one of the Negro denominations, who was born and grew to manhood as a slave, describes his feelings at the news of freedom in these words:

I was ploughing in the fields of Southern Georgia. The whole universe seemed to be exulting in the unrestraint of the liberty wherewith God has made all things free, save my bound and fettered soul, which dared not claim its birthright and kinship with God's wide world of freedom. . . . Suddenly the

---

[1] The Negroes themselves were wiser than we. They well knew that the South was fighting, and would fight to the bitter end to keep them in slavery, and it followed that if the South were defeated it must mean freedom. Further, it seemed to them that at last God's evangel had come. Had they not watched and prayed and waited? Had not the angel of the Lord appeared in night visions and promised that they would be led up out of bondage? Had not their old men fallen asleep bidding them still wait, for the glorious morning of freedom would surely dawn? (Sutherland, Captain George E., U. S. V., in *War Papers, Commandery of Wisconsin,* 1891, pp. 165, 166.)   [2] Gaines, Bishop W. J., *The Negro and the White Man,* p. 71.

news was announced that the war had ended and that slavery was dead. . . .
I realized that all that life meant was mine at last.   Before it had been one long
nightmare, one dark journey of weariness and woe.   From my prison bars I
had caught glimpses of the world of liberty without, but now I could see it,
bathe my spirit in its sunshine and bask in its unobstructed and unclouded
splendor.   Surely it was enough to inspire and transport the heart, and make
it beside itself with the very delirium of joy. . . .
  This picture is not overdrawn.   Thousands whose minds had not been wholly
benighted by the repressing influences of Slavery, and whose natures still
possessed the capability of responding to the blessed boon of freedom felt as
I did. . . .[3]

Freedom to thousands of Negroes, therefore, signified not merely
release from physical bondage but also an opportunity to rise higher
in the human scale.   For, as has been pointed out, the slaves,
while uneducated as a class, were not totally ignorant.   Not only
had a favored few received the benefits of formal training in
varying degrees but the masses had become familiar with the
language of their masters and had absorbed the usages and many
of the ideals of civilization.   In this way they had adopted to a
considerable extent the white man's scale of values.   Thus they
conceived a reverence for the concepts expressed by the words
"freedom" and "education."   As they saw it, those who were
free and those who were schooled were masters of men and of
things, and rose to whatever status their individual abilities
permitted.   Hence opportunities to gain either were eagerly
grasped.   The war meant that freedom was at hand and must be
eagerly embraced whenever the slaves saw its symbol, the blue-
coated Yankee soldiers which Lincoln had sent for their deliverance.   So, wherever the Union armies penetrated the South,
the Negroes flocked to them for refuge; and as they advanced
farther into Confederate territory the number of refugees naturally increased as plantations and farms were abandoned by
their owners, leaving the slaves free to shift for themselves.
What disposition to make of these persons soon became a perplexing problem to the army commanders, for, in strict accordance with the requirements of the Fugitive Slave Law and the
statutes of the several states invaded, they had no right to
harbor the Negroes who took refuge within their lines.[4]   It will
be remembered that at first the Federal Government planned to

    [3] Gaines, *op. cit.*, pp. 72–74.
    [4] For text of the Fugitive Slave Law, see *U. S. Statutes at Large*, Vol. 9, p. 462.

crush the rebellion without interfering with the institution of slavery. One month before the Emancipation Proclamation was issued, President Lincoln in a letter to Horace Greeley, editor of the New York *Tribune*, said in part:

My paramount object in this struggle is to save the Union, and is not either to save or to destroy slavery. If I could save the Union without freeing any slave, I would do it. . . .[5]

This attitude was necessary in order to retain the slaveholding border states in their loyal adherence to the Union by non-interference with slavery and even by promising to prevent the Negroes from freeing themselves.[6] In addition there was an influential element of the population in the North which insisted that the abolition of slavery was not and should not be considered an object of the conflict.[7]

For these reasons the commanders of the Union armies on the front lines along the Mississippi Valley, the Potomac River, and the Atlantic sea coast, where Confederate territory first fell into their hands had to make early decision on this important matter. Some commanding generals refused to permit slaves to enter their lines at all. Halleck in the West [8] and Thomas Williams at Baton Rouge [9] took this position. Hooker and others not only returned fugitives to their owners but permitted masters and agents to enter their camps and search for slaves.[10] Officers in doubt often wrote to their superiors for instructions. For example, a letter written under the date of November 5, 1861, by General C. D. McCook at Nevin, Kentucky, to General W. T. Sherman, his superior officer, raised the problem of the disposition of Negro slaves who had entered his lines, suggested the danger of offending the state of Kentucky by violating its laws, and asked permission to

[5] Quoted in Nicolay, John G. and Hay, John, *Abraham Lincoln*, VI, 152. (Cited hereafter by the abbreviation N. & H.)

[6] General George B. McClelland early in the war, in a proclamation issued to the loyal people of Western Virginia, said, "Notwithstanding all that has been said by the traitors to induce you to believe that our advent among you will be signalized by interference with your slaves, understand one thing clearly; not only will we abstain from all such interference, but we will on the contrary, with an iron hand, crush any attempt at insurrection on their part." (*War of the Rebellion, Official Records*, Series I, II, 46; cited hereafter by the abbreviation *W. R.*)

[7] Commenting editorially upon a speech of Charles Sumner, the *Advertiser* of Springfield, Mass., October 4, 1861, said: "Neither men nor money will be forthcoming for this war, if once the people are impressed with the belief that the abolition of slavery and not the defense of the Union is the object. . . ."   [8] *W. R.*, Ser. I, VIII, 370; *Ibid.*, Ser. II, VII, 659, 660.

[9] *Annual Cyclopaedia*, 1862, p. 756.

[10] N. & H., IV, 391; *W. R.*, Ser. I, IV, 307; McPherson, Edward, *Political History of the United States during the Great Rebellion*, pp. 250, 251.

send the slaves back.[11]   To this communication he received the following reply:[12]

Brigadier General McCook, Camp Nevin.

SIR: I have no instructions from Government on the subject of Negroes. My opinion is that the laws of the State of Kentucky are in full force, and that Negroes must be surrendered on application of their masters or agents or delivered over to the sheriff of the county. We have nothing to do with them at all, and you should not let them take refuge in camp. It forms a source of misrepresentation by which Union men are estranged from our cause. I know it is impossible for you to ascertain in any case the owner of the Negro. But so it is; his word is not taken in evidence and you will send them away.

I am, yours,

W. T. Sherman, *Brigadier General, Commanding*

Such actions were at first condemned in the North, especially by those groups which were agitating the abolition of slavery.[13]

These decisions were in accord with the attitude maintained by the administration at Washington. When, on August 30, 1861, General John C. Fremont in Missouri emancipated by military order and on his own responsibility the slaves in the area under his jurisdiction,[14] President Lincoln requested him to modify the order,[15] and afterwards repudiated it.[16]

The historic emergency solution of the perplexing problem was reached by General Benjamin F. Butler, then in command of the Union forces in the vicinity of Fortress Monroe, Virginia. He took the position that, since slaves could be used against the government of the United States, they belonged to that species of property known as "contraband of war,"[17] and would be treated as such. This was the reason given the Confederate Colonel Mallory who came to him at Fortress Monroe, demanding the return of his slaves who had escaped into the Union lines.[18]   The

---

[11] *W. R.*, Ser. I, IV, 337.   [12] *Ibid.*, p. 347.

[13] Moore, Frank, *Rebellion Record*, Vol. III, Pt. II, p. 183.   [14] *W. R.*, Ser. I, III, 466, 467.

[15] *Ibid.*, 469, 471.   [16] *Ibid.*, 485, 486; McPherson, *op. cit.*, pp. 246, 247.

[17] *W. R.*, Ser. I, II, 659, 660; Moore, *op. cit.*, II, 437; *N. & H.*, IV, 388.

[18] Three slaves of Colonel Mallory, a rebel in arms, escaped into the Union lines at Fortress Monroe. Colonel Mallory, under a flag of truce, demanded the surrender of his slaves. "But," said Butler, "you hold, Colonel Mallory, do you not, that Negro slaves are property, and that Virginia is no longer a part of the United States?" "I do, sir," replied the Colonel. "You are a lawyer, sir," General Butler added, "and I ask you if you claim that the fugitive slave act of the United States is binding on a foreign nation, and if a foreign nation uses this kind of property to destroy the lives and property of citizens of the United States, if that species of property ought not to be regarded as contraband?" Here was coined the word "contraband," which, subsequently applied to slaves, came into general use, and under the shelter of which some humanity was shown before the government awakened to the situation. (Sutherland, *op. cit.*, p. 168.)

policy was approved by the Secretary of War in the following words:

Wash., May 30, 1861

SIR: Your action in respect to the Negroes who came within your line is approved. . . .

Simon Cameron to Major General Butler.[19]

This action solved a perplexing problem and relieved the military officers of their dilemma.

On March 13, 1862 Congress created a new Article of War forbidding officers to use soldiers under their command to return slaves to their owners, under penalty of dismissal.[20] On July 17, 1862 the Confiscation Act was approved, which gave authority to the President to free the slaves and confiscate the property of any one in rebellion,[21] to free all escaping or captured slaves,[22] and to use Negroes in such manner as he deemed best for the suppression of the rebellion.[23]

The change of attitude on the part of the government greatly facilitated the influx of Negroes to those areas in the hands of the Northern armies, thus affording the commanders a much needed labor supply and at the same time increasing greatly the number of fugitives to be cared for. Emancipation, which came in January 1863, more than two years before the end of the war, was a still more powerful stimulus to the Negroes to flee to the Union lines, which they did by tens of thousands.[24] The result was that large concentration camps which were established by the army at convenient points or settlements already in existence were taken over and placed under military control for the aid, direction, and protection of these new wards of the government. It is as wards of the Federal Government that the Negroes as refugees are of immediate interest in this study.

By way of recapitulation it is well to note that the attitude of the Federal Government on the question of the Negro passed rapidly through four stages in the two years from April 1861 to April 1863. First, the Negro was ignored as an issue and not al-

---

[19] *W. R.*, Ser. I, II, 153; McPherson, *op. cit.*, p. 245.

[20] *U. S. Statutes at Large*, Vol. 12, p. 354.

[21] *Ibid.*, Sec. 1, pp. 589–92.   [22] *Ibid.*, Sec. 9.   [23] *Ibid.*, Sec. 11.

[24] George S. Dickerman estimates, on the basis of figures reported by the Freedmen's Bureau, that something less than 400,000 Negroes during the entire period of the war applied for relief, about 3,500,000, or 90 per cent, of the Negroes remaining in the services of their old masters. (*U. S. Bureau of Education Bulletin*, 1916, No. 30, p. 248.)

lowed to enter the Union lines even though the operation of the armies rendered him destitute and homeless. The second stage was reached when the Secretary of War approved Butler's dictum that Negroes were "contraband" and should be received and put to work. The third stage is marked by the Confiscation Act, which not only permitted the army to receive Negroes but ordered it to take them from their masters. The Emancipation Proclamation marks the fourth stage. Through this act the administration at Washington, by declaring the slaves free in those areas held by the Confederate armies, not only changed the status of the Negroes in those areas from fugitive slaves to free men but placed upon the Federal Government the obligation, not only of recognizing and maintaining that freedom, but of making it meaningful. The use of Negro troops to help win the war for the cause of the Union, as victory without them seemed difficult of attainment, strengthened this obligation. The Thirteenth, Fourteenth, and Fifteenth Amendments to the Constitution were the legal enactments raising the Negro from slavery to citizenship. These acts, however, were but the outward signs of emancipation and enfranchisement. Much more was needed to make the transformation real. Those who were in immediate contact with the situation and hence familiar with the conditions of the Negro created first by slavery and then by the war, realized this at once; and with the aid of Northern philanthropy made the first experiments in the mass education of the freedmen while the war was in progress as part of one of the most extensive social service projects ever attempted by any people.

THE WORK OF GENERAL SAXTON IN THE SOUTHEAST

One of the earliest of these experiments arose when the Sea Islands of South Carolina and the neighboring regions were captured and came under the command of General Thomas W. Sherman in October 1861. He found there approximately 40,000 Negroes thrown upon his hands. He at once detailed Brigadier General Rufus Saxton to take charge of the refugees by setting them to work and providing for their general welfare.[25]

For six months he handled successfully a very difficult situation and gained experience which was later to be advantageously

---

[25] Mayo, A. D., "Common Schools in the South," in *U. S. Com. of Ed., An. Rep.*, 1901, I, 416 ff.

utilized in a larger sphere. On April 29, 1862 he was assigned by the Secretary of War to the Department of the South, "to take possession of all the plantations heretofore occupied by the rebels," and to assume general supervision over the inhabitants, mainly Negroes, who remained on them.[26] From this time until the establishment of the Freedmen's Bureau, General Saxton exercised control over all affairs concerning Negroes along the eastern edge of South Carolina, Florida, and Georgia.

In the assignment to his duties General Saxton had received no specific orders concerning the provision of schools for the Negroes coming under his care, but realizing the importance of education to such a people entering upon a new life, especially under such severe handicaps, he communicated with influential groups in Northern cities, describing to them the great opportunity for philanthropy which the situation presented. The result of this appeal to the North among groups already deeply and militantly interested in the cause of the Negro was immediate. It was the signal for the beginning of freedmen's relief organizations of various kinds, some of which continued in existence as late as 1874.[27] As a result of the coöperation of such societies, schools were soon established throughout the area under the supervision of General Saxton, with nearly two thousand children attending regularly under the tutelage of teachers from the North. In one of his reports Saxton, referring to the pupils, says, "They all manifested an intense desire to learn and seemed to have the intuition that it is by means of education that they are to rise in the scale of citizenship. During the harvesting and planting time it is a common sight to see groups of children going to school after having completed their tasks in the field." [28] Thus, for the first time on a large scale, an extensive experiment in the common school was carried on under the supervision of the Federal Government.

Not only was this an experiment in dealing with a complex

[26] Mayo, A. D., "Common Schools in the South," in *U. S. Com. of Ed., An. Rep.*, 1901, I, p. 417.

[27] Prominent among these benevolent societies were the following: New England Freedmen's Aid Society, New York National Freedmen's Relief Association, Pennsylvania Freedmen's Association, Western Sanitary Commission, Friends' Association for Aid of Freedmen of Philadelphia, Friends' Relief Association of Philadelphia, African Methodist Episcopal Church Society, Northwestern Freedmen's Relief Association, Baltimore Association for the Moral and Educational Improvement of the Colored People, American Union Commission, Western Freedmen's Aid Commission, African Civilization Society, Delaware Association, New England Society Branches. (Jones, *op. cit.*, p. 296.)   [28] Mayo, *op. cit.*, p. 419.

social problem by emergency methods, but it was an opportunity to test the capacity of the Negro for advancement under reasonably favorable conditions of freedom. The most important result of this work from the standpoint of this study is that General Saxton pronounced it a decided success. In his final report he says:

> The experiment with the Freedmen in this department is a success. Amid all their obstructions and in spite of all, they have made constant progress and proved their right to be received into the full communion of free men. They have shown that they can appreciate freedom as the highest boon; that they will be industrious and provident, with the same incitements which stimulate the industry of other men in free societies . . . that they are not ignorant from natural incapacity but from the brutishness of their former condition; that they are intelligent, eager and apt to acquire knowledge of letters; docile and receptive pupils; that they aspire to and adopt, as fast as means and opportunity admit, the social forms and habits of civilization; that they quickly get rid of in freedom the faults and vices generated by slavery and in truthfulness, fidelity, and honesty may be compared favorably with men of another color in conditions less unfavorable for the development of those qualities. . . .[29]

THE WORK OF GENERAL EATON IN MISSISSIPPI

A second attempt on the part of the Federal Government to promote the education of the Negroes through the agency of its military force, and hence a test of their capacity to profit by education, was initiated in 1862 when General Grant appointed Chaplain John Eaton[30] to take charge of the colored people in 'the area occupied by the army of the Tennessee, operating along the Mississippi River. Eaton's own description of the conditions that called for immediate attention presents a vivid picture of the Negro's introduction to freedom and hence the point of departure of his educational progress. He says:

> For the first time in the course of its progress the Army of the Tennessee was entering a region densely populated by the Negroes, and was face to face with conditions even more aggravated than any that had confronted the Union forces in the South Atlantic States. With the advance of the forty-five thou-

[29] Mayo, *op. cit.*, pp. 423, 424.

[30] General Eaton had a most distinguished career in the field of education, and was a conspicuous figure in the early provisions of educational opportunities for Negroes. In 1862, while stationed in Tennessee, he was given by General Grant responsibilities as related in the text. In March he was breveted as Brigadier-General of Volunteers and at the close of the war was appointed to serve as Assistant Commissioner of the Freedmen's Bureau for the District of Columbia and the adjacent territory in Maryland, Virginia, and West Virginia. In 1870 General Eaton became United States Commissioner of Education, succeeding Henry Barnard, which position he filled with conspicuous success until 1886 when he withdrew because of ill health. (Ethel Osgood Mason, Introduction to Eaton's, *Grant, Lincoln and the Freedmen*.)

sand troops or more in Grant's command, the cotton plantations were abandoned by their owners, and the Negroes, thrown thus upon their own resources, flocked in vast numbers—an army in themselves—to the camps of the Yankees. Such an influx constituted a menace to soldiers which it is difficult to overestimate. Imagine, if you will, a slave population, springing from antecedent barbarism, rising up and leaving its ancient bondage, forsaking its local traditions and all the associations and attractions of the old plantation life, coming garbed in rags or in silks, with feet shod or bleeding, individually or in families and larger groups,—an army of slaves and fugitives, pushing its way irresistibly toward an army of fighting men, perpetually on the defensive and perpetually ready to attack. The arrival among us of these hordes was like the oncoming of cities. There was no plan in this exodus, no Moses to lead it. Unlettered reason or the mere inarticulate decision of instinct brought them to us.[31]

Without reference to their own desires or inclinations or the policy of the government toward the Negroes, the army officers were compelled to act in the face of this tremenduous human problem. Whether they desired to do so or not there was no alternative if they were to carry on their military operations and protect the health and general well-being of the soldiers for whom they were responsible. Eaton continues:

Their condition was appalling. There were men, women, and children in every stage of disease or decrepitude, often nearly naked with flesh torn by the terrible experiences of their escapes. Sometimes they were intelligent and eager to help themselves; often they were bewildered or stupid or possessed by the wildest notions of what liberty might mean,—expecting to exchange labor, and obedience to the will of another, for idleness and freedom from restraint. Such ignorance and perverted notions produced a veritable moral chaos. Cringing deceit, theft, licentiousness—all the vices which slavery inevitably fosters—were the hideous companions of nakedness, famine, and disease. A few had profited by the misfortunes of the master and were jubilant in their unwonted ease and luxury, but these stood in lurid contrast to the grimmer aspects of the tragedy,—the women in travail, the helplessness of childhood and of old age, the horrors of sickness and of frequent death. Small wonder that men paused in bewilderment and panic, forseeing the demoralization and infection of the Union soldier and the downfall of the Union cause.[32]

Eaton established a concentration camp for the refugees a few miles from the encampment of the army near Great Junction, Mississippi, and immediately set about providing for the most pressing needs of the contrabands, such as caring for the sick, clothing the naked, and feeding the hungry. They were then organized into companies and set to handling the cotton, which at that time was standing in the fields, and performing other labor which partly paid for their support.

[31] Eaton, John, *Grant, Lincoln and the Freedmen*, p. 1.   [32] *Ibid.*, pp. 2, 3.

When General Grant was compelled to fall back upon Memphis, Tennessee, a few weeks after this plan had been put into operation, Eaton had to remove his base to that city, where he continued to work in the same capacity as before. Later still, in the autumn of 1863, he was placed in direct communication with the Secretary of War. On March 5, 1863 he was required to raise colored regiments and to appoint a number of persons to assist him in his work. He thus found himself in charge of approximately 800,000 Negroes in the four states of Tennessee, Arkansas, Mississippi, and Louisiana.[33] As part of his program of uplift he established schools for Negroes in all the cities within the area described, beginning with Nashville and Memphis and extending this service gradually to Vicksburg, Natchez, Little Rock, and Pine Bluff.

Meanwhile the various religious bodies entered the field and began establishing schools. Frequently misunderstanding and conflicts arose which sometimes produced complications. This difficulty was small, however, in comparison with the constant menace of those persons who objected to the establishment of schools for Negroes. For a time it was difficult to maintain such enterprises in places outside the area of immediate protection. In spite of all the obstacles inherent in the situation, the second experiment in educating the Negro under military control was successful as an example of the possibilities of the race, and as a preparation for the more extensive work of the Federal Government through the Freedmen's Bureau.

THE WORK OF GENERAL BANKS IN LOUISIANA

When General N. P. Banks took command in Louisiana in December 1862, he found a problem similar to that already described, which Grant had appointed Eaton to solve. He found within the lines 150,000 Negroes out of a slave population in the whole state in 1860 of 320,000. Those outside the Union lines became free by the Emancipation Proclamation, which became effective January 1, 1863. Those within the lines did not, of course, enjoy emancipation according to law, but being within the area of federal jurisdiction created a serious problem.[34] Banks issued orders requiring able-bodied adults to support themselves and their families. An extract from the order reads:

---

[33] *U. S. Com. of Ed., An. Rep.*, 1900–01, pp. 430, 431.
[34] Banks, N. P., *Emancipated Labor in Louisiana*, p. 5.

The public interest peremptorily demands that all persons without other means of support be required to maintain themselves by labor. Negroes are not exempt from this law. Those who leave their employers will be compelled to support themselves and families by labor upon public works. Under no circumstances can they be maintained in idleness or be allowed to wander through the parishes and cities of the state without employment.[35]

In projecting his program in the interest of coöperation and good feeling, as well as for his own enlightenment, General Banks delegated a selected group of the most intelligent free Negroes in the state to go through the parishes and canvass the desires of the colored people. After visiting parishes all over the state they reported the conditions of labor desired by the Negroes as follows:

First, that their families should not be separated; second, that they should not be flogged; third, that they should not be compelled to labor where they had been abused; fourth, that they should have schools; and fifth, that they should be paid reasonable wages for their toil.[36]

These requests were granted and made effective by a general order dated August 29, 1863, which established a commission of three officers "to regulate the enrollment, recruiting, employment, and education of persons of color." [37] Another order of February 3, 1864 states:

Provision will be made for the establishment of a sufficient number of schools —one at least for each of the police and school districts—for the instruction of colored children under twelve years of age, which when established, will be placed under the direction of the Superintendent of Public Education.[38]

In General Order No. 38 issued at New Orleans, March 22, 1864, eleven regulations were formulated establishing a Board of Education, providing in detail for its proper functioning in promoting education among the Negroes within the area of the Department of the Gulf. The schools were supposed to be supported mainly from taxes on real and personal property.[39] The system was highly thought of by the Negroes but suffered from prejudice as did most early attempts to educate the freedmen.[40] It is spoken of by one of the best students of the problem as the first regular attempt to support free schools in the South by public taxation.[41] The system as set up continued until Decem-

---

[35] Banks, N. P., *Emancipated Labor in Louisiana*, p. 35.
[36] *Ibid.*, p. 7.   [37] *Ibid.*, p. 35.   [38] *Ibid.*, p. 37.   [39] *Ibid.*, pp. 41, 42.
[40] *House Executive Documents*, 41st Congress, 2nd Session, No. 142. (Cited hereafter as *Ho. Ex. Docs.*)
[41] Mayo, A. D., *Southern Women in the Recent Educational Movement in the South*, U. S. Bureau of Education, Circular of Information, 1892, No. 1, p. 80.

ber 1865, during which time more than 50,000 Negroes learned to read.[42]

As the war wore on and the areas under control of the Union armies increased, with the social problem among the Negroes growing more and more difficult, it became evident that the Federal Government was under obligation to take control of the situation by the establishment of an agency for the centralization of authority over matters concerning the freedmen. The translation of this growing realization into statutory enactment was a long and painful process, but finally resulted in the establishment of the Freedmen's Bureau, whose place in the development of the Negro college forms the subject of the next section of this study.

[42] Mayo, A. D., *Southern Women in the Recent Educational Movement in the South*, U. S. Bureau of Education, Circular of Information, 1892, No. 1, p. 80.

CHAPTER IV

THE FREEDMEN'S BUREAU

ORIGIN

IN the preceding section it has been shown how the invasion of the South by the Union armies created a serious social problem because of the necessity of caring for the large numbers of Negroes who fled to the protection of the camps and marching columns of the Union armies or who were left by their fleeing masters on abandoned plantations. The efforts made to meet this unprecedented situation by the army commanders, the Federal Government, and the philanthropic organizations from the North have also been briefly indicated. As the number of refugees increased the problem grew correspondingly larger; and as the number of agencies engaged in relief multiplied the work became increasingly complicated and confused. It soon became evident to many persons of judgment and influence that the Federal Government would be compelled to take some steps to handle this growing problem in a large and systematic way. The plan most generally conceived by those who gave the question serious thought was the establishment of some sort of federal agency with large powers, to take entire charge of the affairs of the freedmen. Its function would necessarily include, first, the supervision of their material affairs, including employment, transportation, housing, food, and clothing; and second, the provision of means for their mental and spiritual improvement.

The statement quoted below expresses clearly and concisely the justification of federal action on behalf of the freedmen as conceived by its advocates:

Mr. Speaker, it is not often given to a legislature to perform an act such as we are now to pass upon. We have four million people in poverty because our laws have denied them the right to acquire property; in ignorance because our laws have made it a felony to instruct them; without organized habits because war has broken the shackles which bound them, and has released them from the plantations which were destined to be their world.

We are to organize them into society; we are to guide them, as the guardian

31

guides his ward, for a brief period, until they can acquire habits and become confident and capable of self-control; we are to watch over them, and, if we do, we have, from their conduct in the field and in the school, evidence that they will more than repay our labor.   If we do not, we will doom them to vagrancy and pauperism, and throw upon another Congress, and perhaps upon another generation, the duty or the effort to reclaim those whose hopes we will have blasted, whose usefulness we will have destroyed.[1]

As a result of petitions to the President [2] and to Congress and of general publicity through the press urging the need of such governmental organization, Representative Thomas D. Eliot of Massachusetts, on January 12, 1863, introduced a bill in the House creating a "Bureau of Emancipation," thus making the first formal step in Congress toward the creation of the desired agency for promoting and coördinating the efforts designed for the uplift of the freedmen.   One such petition from the officers of the private freedmen's aid societies of the country to President Lincoln placed before the House by Mr. Eliot on February 9, 1865, reads, in part, as follows:

It is the magnitude, not the nature of the work that appalls us, and drives us to the Government for aid and support.   We have found the freedman easy to manage beyond even our best hopes; willing and able to fight as a soldier; willing and able to work as a laborer; willing and able to learn as a pupil; docile, patient, affectionate, grateful, and although with a great tribal range of intellect from nearly infantile to nearly or quite the best white intelligence, yet with an average mental capacity above the ordinary estimates of it.

We have no doubts of the aptitude of the slave for freedom under any fair circumstances.   But we see that these circumstances must inevitably be unfair under the best arrangements the Government can make, and that, independently of a great paternal care on the part of the Government, they will be so bad as to wring cries of shame and indignation from the civilized world, dishearten the friends and advocates of emancipation at home, and give new vitality to the disloyal suggestions of the slaveholders' allies in the North and West. . . .

While anything remains undone within the power of the nation or the Government to do to alleviate or diminish this misery, the Christian principle and pity of our people will allow none who are responsible for it to rest in peace.

From this date to March 3, 1865, when the bill establishing the bureau finally became a law, a bitter fight was waged in both the Senate and the House over its provisions.   Eliot's first bill died in committee before the close of the session.[3]   The Secretary of War looked with favor upon the plan proposed, and recom-

---

[1] *Congressional Globe*, 38th Congress, 2nd Session, p. 693.   (Speech in favor of the Freedmen's Bureau bill, by William D. Kelly.)

[2] *Cong. Globe*, 37th Cong., 3rd Sess., p. 282.   [3] *Ibid.*, pp. 281–82.

mended that there be set up a permanent federal body for the purpose of caring for the freedmen.[4] On December 22, 1863 Eliot again introduced a bill providing for a bureau of freedmen's affairs under the War Department. This bill, after amendment, passed the House by a vote of 69 to 67, which indicates how evenly divided that body was on this measure.[5]

The bill was reported to the Senate from its committee on slavery and freedmen on May 25 by its chairman, Charles Sumner,[6] who ardently and ably championed the plan in general until the final legislative step was taken in its progress through Congress. An important amendment to the bill, however, had been made in the Senate committee, placing the proposed bureau under the Treasury Department instead of the War Department. Opinion varied greatly as to the department under which the bureau, if established, should operate. Some favored the War Department because the military power would be needed to make the proposed work effective.[7] The fact that much of its activity would be concerned with the administration of justice caused some to believe that the Judiciary Department was the proper authority.[8] The Department of the Interior was considered the logical controlling body for such work by those who thought the proposed functions of the bureau similar to those already being performed by the Bureau of Indian Affairs.[9] The leaders of the Senate, however, favored the Treasury Department since great areas of abandoned plantations upon which the freedmen would have to live were already under its jurisdiction.[10] That this amendment to the House bill was a tactical blunder by its proponents is indicated by the fact that although the bill as amended passed the Senate on June 28,[11] the House refused to concur and the whole matter was postponed until the following session of Congress.[12]

At the second session of the 38th Congress a conference committee was appointed on December 20.[13] Its report was accepted by the House on February 9, 1865, and rejected by the Senate on February 22. As a result of the appointment of a second conference committee,[14] a new bill was proposed on February 28, creating a "Bureau of Refugees, Freedmen, and Abandoned Lands"

[4] *Ho. Ex. Docs.*, 38th Cong., 1st Sess., Vol. 5, No. 1, p. 8.
[5] *Cong. Globe*, 38th Cong., 1st Sess., p. 895.   [6] *Ibid.*, p. 2457.   [7] *Ibid.*, p. 572.
[8] *Ibid.*, pp. 571, 2932.   [9] *Ibid.*, pp. 573, 2931.   [10] *Ibid.*, p. 2931.
[11] *Ibid.*, p. 3350.   [12] *Ibid.*, p. 3397.   [13] *Ibid.*, p. 80.   [14] *Ibid.*, p. 1004.

under the War Department.[15] After much debate the bill was passed by both houses on March 3, 1865,[16] and became a law when President Lincoln signed it on the same day, thus performing one of his last important official acts. Thus, after two years of parliamentary struggle and vigorous debate on the part of some of the ablest statesmen of the day in both houses of Congress, there was created an agency of the Federal Government which, until its formal discontinuance on June 30, 1872, was to hold a virtually absolute guardianship over the 4,000,000 Negroes who had suddenly attained the status of freedmen as a result of the Civil War.

The first section of the act creating the bureau reads as follows:

An Act to establish a Bureau for the Relief of Freedmen and Refugees. Be it enacted. . . . That there is hereby established in the War Department, to continue during the present war of rebellion, and for one year thereafter, a bureau of refugees, freedmen, and abandoned lands, to which shall be committed, as hereinafter provided, the supervision and management of all abandoned lands, and the control of all subjects relating to refugees and freedmen from rebel states, or from any district or country within the territory embraced in the operations of the army, under such rules and regulations as may be prescribed by the head of the bureau and approved by the President. The said bureau shall be under the management and control of a commissioner to be appointed by the President, by and with the advice and consent of the Senate. . . . And the commissioner and all persons appointed under this act, shall, before entering upon their duties, take the oath of office prescribed in . . . (the act of July 2, 1862). . . . [17]

By the act, legislative, executive, and judicial authority was given to a commissioner over millions of people, and large resources were placed at his command to carry out his plans.[18] Because of the vast powers vested in the office of commissioner, the great amount of wealth intrusted to his care in the form of lands, materials, and congressional appropriations, the extensive area involved, the number of subordinate officers engaged in so many varied activities, the many benevolent organizations, religious and otherwise, whose differences had to be composed, and above all the chaotic social and economic conditions in the South at the close of the war—because of this unusual combination of cir-

[15] *Cong. Globe*, 38th Cong., 1st Sess., p. 1307.   [16] *Ibid.*, pp. 1348, 1402.

[17] *U. S. Statutes at Large*, Vol. 13, pp. 507–09.

[18] See *Report of Commissioner of Freedmen's Bureau*, February 1870, for Oliver O. Howard's view of this responsibility; *Ho. Ex. Docs.*, 41st Cong., 2nd Sess., No. 142, p. 4.

cumstances, it was of the highest importance to select the right man as commissioner of the newly created bureau.[19]

On May 7, 1865, by order of General Grant, General Oliver O. Howard was detached from his command with Sherman's army, then on its way to Washington from Petersburg, and ordered to report to the Secretary of War. Reporting to Mr. Stanton on May 10, he was offered the responsibility of heading the newly formed "Bureau of Refugees, Freedmen and Abandoned Lands." In explanation the Secretary said:

> We have been delaying the execution of this law because it has been difficult to fix upon the commissioner. You notice that he can be detailed from the army. Mr. Lincoln, before his death, expressed a decided wish that you should have the office; but he was not willing to detail you before you could be spared from the army in the field. Now, as the war is ended, the way is clear. The place will be given you if you accept it.[19]

General Howard, after studying the matter, accepted the offer and was formally appointed by President Andrew Johnson on May 12, entering upon his duties on May 15 at the age of thirty-four.[20] The announcement of the selection met with the general approval of the country.[21] General W. T. Sherman, one of whose columns had been under Howard's command in the "March to the Sea," on learning of the appointment wrote to the new commissioner as follows:

> I hardly know whether to congratulate you or not, but of one thing you may rest assured, that you possess my entire confidence, and I cannot imagine that matters that involve the future of 4,000,000 souls could be put in more charitable hands. So far as man can do I believe you will, but I fear you have Hercules' task. God has limited the power of man, and though in the kindness of your heart you would alleviate all the ills of humanity, it is not in your power to fulfill one-tenth of the expectation of those who formed the Bureau for the Freedmen and Refugees and Abandoned Estates. It is simply impracticable. Yet you can and will do all the good one man may, and that is all you are called on as a man and a Christian to do, and to that extent count on me as a friend and fellow soldier for counsel and assistance.[22]

ORGANIZATION

With headquarters in Washington, the commissioner set about the organization of the bureau, dividing the area included in its jurisdiction into ten districts over each of which was placed an

---

[19] Howard, Oliver O., *Autobiography*, II, 206, 207; Peirce, Paul S., *The Freedmen's Bureau*, *passim*.   [20] Howard, *op. cit.*, II, 209.

[21] *Annual Cyclopedia*, 1865, p. 371; Blaine, James G., *Twenty Years in Congress*, II, 164.

[22] Howard, *op. cit.*, pp. 209, 210.

assistant commissioner.   For each position he selected an army officer whose experience with the conditions with which he would have to deal gave promise of success.[23]   Many changes were made in the personnel of the assistant commissioners during the life of the bureau, but all incumbents were military men.[24]

The central office was organized into four divisions in order to handle most effectively the work for which the bureau was responsible.   The Division of Records, under the direction of the adjutant general of the bureau had charge of the correspondence, supplies, labor, and schools.[25]   The Land Division attended to all matters concerning abandoned lands and those confiscated by the government.   The Finance Division, as the name implies, collected and disbursed all monies handled by the bureau.   The Medical Division, under the direction of an army medical officer, directed the colonies and supervised the hospitals and asylums which had been established throughout the area included in the act creating the bureau.   Later, divisions of commissary supplies and quartermaster supplies were added.[26]

The activity of the various benevolent organizations in urging the establishment of the bureau has already been noted.   It was natural, therefore, that these bodies should become actively associated with the commissioner as soon as he took office.   At the very opening of his headquarters in Washington he found that "at least thirty Northern benevolent societies had written letters" acknowledging him as their ally and declaring that their workers in the field looked upon him "as their friend and coadjutor." [27]

[23] The districts, assistant commissioner, and headquarters were as follows:

District	Assistant Commissioner	Headquarters
District of Columbia (Including Maryland, Alexandria, Fairfax, and Loudon Counties, Va.)	Colonel John Eaton, Jr.	Washington
Virginia	Colonel Orlando Brown	Richmond
North Carolina	Colonel E. Whittlesey	Raleigh
South Carolina and Georgia	General Rufus Saxton	Beaufort, S. C.
Florida	Colonel T. W. Osborne	Tallahassee
Alabama	General Wager Swayne	Montgomery
Louisiana	Chaplain T. W. Conway	New Orleans
Mississippi	Colonel Samuel Thomas	Vicksburg
Kentucky and Tennessee	General C. B. Fiske	Nashville
Missouri and Arkansas	General J. W. Sprague	St. Louis
Texas (later)	General E. M. Gregory	Galveston

(Peirce, *op. cit.*, p. 48.; *Ho. Ex. Docs.*, 39th Cong., 1st Sess., No. 11.)

[24] See list of changes in these offices, in Peirce, *op. cit.*, Appendix, pp. 172–74.
[25] *Ho. Ex. Docs.*, 39th Cong., 2nd Sess., Vol. 3, No. 1, p. 705.   [26] Howard, *op. cit.*, p. 219.
[27] *Ibid.*, p. 218.

On May 19 General Howard issued a public announcement, stationing the assistant commissioners and giving them control of all matters in their respective districts concerning refugees, freedmen, and abandoned lands. It was made clear in this order that all agents, whether appointed by the government or by private organizations, must report the condition of their work from time to time to the assistant commissioner in charge of the area in which they were located. "It is not the intention of the government," the statement continued, "that the bureau shall supersede the various benevolent organizations in the work of administering relief. This must still be afforded by the benevolence of the people through their voluntary societies, no government appropriations having been made for this purpose." [28] Thus an early understanding was reached concerning the relationships between the benevolent bodies and the bureau in dealing with the relief of the Negroes, which was their common concern. The bureau could not have assumed other relationships under the law as originally passed.

The bill creating the bureau did not include the promotion of education among the Negroes as one of its functions. General Howard, therefore, in his first report, called attention to the necessity for further legislation not only covering this point but broadening the powers of the bureau in other ways.[29] On January 5, 1866 Senator Trumbull of Illinois introduced a bill in the Senate amending the original Bureau act. Among other provisions was one that the bureau should continue in operation until otherwise provided by law and another to the effect "that the commissioner procure land and erect suitable buildings, asylums, and schools for dependent freedmen and refugees in accordance with recommendations to be made by Congress." [30] The bill passed both houses by substantial majorities,[31] but was vetoed by President Johnson.[32] The friends of the bill were unable to muster the necessary number of votes to override the veto.[33]

[28] Howard, *op. cit.*, pp. 219, 220.   [29] *Ho. Ex. Docs.*, 39th Cong., 1st Sess., Vol. 1, No. 2, p. 34.
[30] *Cong. Globe*, 39th Cong., 1st Sess., pp. 77, 104, 135.
[31] *Ibid.*, pp. 339, 362; *ibid.*, pp. 512, 688.
[32] By this time President Johnson had reached the disagreement with the Progressives in Congress over the method of reconstructing the seceding states which finally led to his impeachment. He therefore opposed each of the Freedmen's Bureau bills, which naturally were sponsored by his opponents.
[33] There was a considerable number of congressmen who, while favorable to the Negro and sympathetic with efforts toward his uplift, feared the bureau as a potential political machine and hence voted against it.

On May 22, 1866 Mr. Eliot introduced in the House a new bill intended to avoid the objectionable features pointed out in the President's veto message.[34]   After amendment by the Senate and agreement by a conference committee, both houses passed the bill.[35]   This bill also was vetoed by the President,[36] but was passed over the veto and became a law July 16, 1866.   By the provisions of this bill, education became one of the authorized functions of the bureau, and much of the anxiety of the friends and promoters of the bureau was removed and the work was permitted to take on new life.[37]

By this bill the activities of the bureau were extended for two years, terminating on July 16, 1868, although by further action, not then contemplated, the life of the bureau was extended to June 1872.   It was necessary, therefore, to put through its program at a feverish pace.   In his report of November 1867 the commissioner, realizing that even with the provision of sufficient funds only a beginning in educational work could be made in two years, recommended among other things that the work of education continue until the bureau itself had expired by law; and that it be then transferred to the Department of Education or some other governmental agency, with power to extend the system, and "that the school buildings upon lands purchased by regularly incorporated institutions of learning, be transferred to the corporate body having those institutions in charge."   He also expressed the belief that the reconstruction of the states would be completed by July 1868 and that thereafter, with military protection available and educational assistance provided, the colored people would be able to make their way without the assistance of such an agency as the bureau.[38]

Between November 1867 and July 1868, on which date the matter was formally taken up in the House, Howard had said:

Since writing the report in question (November 1868) I have attempted to discharge all officers and agents in certain states and in part from certain other states.   A reaction against the interests of freedmen immediately followed. This I did not anticipate. . . . Officers and agents of the bureau are required to bring all cases involving a violation of the civil rights act before the United States courts. . . . Again, the practical effect of discharging the officers and

[34] McPherson, Edward, *Political History of the United States during the Period of Reconstruction*, p. 149.
[35] *Ibid.*, p. 151.   [36] *Cong. Globe*, 39th Cong., 1st Sess., p. 3851; Howard, *op. cit.*, p. 282.
[37] Howard, *op. cit.*, p. 282.   [38] *Cong. Globe*, 40th Cong., 2nd Sess., p. 473.

agents has been to close up the schools; to intimidate union men and colored people; and, in fact, to paralyze almost completely the work of education.[39]

On the basis of these recommendations a bill was passed, again over the President's veto, continuing the bureau to July 1869.[40] Wherever the bureau had been discontinued the Secretary of War was empowered to restore it and, with the consent of Congress, to discontinue it in those areas where reconstruction had been completed. In no case, however, should the educational work be interfered with until the state had made provisions for the education of Negroes.[41] Another bill was passed over the President's veto on July 25, 1868 providing, among other things, "that the educational work . . . should continue unless otherwise ordered by Congress." [42] On June 10, 1872 an act was passed setting June 30, 1872 as the date when the bureau should end its work.[43] On that date its affairs were closed and, after a stormy career, the bureau actually came to an end.

GENERAL EDUCATIONAL ACTIVITY

During the first year of the life of the bureau the work done in the promotion of education was relatively unimportant. The act creating the bureau made no provision for education, although this need was often spoken of in debates in Congress. General Howard, however, realized fully the need of schools as a necessary agency in the uplift of the freedmen. His attitude is set forth in Circular Number 2 of the bureau, released March 19, 1865, at the very beginning of his administration. In that circular he says:

The education and the moral conditions of the people will not be forgotten and the utmost facility will be offered to benevolent and religious organizations and state authorities in the maintenance of good schools for refugees and freedmen until a system of free schools can be supported by the reorganized local governments. It is not my purpose to supersede the benevolent agencies already employed in the work of education but to sympathize with and facilitate them.

Not only did the act originally creating the bureau make no provision for education, but it made none for the financial support of the bureau itself through congressional appropriation, it being

---

[39] *House Miscellaneous Documents* (cited hereafter as *Ho. Misc. Docs.*), 40th Cong., 2nd Sess., No. 44.

[40] *Cong. Globe*, 40th Cong., 2nd Sess., p. 1998.   [41] *U. S. Statutes at Large*, Vol. 15, p. 83.

[42] *Cong. Globe*, 40th Cong., 2nd Sess., p. 3424; *U. S. Statutes at Large*, Vol. 15, p. 193.

[43] *U. S. Statutes at Large*, Vol. 18, p. 366.

assumed by Congress that the funds derived from crops, the sale and rental of seized and abandoned property of the confederates, school taxes, and other miscellaneous sources would be sufficiently large to cover the costs of operation.   This was true at the beginning when the activities of the organization were limited.   So far as education was concerned, however, it was clearly seen during that first year that with the number of schools already in existence which were precariously maintained by philanthropy, and in view of the constantly growing need of the extension of educational opportunities for the freedmen, something more substantial would be needed from the bureau than sympathy, protection, and supervision.   The commissioner, in spite of the absence of legal authority had acted in accordance with his convictions as expressed in the declaration just quoted.   Referring to this action later he writes:

Though no appropriation had been granted by Congress for this purpose, by using the funds derived from rent of "abandoned property," by fitting up for school-houses such government buildings as were no longer needed for military purposes, by giving transportation for teachers, books and school furniture, and by granting subsistence, I was able to give material aid to all engaged in educational work.   With the aim to harmonize the numerous independent agencies in the field, and to assist all impartially, I appointed a superintendent of schools for each state, who should collect information, encourage the organization of new schools, find houses for teachers, and supervise the whole work.[44]

Under the justification of emergency measures and as a means of organizing the educational work, a general superintendent of education was actually appointed during the first year to supervise the state superintendents, with authority to coördinate the various educational activities and to give such aid as was found feasible, with the hope that future legislation would endorse the action.[45]

Many buildings used for schools up to that time had been abandoned or confiscated property.   The reconstruction program, however, restored these properties to their former owners, left the benevolent organizations in many cases without buildings or lands, and thus threatened to hamper seriously their program. Because of this menace and with the backing of the officials of the bureau, these bodies urged Congress to make some provision for a more adequate and dependable program for the support of the

[44] *Ho. Ex. Docs.*, 41st Cong., 2nd Sess., No. 142, p. 11; *Report of Com. of Freed. Bur.*, October 20, 1869.   [45] *Ho. Ex. Docs.*, 39th Cong., 1st Sess., No. 11, p. 49.

education of the freedmen by liberal federal appropriation.[46] Favorable legislation followed, with the result that the army appropriation bill for the fiscal year ending June 1867 included a sum of $521,000 to be used for educational purposes out of a total of $6,944,450 for the entire work of the bureau.[47] Of this amount $21,000 was for the salaries of school superintendents and $500,000 for school buildings and asylums.[48] In June 1868 congressional authorization was given the bureau to use, for educational purposes, any unexpended balances not legally required for other purposes.[49] Thus, Congress granted to the commissioner not only the authority but the means to carry forward an extensive educational program in coöperation with the benevolent agencies already engaged in such work.

INTIMIDATION

This favorable attitude of the Federal Government as expressed through the bureau gave great encouragement to the denominational missionary organizations; for the support of this strong ally backed by the physical protection of the army, which still remained scattered throughout the South at strategic points, relieved them of the menace of violence which had constantly threatened the success of their work from the beginning and increased rather than diminished as the reconstruction measures of Congress grew more and more irksome to the South.[50] Expansion went forward, however, with increasing zeal and better organization until schools had been established in places throughout the South which had hitherto been unreached.[51]

The nature of the opposition varied from the very beginning of educational efforts in behalf of the freedmen to the restoration of "home rule" in the South in the seventies. The menace of this opposition was quite evident at the close of the war and the bureau officials looked upon the actual physical protection of Negro schools as an important part of their function. In concluding his report of January 1866, after a tour of inspection through the South, the general superintendent of education, J. W. Alvord, referred to this aspect of the situation as follows:

[46] Alvord, J. W., *Semi-Annual Report on Schools for Freedmen*, Jan. 1, 1868, p. 1; Senate Documents, 1865–66, No. 27, p. 108.
[47] *Ho. Ex. Docs.*, 39th Cong., 2nd Sess., Vol. 3, No. 1, p. 714.   [48] Howard, *op. cit.*, p. 282.
[49] *U. S. Statutes at Large*, Vol. 14, p. 434, Sec. 3.   [50] Howard, *op. cit.*, pp. 374 ff.
[51] *Ho. Ex. Docs.*, 40th Cong., 2nd Sess., No. 1, p. 651.

Permit me distinctly to call attention to the fact that this whole educational movement among the freedmen must, for the present, be protected by the general government. I need not repeat what appears all through this report, viz: that military force alone can save many of our schools from being broken up, or enable us to organize new schools. Such is the improper spirit in many parts of the South, that where as yet there have been no atrocities attempted against the schools, protecting power is called for to give that sense of quiet and consciousness of security which the calm duties of both teacher and pupil require.[52]

It was thought, however, that there was a decline rather than an increase in the opposition after the close of the war. This at least was the opinion of the commissioner himself in November 1866, with reports from the whole field before him as submitted by the assistant commissioners. He expressed the opinion that the "sentiment of the white South to the education of the Negro had appreciably improved especially among the better class, who conceded that education must be universal." [53]

By 1868, however, it was evident that the opposition had become organized. Workers in Charleston, West Virginia, early in that year received a note from the Ku Klux Klan warning them that their efforts were unwelcome and must be stopped on pain of reprisal. No white family in the community could be found who would offer living accommodations to Northern women who taught Negroes. A male teacher at Frostburg was ordered to leave town or suffer violence, but he was protected by friendly citizens and allowed to remain. In Maryland a teacher was forced to discontinue the work of teaching Negroes and leave the vicinity. A Negro teacher at Hawkinsville, Georgia, was seriously wounded, and the state superintendent of the Bureau reported that during April, May, and June of 1868 opposition to the education of Negroes had increased and that a number of those engaged in the work had received threats, some anonymous and some with no effort at concealment.[54]

Along the seacoast, or wherever the military authorities ruled with a strong hand, such violence was generally suppressed. It had full sway, however, in the interior counties of Texas, Alabama, Mississippi, Louisiana, Kentucky, and Maryland.[55] John Dunlap, a teacher in Shelbyville, Tennessee, was flogged and driven away but returned under protection of a guard which fired upon and dispersed the mob who sought the object of their

[52] Alvord, *op. cit.*, Jan. 1, 1866, p. 14.   [53] *Report of Com. of Freed. Bur.*, 1866, p. 67.
[54] Howard, *op. cit.*, II, 376.   [55] *Ho. Ex. Docs.*, 39th Cong., 1st Sess., No. 70, p. 159.

wrath with the announcement that they "wanted Dunlap and fried meat." [56]   A school building was burned at Carthage, Tennessee, and schools were broken up in other parts of the state by insults and other outrages meted out to those who had the schools in charge.   At Rock Springs, Kentucky, the Ku Klux Klan, forming a mob, drove the Negro teacher, James Davis, from the county and completely destroyed the school building by fire.[57] Descriptions of such outrages frequently appear in the reports of the bureau superintendents throughout the South during this period, in the reports of the denominational organizations, and in the report to Congress of the Ku Klux Klan investigation.[58] Such reports furnished additional arguments to those favoring continued government supervision and military protection for the Negroes in the South.[59]

It was in the midst of such conditions that the Negro colleges were founded.   And the fact that the more remote sections offered less protection to the promoters of education for Negroes may explain in part why the larger and stronger schools which ultimately grew into colleges are located in the more populous centers.   Another reason, of course, and probably the principal one, is that the cities offered decidedly greater opportunities for service than the rural areas.

General Howard himself, long after these events had occurred and therefore with a better perspective of the whole situation, expressed his opinion that:

The operations of the Ku Klux Klan were directed principally against the Negroes and those who were supposed to especially lend them countenance, by murders, whippings, and other acts of violence to inspire them with such terror as to render unavailable their newly conferred political privileges.

But the hostility to education was rather incidental than otherwise.   The grand object of the "Solid South," so called, was to prevent what was denominated "Negro domination."   The secret societies turned their machinery against Union Southerners to silence or convert them; against "carpet baggers" (which included the Northern teachers of colored schools) to banish them; and against all Negroes to so intimidate and terrorize them that they would not dare to vote except as their new masters directed.[60]

It should be noted, however, that this campaign of terrorism against the Negro schools was not unanimously endorsed by the

[56] Howard, *op. cit.*, II, 379.   [57] *Ibid.*, p. 381.
[58] The reports of this investigation are available in thirteen volumes as *House Miscellaneous Documents*, 42nd Cong., 2nd Sess., under the title "Ku Klux Klan Investigation."
[59] *Sen. Ex. Docs.*, 39th Cong., 1st Sess., No. 27, pp. 108–20.   [60] Howard, *op. cit.*, p. 388.

most cultured and enlightened people of the South even at the period when their resentment toward the Northern scheme of reconstructing the Southern states was most bitter. As early as 1866 many of the more intelligent and influential men of the South believed that the education of the Negro was necessary as a means of making him a more desirable citizen.[61]

The following estimate of the education of the Negro of the period under discussion is appropriate here as giving the view of a Southern man, Dr. J. L. M. Curry, distinguished for many years for his devoted activity in behalf of the Negro. Dr. Curry was for twelve years the executive agent of the John F. Slater Fund,[62] during which period he added immensely to his intimate knowledge of the conditions of the Negro schools and was thereby enabled to render an opinion demanding the respectful consideration of earnest students of this subject. He said in 1890:

I have very little respect for the intelligence or the patriotism of the man who doubts the capacity of the Negro for improvement or usefulness. The progress made by the Negroes in education, considering their environments, their heredity, the abominable scoundrels who have come here from other quarters to seduce and lead them astray, is marvelous. . . . It is not just to condemn the Negro for the education which he received in the early years after the War. That was the period of reconstruction, the saturnalia of misgovernments, the greatest possible hindrance to the progress of the freedmen, an immitigable curse, the malignant attempt to use the Negro voter as a pawn in the corrupt game of manufacturing members of Congress. The education was unsettling, demoralizing, pandered to a wild frenzy for schooling as a quick method of reversing social and political conditions. Nothing could have been better devised for deluding the poor Negro, and making him the tool, the slave of corrupt taskmasters. Education is a natural consequence of citizenship and enfranchisement, I should say, of freedom and humanity. But with deliberate purpose to subject the Southern States to Negro domination, and secure the states permanently for partisan ends, the education adopted was contrary to common sense, to human experience, to all noble purposes. The curriculum was for a people in the highest degree of civilization; the aptitude and capabilities and needs of the Negro were wholly disregarded. Especial stress was laid on classics and liberal culture to bring the race *per saltum* to the same plane with their former masters, and realize the theory of social and political equality. A race more highly civilized, with best heredities and environments, could not have been coddled with more disregard of all the teaching of human history and the necessities of the race. Colleges and universities, established and conducted by the Freedmen's Bureau and northern churches and societies, sprang up like mushrooms, and the teachers, ignorant,

[61] *Report of Joint Committee on Reconstruction*, Pt. I, p. 112; Pt. II, pp. 74, 87, 115, 126, 130, 137, 165, 232, 243, 290.   [62] See "Organized Philanthropy" in a later section of this study.

fanatical, without self-poise, proceeded to make all possible mischief. It is irrational, cruel to hold the Negro, under such strange conditions, responsible for all the ill consequences of bad education, unwise teachers, reconstruction villanies, and partisan schemes. To educate at all, slowly, was a gigantic task.[63]

HIGHER EDUCATION

In the last months of the year 1865, the General Superintendent of Education made an extended tour of inspection of the Southern states to observe the educational situation among Negroes including not only the larger centers of population but the interior areas as well. In his report of June 1866 he noted particularly the eagerness of the freedmen for knowledge and their willingness to sacrifice for its attainment, calling attention to figures which indicated that in the District of Columbia 75 per cent of the Negro children attended school as against only 41 per cent of the white children; that in Memphis, Tennessee, 72 per cent of the Negro children attended school, in Alabama 79 per cent, and in Virginia 82 per cent. He compared these figures with an attendance of 43 per cent in the public schools of New York State and 93 per cent in Boston, which probably ranked first in this respect among the cities of the entire country.[64] He remarked upon the large number of schools in certain districts conducted by the Negroes themselves, noting particularly the situation in Charleston, South Carolina, Savannah, Georgia, and New Orleans, Louisiana. One school visited in the latter place, where three hundred pupils were taught entirely by cultured colored men, could be favorably compared with any ordinary school in the North. "Very creditable specimens of writing were shown, and all the older classes could read or recite as fluently in French as in English."[65]

This combination of desire and ability, in the opinion of the general superintendent, was rapidly creating the problem of supplying teachers in sufficient numbers to meet the growing demand for more extended training. The solution of the problem, of course, could be found only in the provision of higher schools where the colored people could be trained to supply their own schools with competent instructors. He calculated that 20,000 teachers were immediately needed for the one million or more

---

[63] *Montgomery Conference on Race Problems (1900)*, p. 108. (A Southern View, from the address of Dr. J. L. M. Curry.)

[64] Alvord, *op. cit.*, Jan. 1, 1866, p. 2.   [65] *Ibid.*, pp. 16, 17.

Negro children at that time ready and eager to attend school.[66]
Here, then, was an official forecasting of the need of institutions of
higher learning whose encouragement constituted such an important contribution of the Freedmen's Bureau to the education of
the Negro.

A year later the superintendent mentions 581 students enrolled
in eleven "high or normal" schools, as part of the 1,208 schools
and 77,998 pupils reported.[67]   While the terms "high school"
and "normal school" must be interpreted in terms of the entire
educational situation of the time, a definite lifting of the level of
instruction is indicated.   In many places a decided preference for
colored teachers was shown.   This was due partly to the pride of
the race in having their own members elevated to positions which
to them seemed important and influential, and partly to the feeling of the white Southerner that, since Negro schools were inevitable, Negro teachers were preferable to white teachers from
the North.

It is evident that the freedmen are to have teachers of their own color.
Many such are already employed. . . . The planters promise protection and
help in their work; and where they are employed the schools will become very
soon self-supporting.   From a number of the states, officers of this bureau ask
us to send teachers of this description.   One says, "I want fifty"; another wants
thirty; another twenty; all urging special reasons for their employment.   These,
of sufficient capacity, are not to be had at present, but such demands show the
drift of feeling and sentiments on the subject.[68]

The inspector urged the improvement and enlargement of the
normal schools and made the first suggestion that higher institutions should be endowed to insure their permanency.   Scholarship funds were also suggested to enable competent but indigent
young Negroes to prepare for service commensurate with their
abilities.[69]   General Howard mentions in his reports a number of
institutions of higher learning definitely encouraged and substantially aided by the bureau, most of which are now included among
the permanent colleges and universities for Negroes.[70]   His zeal
and that of his assistants in promoting such work is the basis for
part of the charges which were brought against him in connection
with his administration of the bureau.[71]   The report of July 1,
1867 shows that Howard University at Washington had been

[66] Alvord, *op. cit.*, Jan. 1, 1866, pp. 16ff.   [67] *Ibid.*, 1867, p. 4.   [68] *Ibid.*, p. 36.   [69] *Ibid.*
[70] *Report of Com. of Freed. Bur.*, sections on Education, *passim*.
[71] *Ho. Ex. Docs.*, 41st Cong., 2nd Sess., No. 121, p. 2.

chartered and had begun its work.[72] At Harper's Ferry, West Virginia, efforts were in progress to establish a normal school and college, a board of trustees having already been incorporated and about $20,000 raised.[73] A fund of $50,000 had been raised and an act of incorporation secured for St. Augustine's Normal and Collegiate Institute at Raleigh, North Carolina.[74] From Missouri came the report of Lincoln Institute, located at Jefferson City, which had its origin in the voluntary contributions of $6,325 from the 62nd and 65th regiments, United States colored troops. It had been incorporated by the state for the education of the colored people especially for the teaching profession. The school opened in September with two pupils and closed in June with one hundred and fifty. The site of the school included 365 acres of land, about three miles out of Jefferson City.[75]

In Tennessee the report indicates that Fisk University at Nashville had been opened in an old military hospital and that the Central Tennessee College of the Methodist Episcopal Church had opened classes in an old gun factory in the same city.[76]

In January 1868 the General Superintendent reported:

Higher schools, and those for the preparation of teachers, have been aided in equal distribution through the several states. The principal of these, as assisted by the bureau, all of them made permanent institutions by charter of the respective states where they are located, are as follows: National Theological Institute, Washington, D. C.; Howard University, Washington D. C.; Saint Martin's School, Washington, D. C.; Normal School, Richmond, Va.; Berea College, Berea, Ky.; St. Augustine's Normal School, Raleigh, N. C.; Wesleyan College, East Tennessee; Fisk University, Nashville, Tenn.; Storer College, Harper's Ferry, W. Va.; Atlanta University, Atlanta, Ga.; Robert College, Lookout Mountain, Tenn.; Marysville College, Tenn.; Alabama High and Normal Schools; St. Bridgit's Parochial School, Pittsburgh, Pa.; South Carolina High and Normal Schools. The total amount granted to these institutions is $168,000.[77]

The successive reports of the commissioner show that the bureau substantially aided these and other institutions above elementary grade in every way save in supplying teachers' salaries, and thereby made a permanent contribution to the Negro college at the time when the very life of these schools depended upon just the aid which the bureau was permitted by law to give. In a

[72] Alvord, *op. cit.*, July 1, 1867, p. 8.   [73] *Ibid.*, p. 10.   (Now Storer College.)
[74] *Ibid.*, p. 22.   (Now St. Augustine's College.)
[75] *Ibid.*, p. 62.   (Now Lincoln University of Missouri.)   [76] *Ibid.*, p. 66.
[77] Alvord, *op. cit.*, Jan. 1, 1868, p. 23.

later section of this study it is remarked that without the denominational boards it is difficult to see how the Negro college could have had its beginning. It is appropriate here to say that without such a federal organization as the Freedmen's Bureau it is equally difficult to see how the denominational boards could have carried forward their educational activities in the South for the five years following the close of the Civil War.

By the end of the year 1870 the bureau had about completed the most important task of encouraging, aiding, and protecting the benevolent organizations in the promotion of education for the freedmen. As has been indicated, its life had repeatedly been prolonged by congressional action; but now, removed by five years from the close of the war and the pressing emergency, it began to withdraw from the field and permit the educational responsibility to rest upon the churches, the several states, and the Negroes themselves. General Howard, while reporting a continued and increasing interest in education on the part of the Negroes, expressed regret that the Federal Government could not offer further assistance. In spite of this fact, the number of high or normal schools and industrial schools had increased, and for the first time the number of colored teachers exceeded the number of white. Attention is called to the fact that:

> The people of the Southern States have been too much occupied with material interests, the restoration of industrial order, and political reconstruction, to give to the subject of education the attention which its importance demands. In two or three states a good beginning has been made; but no Southern State is fully prepared with buildings, teachers, funds, and intelligent officers to set in operation and sustain an efficient free school system. Even for the white children no adequate provision is made.[78]

The operations of the bureau had been under constant criticism since its organization. In 1870 Fernando Wood of New York offered a resolution in the House calling for an investigation of the bureau on the basis of fifteen charges which he brought against the commissioner.[79] After an investigation by a committee, General Howard was exonerated and commended for his administration of the bureau and the faithful discharge of his difficult task.[80] Congress itself passed a resolution freeing him from all blame and praising his record.[81]

[78] *Report of Com. of Freed. Bur.*, Oct. 20, 1870; *Ho. Ex. Doc.*, 41st Cong., 3rd Sess., No. 2, p. 317.
[79] *Ho. Ex. Docs.*, 41st Cong., 2nd Sess., No. 121, p. 1.		[80] *Ibid.*, p. 27.
[81] *Cong. Globe*, 41st Cong., 3rd Sess., p. 1850.

But the matter was not allowed to end there. Further attacks were made through military channels, since many of the officers involved in the alleged irregularities were soldiers. As a result of such charges, a military court of inquiry, with General William T. Sherman presiding, conducted an investigation for a period of forty days.[82] General Howard was again exonerated with praise. Although the question was again raised in Congress two years later, upon the appeal of Senator George B. Hoar it was dropped.[83]

HOWARD UNIVERSITY

Howard University at Washington, named in honor of the Commissioner of the Freedmen's Bureau, is the largest of the colleges in the group under consideration. Because of the place it holds in the higher education of the Negro, a somewhat detailed account of its evolution in connection with the discussion of the Freedmen's Bureau seems appropriate, especially since its organization and early history were so largely influenced by that organization.

The abolition of slavery in the District of Columbia and later throughout the South resulted in a large influx of freedmen into the District until they formed one-third of its population, thus constituting the largest urban group of Negroes in the world.[84] The educational problem presented by this group was quickly realized by various freedmen's aid organizations and philanthropic individuals, with the result that day and night schools, providing instruction in the elementary studies, were immediately established for persons of all ages.[85] It was realized also that there would soon be a pressing need for Negroes educated on the higher levels to take places of leadership as teachers and preachers in the regeneration of the recently emancipated race. It was for the purpose of helping to supply this need that a small group of men in November 1866 took the first steps that led to the founding of

[82] *Court of Inquiry in the Case of Brig. Gen. Oliver O. Howard, Proceedings, Findings, and Opinions*, pp. 601, 602.

[83] *Cong. Globe*, 44th Cong., 1st Sess., p. 3930.

[84] See Mayo, A. D., in *U. S. Com. of Ed. An. Rep., for 1902*, I, 410 ff.

[85] Probably the most famous of these early schools was the normal school for girls opened by Miss Myrtilla Miner, December 3, 1851, and chartered under the name "Institution for the Education of Colored Youth," under the Miner Board. In 1879 it was taken over by the public school system of the District as the Myrtilla Miner Normal School. From 1871 to 1876 it worked coöperatively with the Normal Department of Howard University. After operating for many years as the city normal school, in 1931 it became the Miner Teachers' College with a four-year course leading to the Bachelor's degree.

Howard University.[86]   These men were members of the First
Congregational Church of Washington and all were convinced
at first that the proposed institution should concentrate upon the
preparation of ministers.   At a later meeting, a committee appointed to bring in a plan of organization recommended that a
night school be opened at first; that application be made to the
Commissioner of the Freedmen's Bureau for quarters, fuel, and
light for the school;[87] and that three chairs of instruction be
established.[88]   These recommendations were adopted, and the
first faculty appointed consisted of professors of Evidences and
Biblical Interpretation, Biblical History and Geography, and
Anatomy and Physiology.   Thus was the university born in the
minds of its founders without a location or a name.   It was
styled a "Theological Institute" and its aim was "the education
of the colored youth for the ministry."   The name was soon
expanded into "Theological and Normal Institute" and finally to
"The Howard University," under which title it was chartered.[89]

The development of plans for this new educational center was
rapid.   Senator Pomeroy of Kansas, who had become greatly
interested in the movement, suggested at first an extension of the
original idea to include the training of teachers.   Later he made
a motion that the doors be thrown open to all who wished to
enter, a motion which was heartily approved.   At a later meeting
held to consider the charter, it was decided to include in that
instrument university privileges and to provide for departments
of theology, law, and medicine.[90]   When the question of a name
for the new university was reached, several were suggested and
rejected.   Finally, Dr. D. B. Nichols made the motion that the
university bear the name of General Howard, a suggestion which
was enthusiastically adopted with but one dissenting vote, that
of the General himself, who felt that his usefulness to the new
institution would be greater if it bore another name than his.[91]

The act of incorporation was drawn by Senator Pomeroy and
presented to the Senate on January 23, 1867 [92] by Senator Henry

[86] *Annual Report of the President of Howard University for 1868–69*, p. 3.

[87] This recommendation marked the beginning of the relationship between Howard University
and the Freedmen's Bureau.   In this relationship, the university, at that time, was merely one
of a number of such schools aided by the bureau.   Regular federal appropriations began at a
later date and gave the university a relationship with the government shared by no other
private institution.   [88] *Minutes of the Meeting of Jan. 8, 1867.*

[89] Nichols, Danforth B., *The Genesis of Howard University* (1892), pp. 5, 6.

[90] *Minutes of the Meeting of Jan. 29, 1867.*   [91] Howard, *op. cit.*, p. 397.

[92] *Congressional Globe*, 32nd Cong., 2nd Sess., pp. 1127, 1701, 1725.

Wilson of Massachusetts, afterwards Vice-President of the United States under President Grant. The bill incorporating the institution, after amendment, passed both houses of Congress and became a law when President Andrew Johnson affixed his signature, March 2, 1867.[93] At the first meeting of the corporation the board of trustees was formed, which included the seventeen incorporators with the addition of General G. W. Balloch who was elected treasurer.[94]

The preliminaries disposed of, the university began its work by opening classes in the normal and preparatory departments united on the first of the following May. The first student body of five pupils consisted entirely of young white women, the daughters of trustees Robinson and Nichols.[95] The recitations were held in a rented frame building, previously used as a German dance hall and saloon, which stood on the east side of what is now Georgia Avenue, a short distance south of W Street.[96] The building and lot were purchased by the university but later sold when the classes were removed to their permanent home.

The selection of the permanent site for the university is due largely to the fortunate combination of judgment, persistence, and faith characteristic of General Howard. He, acting with General E. Whittlesey as a committee on the selection of a site, wished to procure the commanding elevation in the northern part of the city where the university now stands. This was part of the tract of one hundred and fifty acres known as "Effingham" and owned by John A. Smith. On the plea that the location of a Negro school would depreciate the remainder of his property, the owner refused to sell any part of it. After much argument, General Howard asked him to state his price for the whole farm. The rate given was $1,000 an acre, making a total valuation of $150,000, a staggering sum under the circumstances. Undaunted, however, General Howard closed the bargain, although the treasury of the university was without a single dollar. Adjustments brought the final purchase price for the property

[93] *Ibid.; U. S. Statutes at Large*, Vol. 14, pp. 438, 439.

[94] *Minutes of the Board of Trustees Meeting*, March 19, 1867; Howard, *op. cit.*, p. 397.

[95] Johnson, James B. (secretary-treasurer of Howard University), *Address at the 25th Anniversary of Howard University*, 1892, p. 18. It is possible, however, that night classes were held as early as February even before the charter was granted. (See Dyson, Walter, "The Founding of Howard University," *Howard University Record*, Vol. XV, No. 8, June 1921, pp. 434, 435.)

[96] Patton, William M., *The History of Howard University*, 1893, p. 30; Howard, *op. cit.*, pp. 398–99.

down to $147,500, for which the corporation made itself responsible.[97]

This transaction was approved by the board but not with enthusiasm. A few gifts had been received, but these were negligible in face of the obligation created. It was part of the plan to subdivide and sell that part of the property not needed for educational purposes and thereby realize enough to pay off the purchase price. But ready cash was needed for meeting the first payment on the property and making a survey. How the initial difficulty was met can best be told in General Howard's own words:

The university treasurer showed that the first amount to be paid to Mr. Smith was twenty thousand dollars ($20,000). To meet that and other expenses in starting this enterprise, there was in the hands of the Bureau disbursing officer a residue of "the refugees and freedmen's fund." And as I had the authority of law in the Appropriation Act for March 2, 1867, to use it at my discretion for education, after reflection, I resolved to transfer thirty thousand dollars ($30,000) to the Howard University treasury, and did so by a carefully drawn order dated April 15, 1867. The university treasurer, being duly authorized by the trustees, receipted for the same. Thus the treasurer now had ample means to meet the first payment.

July 2nd of this same year the executive committee of Howard University wrote to the board: The number of lots sold is 245, and their average value, as estimated by Mr. R. M. Hall, their agent, is six hundred dollars ($600) each, and the total value one hundred and forty-seven thousand dollars ($147,000), so that the university treasury was fairly well supplied, as the deferred payments from lots from time to time came in.[98]

The amount realized from the sale of lots amounted to more than $172,000 by 1870, according to General Howard's statement made in answer to charges preferred against him and heard before the Congressional Committee on Education and Labor,[99] showing that the purchase was an excellent investment. The part of the property reserved for educational purposes consisted of the main campus, later occupied by the academic buildings, dormitories, and residences, the site of the Medical School and the old Freedmen's Hospital and a park between the two covering four city blocks.[100]

---

[97] Howard, *op. cit.*, p. 379. [98] *Ibid.*, pp. 400, 401.

[99] *Ho. Ex. Doc.*, 41st Cong., 2nd Sess., No. 121, p. 2.

[100] This park was at one time surrendered to the Federal Government for the remission of back taxes and exemption from further taxation. Later, when the new Freedmen's Hospital was about to be erected on that site the ground was transferred back to the University and leased by the government for a nominal sum.

The main part of the purchase price for the property was supplied by the Freedmen's Bureau, while the funds from the sale of the property not needed for university purposes were placed in the treasury to be used for the construction of buildings.[101] The corporation received additional grants from the Freedmen's Bureau, bringing the sum obtained from this source to about $500,000.[102] With these funds, several residences for professors and four large buildings were erected, namely, University Hall, Miner Hall, Clark Hall, and the Medical Building. Clark Hall, the boys' dormitory, was named in honor of David Clark of Hartford, Connecticut, who contributed $25,000 toward the support of the university. Miner Hall, the dormitory for girls, was named in honor of Miss Myrtilla Miner, one of the pioneers in the education of colored girls in the District of Columbia.[103] The close relationship of Howard University with the Freedmen's Bureau is thus clearly indicated. It should further be noted that after two brief administrations under Dr. Charles B. Boynton and Dr. Byron Sunderland[104] General Howard became president of the university on September 21, 1868, less than two years after its incorporation, and continued to administer its affairs, along with his duties as commissioner of the Freedmen's Bureau, until 1873. Because of this active interest during these early years, General Howard is generally looked upon as the founder of the university which bears his name.

The catalog of the university for 1868–69 shows that from the beginning those in charge actually established the departments called for in the charter and set up standards of admission which they considered justifiable in academic circles. The "Normal and Preparatory Department" in combination prepared students for college and trained them for teaching. In the "Preparatory Course," eleven students were enrolled for that year and in the "Normal Course" twenty-five. The "Model School," consisting of graded classes providing practice facilities for prospective teachers, enrolled 103 pupils. For the combined department, a

---

[101] Patton, *op. cit.*, p. 17.

[102] Among the fifteen charges made against General Howard which led to the investigations already referred to were the following: "First, that he has taken from the appropriations made for, and the receipts of, that bureau more than five hundred thousand dollars, improperly and without authority of law, for the Howard University hospitals and lands. Second, that portions of the land supposed to have been sold for the benefit of the Howard University fund were disposed of improperly to members of his own family and officers of his staff." (*Ho. Reports,* 41st Cong., 2nd Sess., No. 121, *passim.*)   [103] Referred to in footnote 85, page 49.

[104] Patton, *op. cit.*, pp. 26, 27.

faculty of eight persons was provided, two of whom were registered at the same time as college students.[105]

The "College Department," with a faculty consisting of the president and two professors, enrolled only a freshman class of four students.[106] The requirements for admission to the freshman class, however, were about the same as for the standard classical colleges of that period. These requirements, as outlined, were two books of *Caesar*, six orations of *Cicero*, the *Bucolics*, the *Georgics*, six books of Vergil's *Aeneid*, Sallust's *Cataline*, two books of Xenophon's *Anabasis*, and the first two books of Homer's *Iliad*. In addition to these requirements, the student was required to pass examinations in higher arithmetic, algebra to quadratics, the history of Greece and Rome, ancient and modern geography, and English grammar.[107]

It should be noted in passing that these requirements were not peculiar to Howard University among the Negro institutions, but were set up at Fisk University, Atlanta University, and other institutions of similar grade. This fact largely accounts for the paucity of students enrolled in college courses for the first twenty-five years of the existence of these schools, and the large number enrolled in the subcollegiate grades. Because of the absence of public high schools, every institution of higher learning was compelled to prepare its own college students, beginning often with the elementary grades and carrying them through the three-year preparatory courses of highly classical content here described.

In addition to these departments, a law department was in operation in 1868–69, enrolling twenty-one students under a faculty of two; and a medical department with eight students and a faculty of eight.[108] Whereas the original intention of the founders was that the training of preachers should be an important function of the university, no students in this field were enrolled during 1868–69, although some lectures in theology were given and an announcement was made of the intention of the trustees to establish a "Theological Department" in the near future.[109]

The early financial management of the university soon brought it into difficulties. The hopeful spirit of the times and the enthusiasm and faith of those in charge of the enterprise were responsible for the too rapid expansion of the first few years of the

---

[105] *Catalog of Howard University*, 1868–69, pp. 6–10.   [106] *Ibid.*, p. 11.
[107] *Ibid.*, p. 22.   [108] *Ibid.*, pp. 12, 13.   [109] *Ibid.*, p. 35.

existence of the institution which resulted in a constantly growing deficit. A financial statement for the first eight years up to June 30, 1875, leaving out of account the value of lands and buildings given by the government and of borrowed funds, shows receipts of $645,067.30 and expenditures of $744,914.56, leaving a deficit of nearly $100,000.[110] At the annual meeting of the trustees, May 31, 1873, it was decided that a retrenchment of one-half the current expenses would be necessary in order to avert disaster. To effect this the management had to make radical readjustment in the faculties and in the salary schedule. To this end every salaried officer in the university resigned upon the request of the trustees.[111]

In reëstablishing the faculties, the basis was one of rigid economy, the only way by which the institution could be saved; for the nation-wide financial crisis of 1873 and the lean years that followed precluded the possibility of any increase in the income. The success of this measure is indicated by the fact that the academic expenses of the university were reduced from $57,160.40 in 1872 to $9,446.19 in 1877.[112] Former President Patton thus comments upon these drastic measures:

This heroic treatment, far too long delayed, saved the institution, but it cost it much in professors, in students,[113] and in prestige. The vessel escaped shipwreck with loss of many of the crew and passengers and a lot of her cargo. The professional departments were cut off from any support from the general funds, and were limited in expenditures to receipts from tuition fees and special donations. College professorships were reduced in salary from $2,500 to $1,200 and a residence worth $300; and the salaries of other officers were simi-

[110] Patton, *op. cit.*, p. 22.   [111] *Ibid.*   [112] *Ibid.*
[113] The following table, compiled from catalogs for the years indicated, shows the rapid decrease in enrollment during the period of financial stress.

Department	1872–73	1875–76	1876–77
Normal	238	175	97
Preparatory	100	39	18
College	35	33	22
Theological	26	25	32
Law	67	13	6
Medical	45	24	50
Commercial	84	..	..
Music	21	..	..
Total	616	309	225
Duplicates	49		
Net totals	567	309	225

larly lowered. Incidentals were brought down to the lowest living figure, and finally, with half the main building and a large part of the dormitories closed, the point was reached at which the income covered expenses.[114]

When, in 1873, General Howard resigned from the presidency of the university to take up active military duties, the trustees granted him an indefinite leave of absence.[115] At the same meeting it was decided to revive the office of vice-president, which had been discontinued, and John M. Langston, dean of the Law School, was elected to that position.[116] The opinion prevailed that the experiment of placing an able colored man in charge of the university would stimulate both the Negro race and white philanthropists to contribute more generously to the support of the institution. But increased income from outside sources failed to materialize. Convinced that a permanent president must be at once secured, Mr. Langston resigned the vice-presidency in 1875.[117]

The second epoch in the history of the university began when Doctor William W. Patton was elected president in the spring of 1876. His administration, lasting over a term of twelve years, was a period of recovery and consolidation and an era of good feeling. Carefully administering the affairs of the institution, he was able to restore confidence in the minds of the public and of Congress. This accomplished, he felt justified in arguing for federal aid on the ground that through this means alone was it possible to make the best use of the large and expensive plant which the government had already provided. The result was that for the year beginning July 1, 1879, Congress appropriated $10,000 toward current expenses.[118] Since that date federal appropriations have been regularly made toward the support of the university.[119]

The Patton administration, which extended to May 1889, stands out as one of the most important in the history of Howard University, because of two vital contributions: first, the solvency of the university, so seriously threatened, was preserved; second, the Federal Government inaugurated the practice of making

[114] Patton, *op. cit.*, p. 24.

[115] The resignation was accepted the following year after General Howard had been appointed to the command of the Department of the Columbia.

[116] *Minutes of the Board of Trustees*, Dec. 1, 1873.   [117] *Ibid.*, June 16, 1875.

[118] *U. S. Statutes at Large*, Vol. 21, p. 273.

[119] These annual appropriations have not always been unopposed. (See, for example, *Minority Report to Accompany House of Representatives Bill*, 10604, Jan. 21, 1925.)

annual appropriations, which totaled $215,900 during Patton's administration from 1879 to 1889,[120] and marked the beginning of annual grants that have continued for fifty-four years (1933).

The next important era in the evolution of the university began when the Reverend Wilbur P. Thirkield [121] became president in 1906. With keen insight, he realized at the very beginning of his term of office that the great and basic need of the university was material expansion. He saw the necessity of a more extensive plant with modern equipment and served by a larger faculty. He sought, therefore, to bring the university into a still closer alliance with the Federal Government. So successfully was the case presented that during his administration of six years he succeeded in raising the annual congressional appropriations for current expenses from less than $50,000 in 1906 to nearly $100,000 in 1912,[122] the peak for his administration being reached in 1910 with an appropriation of $194,700, which included $80,000 for a science hall. In 1909 a library was erected at a cost of $50,000, the gift of Mr. Andrew Carnegie.

Possibly the most striking result of the educational awakening under President Thirkield was the rapid growth of the college department. In 1876, for example, the roster of the department showed thirty-five students and four graduates. In 1907 the corresponding figures were seventy-five and eight, a gain of about 100 per cent in thirty years. In 1911 these figures had grown to 243 and thirty-one respectively, a gain, during the period of six years covered by this administration, of about 240 per cent in students and nearly 300 per cent in graduates.[123]

In 1918 the Reverend J. Stanley Durkee became president of the university. His inauguration was the beginning of a period of expansion and readjustment that marks his administration of seven years as one of the most significant in the history of the institution. At the beginning of his term of office he effected a

---

[120] Dyson, Walter, *A History of the Federal Appropriations for Howard University.* Howard University Studies in History, No. 8, Nov. 1927, p. 12.

[121] Dr. Thirkield served as the first president of Gammon Theological Seminary, Atlanta, Georgia, from 1883 to 1889, during which time he secured endowment for that institution to the amount of $600,000. He was called to the presidency of Howard after several years of successful service, first as a General Secretary of the Epworth League and later as General Secretary of the Freedmen's Aid and Southern Educational Society of the Methodist Episcopal Church. He resigned the presidency of Howard on his election to the bishopric in the Methodist Episcopal Church.

[122] *Report of the President of Howard University to the Secretary of the Interior,* June 1906, pp. 9–11; *ibid.,* June 1912, p. 13.   [123] See annual catalogs for the years mentioned.

reorganization of the academic work by discontinuing all studies below collegiate grade and organizing all the work of the first two years into a junior college as a basis for an upper division consisting of schools of Applied Science, Commerce and Finance, Education, Journalism, Liberal Arts, and Music.[124] A registrar's office was also set up to centralize the handling of academic records, and the offices of secretary and treasurer were combined under one person.[125] The beginning of graduate work in the academic subjects under a committee on graduate studies was also part of the program of academic improvement.[126] This organization of the academic work was later seen to be too elaborate, and was therefore abandoned in 1925 and the work placed under four colleges, each covering four years.[127] Meanwhile the professional schools remained organized as before.

Definite efforts were made to bring the university before the public generally and to gain the active coöperation of the alumni in promoting the program of expansion.   To this end, the office of field and alumni secretary was established for publicity purposes.[128] Even more significant was the establishment of three alumni trusteeships by act of the board of trustees, one of which is filled each year by the board from three names selected by the alumni.[129]

During his administration, President Durkee succeeded in persuading the Federal Government to increase its appropriations to the university by more than 400 per cent, from $117,937 in 1918–19 to $591,000 in 1925–26.   Included in the appropriations for this period are the sums of $201,000 for a dining hall, $197,500 for a gymnasium and athletic field, and $390,000 for a medical building.[130]   The interest of the General Education Board was also gained to the extent of a contribution of $130,000 to equip the medical building and a conditional pledge of $250,000 toward a $500,000 endowment for the medical school.[131]

In 1921 the College of Liberal Arts was placed on the approved list of the Association of Colleges and Preparatory Schools of the Middle States and Maryland; and during the next year the College of Dentistry was registered by the New York State Board of Regents.[132]

[124] See *Catalog of Howard University*, 1918–19, p. 59.
[125] *Ibid.*, 1919–20, p. 21; also *Minutes of the Board of Trustees*, June 4, 1919.
[126] *Ibid.*, 1920–21, p. 116.   [127] *Ibid.*, 1925–26, pp. 102–15.
[128] *Minutes of the Board of Trustees*, Feb. 8, 1920.   [129] *Ibid.*
[130] *Facts* (pamphlet published by Howard University, 1926), pp. 12, 18.   [131] *Ibid.*, p. 19.
[132] *Ibid.*, p. 16.

The student enrollment from 1919 to 1925 followed the general trend of the period following the World War by increasing rapidly. For 1917–18 there were 1,080 students registered, exclusive of those of sub-collegiate grades and those taking correspondence courses.[133]   In 1925–26, the last year of the Durkee administration, the corresponding figure was 2,123, showing a gain of almost exactly 100 per cent.[134]

After the resignation of President Durkee in 1926, the trustees decided, for the first time in the history of the university, to entrust its direction to a Negro and elected the Reverend Mordecai W. Johnson to the presidency.

The new president realized early in his administration that the greatest immediate need of Howard University was a comprehensive plan of systematic development which would insure the generous financial support of the Federal Government and philanthropy.   The chief obstacle to such a plan was the insecure grounds upon which the federal appropriations to Howard University had rested up to that time.   For, until 1929, there had been no basic legislation permitting such grants.   Hence the Howard University appropriation could be stricken from the Department of the Interior bill, when under consideration, by a point of order raised by any member of Congress who objected to it.

To avoid this embarrassment, Congress passed a law, approved December 13, 1928, which reads as follows:

Be it enacted by the Senate and the House of Representatives of the United States of America in Congress assembled, that section 8 of an act entitled "An Act to incorporate Howard University in the District of Columbia," approved March 2, 1867, be amended to read as follows: Section 8.   Annual appropriations are hereby authorized to aid in the construction, development, improvement, and maintenance of the university, no part of which shall be used for religious instruction.   The university shall at all times be open to inspection by the Bureau of Education and shall be inspected by the said Bureau at least once each year.   An annual report making a full exhibit of the affairs of the university shall be presented to Congress each year in the report of the Bureau of Education.[135]

With the legislative difficulty out of the way, the president was able to persuade the Secretary of the Interior to call a conference, on February 11, 1929, composed of representatives of both houses of Congress, of the United States Bureau of Education, of the

[133] *Catalog of Howard University*, 1917–18, p. 280.   [134] *Ibid.*, 1925–26, p. 405.
[135] *U. S. Statutes at Large*, 70th Cong., Vol. 45, p. 1021.

Bureau of the Budget, of the Julius Rosenwald Fund, and of Howard University. At this conference, a working plan was tentatively established for the development of the university over a period of ten years or more. The plan as recommended by the Office of Education of the Department of the Interior was substantially as follows:

That for a period of ten years, or until the physical plant development program is completed, the Congress of the United States will contribute to the support, maintenance, and development of Howard University, annual sums not to exceed 66.4 per cent of the total budget—the median line percentage of public support now granted to 52 land-grant colleges and universities—it being understood that, immediately after the completion of the physical plant development program, the Trustees will undertake to increase the private endowment of the university at such a rate as, within a period of ten and not to exceed fifteen years, shall reduce the proportion of Government support to less than 50 per cent of the total budget.

That as part of such annual contribution the Federal Government will appropriate an average sum of $1,100,000 toward each of ten successive steps in the physical plant development program of the university—the Trustees of the university to supplement from private contributions or otherwise each such Federal appropriation to the extent of one-third thereof. The use of supplementary funds, however, shall not be restricted necessarily to the project or projects involved in the immediate governmental appropriation.[136]

The unusual world economic situation naturally affected the promotion of the proposed program. Financial pressure halted the growth in enrollment of students with a peak registration of 2,447 students in 1929–30, followed by a rapid decline, thus delaying the program. The tentative agreement, however, indicates the determination on the part of those who control the funds to develop Howard into a university of high standing by supplying and maintaining an adequate physical plant and insuring a steady income large enough to support a staff as numerous and as well trained as is required by the kind of university planned.

During the administration of President Johnson, the university in certain respects has made the greatest advances in its history and in others has moved definitely forward. The total assets of the institution increased from $2,649,803.02 in June 1926 [137] to $7,828,952.90 in June 1932.[138]

[136] *A Report to the Board of Trustees of Howard University and to the Congress of the United States on a Program of Development of Howard University from 1931–32 to 1940–41*, p. 46.

[137] *Howard University Bulletin: Financial Report of Howard University*, 1925–26, Vol. VI, No. 3, pp. 21, 22, Nov. 1926.   [138] *Ibid.*, Vol. XII, No. 5, p. 11, 1933.

Table I, which shows the appropriations made by the Federal Government for Howard University from 1926–27 to 1931–32, strikingly illustrates the upturn in the figures after 1926–27 for which the preceding administration was responsible.

TABLE I

FEDERAL APPROPRIATIONS FOR HOWARD UNIVERSITY FOR FISCAL YEARS
1926–27 TO 1931–32

	Fiscal Year					
	1926–27	1927–28	1928–29	1929–30	1930–31	1931–32
	Congress and Session					
	69th, 1st	69th, 2nd	70th, 1st	70th, 2nd	71st, 1st	71st, 2nd
Salaries..............	$153,000	$150,000	$160,000	$225,000	$350,000	$450,000
General Expenses......	65,000	68,000	80,000	95,000	160,000	225,000
Total Current Expenses...........	$218,000	$218,000	$240,000	$320,000	$510,000	$675,000
Buildings...........	....	150,000	150,000	280,000	739,000	885,000
Total.............	$218,000*	$368,000†	$390,000‡	$600,000§	$1,249,000**	$1,560,000††

* *U. S. Statutes at Large*, Vol. 44, Pt. 1, p. 495. § *Ibid.*, p. 1606.
† *Ibid.*, p. 971. ** *Ibid.*, Vol. 46, Pt. 1, pp. 324, 1159.
‡ *Ibid.*, Vol. 45, Pt. 1, p. 242. †† *Ibid.*

The most significant fact revealed in this table is that the amount allocated for salaries during the period considered increased about 200 per cent, reaching $450,000 for 1931–32. This remarkable increase, resulting in the enlargement of the faculty and the improvement in its quality, touches the work of the university at the vital spot, since the quality of the work done by a school depends upon the quality of its teachers.

Not only were government appropriations increased but the total income of the university was lifted far above any sum received before. For the fiscal year ending June 30, 1926, immediately preceding the Johnson administration, the total income of the university was $682,777.03.[139] The corresponding figures for successive years are: $730,727.76 in 1927;[140] $787,013.56 in 1928;[141]

---

[139] *Howard University Bulletin: Financial Report of Howard University*, Vol. XII, No. 5, p. 11, Nov. 1926.

[140] *Ibid.*, Vol. VII, No. 2, p. 11, Dec. 1927.   [141] *Ibid.*, Vol. VIII, No. 3, p. 11, Dec. 1929.

$735,444.87 in 1929; [142] $915,714.02 in 1930; [143] $1,595,875.71 in 1931; [144] and $1,745,197.55 in 1932.[145]

In 1928-29 the Julius Rosenwald Fund appropriated $80,000 to be distributed over a five-year period for the development of research and graduate study in zoölogy. The General Education Board granted $80,000 to be used over a period of four years for increasing salaries. The Rockefeller Foundation and the Julius Rosenwald Fund gave $29,000 for promoting advanced study by teachers of mathematics and the natural sciences. For the two-year period from 1927 to 1928, the sum of $60,000 was contributed by private sources for the libraries of the university.[146]

Realizing the need of the future extension of the physical plant of the university, the president in 1928 procured grants of $600,000 from the General Education Board and $300,000 from the Julius Rosenwald Fund, a total of $900,000, for the purchase of real

TABLE II *

NUMBER OF STUDENTS ENROLLED AND NUMBER OF GRADUATES IN HOWARD UNIVERSITY, 1931-32

School or College	Number Enrolled	Number of Graduates
College of Liberal Arts............	678	98
College of Education.............	746	131
College of Applied Science........	68	6
School of Music:		
Degree students...............	61	3
Special students...............	21	
School of Medicine:		
College of Medicine............	221	55
College of Dentistry............	53	17
College of Pharmacy............	33	9
School of Law:		
Degree students...............	62	17
School of religion:		
Degree students...............	45	8
Correspondence................	282	
Graduate Division...............	194	18
Total........................	2,464	362

* *Report of the President of Howard University to the Secretary of the Interior for the Fiscal Year Ending June 30, 1932,* p. 1.

[142] *Howard University Bulletin: Financial Report of Howard University,* Vol. IX, No. 3, p. 11, Dec. 1930.   [143] *Ibid.*   [144] *Ibid.,* Vol. XII, No. 5, p. 13, Feb. 1933.   [145] *Ibid.*
[146] *Annual Report of the President of Howard University to the Secretary of the Interior for Fiscal Year Ended June 30, 1929,* p. 4.

estate in the vicinity of the university campus. By 1932 property costing $805,229 had been added to the assets of the university from this fund.[147]

During the administration under consideration, three dormitories for women have been erected at a cost of $729,000 to the Federal Government.[148] Appropriations have also been procured for a chemistry building to cost $390,000; [149] an educational classroom building to cost $460,000; [150] a library to cost $800,000; [151] and a central heating plant to cost $400,000. In addition, have been spent $200,000[152] in beautifying the grounds and $225,000 for the construction of conduits for the distribution of heat and power.[153]

The enrollment of students in Howard University and the number of graduates for 1931–32 distributed by schools and colleges are shown in Table II.

[147] *Annual Report of the President of Howard University to the Secretary of the Interior for Fiscal Year Ended June 30, 1930*, p. 14; 1931, p. 16; 1932, p. 19.
[148] *U. S. Statutes at Large*, Vol. 44, Pt. 2, p. 495; Vol. 45, Pt. 2, p. 904; Vol. 46, Pt. 1, p. 324.
[149] *Ibid.*, Vol. 45, Pt. 1, p. 1606.   [150] *Ibid.*, Vol. 46, Pt. 1, pp. 324, 1151.
[151] *Ibid.*, Vol. 46, Pt. 2, p. 1159.
[152] Special appropriations to relieve unemployment.
[153] *U. S. Statutes at Large*, Vol. 46, Pt. 2, p. 1159.

PART III

THE EMERGENCE OF THE COLLEGE

CHAPTER V

THE DENOMINATIONAL BOARDS

EARLY ATTITUDES OF THE NORTH AND SOUTH RELATIVE TO THE
EDUCATION OF THE NEGRO

As already related, many organizations were engaged in the task of aiding the refugees and freedmen during and immediately following the Civil War. Even before the close of the war, some of these agencies merged for increased efficiency, others went out of existence entirely, while still others continued as permanent organizations for the performance of the more arduous and continuous task of giving to the newly made citizens the opportunity to procure an education extending beyond the rudiments of learning. Such permanent organizations were naturally confined to those representing the religious denominations which were themselves permanent and which considered it a duty to give the Negro a chance, through Christian education, to rise in the human scale. The Northern religious bodies which were most prominent in the pursuit of this objective at the beginning of this crusade and which are most largely responsible for the establishment and maintenance of the colleges for Negroes that exist today are the Congregationalists, the Baptists, the Methodists, and the Presbyterians. Several other Northern denominational bodies promoted schools of sub-collegiate grade and in recent years the Protestant Episcopal Church and the Roman Catholic Church have expanded their educational program for Negroes to include four years of college work.[1] Several Negro denominational boards have also established and maintained schools, some even before the Civil War, which developed into colleges. These include the African Methodist Episcopal Church, the African Methodist

---

[1] Saint Augustine's College at Raleigh, N. C., established by the Protestant Episcopal Church in 1867, has become, in recent years, a four-year college. In 1915 the Xavier High School, a Catholic institution in New Orleans, purchased the plant of Southern University, the state school for Negroes, which had moved to Baton Rouge. In 1917 a normal department was opened and in 1925 it was expanded into a teachers college and a college of liberal arts with a curriculum covering four years.

Episcopal Zion Church, the Colored Methodist Episcopal Church, and the Negro Baptist Conventions.[2]

The objectives and procedures of the boards representing the Northern denominational organizations in dealing with the freedmen must be interpreted and evaluated in view of the social obligation implied in Christian duty as they saw it. The difficulties which they encountered in the form of opposition and criticism must be taken as the result of the different social philosophy with reference to the Negro which was prevalent in the South at the close of the Civil War. It must be remembered that the ending of the war and the defeat of the South left bitterness and resentment on the one side and on the other elation and a feeling that the North was the champion of a great cause not yet completed. As has been shown, the North felt that the disappointed Southerners would vent their resentment upon the defenceless Negroes if protection were withdrawn. The leaders of that section, whatever they had felt about the Negro when the war began, had naturally become anti-slavery by the end of the conflict and were, for the most part, zealous in their desires to protect him. This attitude was extremely irritating to the South in all of its manifestations and in none more so than that concerning the education of the Negroes. This means that, making due allowance for many exceptions, there was in general a complete divergence of opinion between the North and South on this subject. The beliefs of the North in general, as expressed by the missionary bodies of the churches and the Freedmen's Bureau, can fairly be stated as follows: First, the Negro, having been rescued from the hell of slavery and two and a half centuries of unrequited toil, was worthy of everything the nation could bestow upon him by way of recompense, including citizenship and all the necessary means to meet its requirements.[3] Second, it was the plain duty of a Chris-

---

[2] Jones, Thomas Jesse, *Negro Education: A Study of the Private and Higher Schools for Colored People in the United States.* U. S. Bureau of Education Bulletin, 1916, No. 38, pp. 303ff. (Cited hereafter as *U. S. Bur. of Ed. Bul.*)

[3] At the annual meetings of the denominational boards during the decade following the Civil War, this view was frequently stressed in such terms as these, "The Freedmen, though of African origin, have for the most part been born on our soil (and) reared under our institutions. . . . Their injuries appeal to our sense of justice, we must not forget that we are implicated in slavery. Our fathers covenanted to protect it. . . . The benefits they have conferred upon us appeal to our gratitude. By their unpaid toil they and their fathers contributed largely to the wealth of our country. By their aid during the rebellion they contributed to the preservation of the Union. . . ." (*Annual Report of the Freedmen's Aid Society of the M. E. Church*, 1868, p. 14, Address of Bishop Thompson.)

tian nation to discharge this obligation to the freedmen promptly by providing them with the same means of mental and moral development that has proved effectual in the advance of white people.[4] Third, the Negro possessed the same mental capacity as the white man, his apparent mental inferiority being due to the debasing effect of slavery.[5] Fourth, without education the freedmen would rapidly degenerate and become a national menace not only to the South but to the entire nation.[6] Fifth, the South had neither the means nor the inclination to offer to the Negro the educational opportunities that he needed and deserved to fit him for citizenship.[7] Sixth, on the above assumptions, the people in the North must of necessity undertake to promote the education of the Negro in the South.

The South, on the other hand, held mixed views on the subject, practically all of which, in the beginning, opposed those held by the Northern philanthropists. Its position may fairly be described as follows: First, the ignorant whites opposed any kind of education for the Negro because they themselves were ignorant and unschooled and could not bear the idea of the Negro receiving education which had been, up to that time, the prerogative of the

---

[4] But in addition to all this, the freedmen have a still stronger claim upon us. They have for centuries been wronged by us; stolen from their homes, sold in the shambles like cattle, degraded by slavery, their earnings wrested from them, the relations of husband and wife, parent and child trampled in the dust, their souls shut up in ignorance and everything dear to their hearts and their homes ruthlessly crushed. We have participated in these flagrant crimes, and we are involved in this terrible guilt.

"Let us atone for our sins, as much as possible, by furnishing schools and the means of improvement for the children, upon whose parents we have inflicted such fearful evils. Let us lend a helping hand in their escape from the degradation into which we have forced them by our complicity with oppressors. Justice, stern justice, demands this at our hands. Let us pay the debt we owe this race before we complain of weariness in the trifling sums we have given for schools and churches." (*Annual Report of Freedmen's Aid Society of the M. E. Church*, 1871, p. 15.)

[5] "This society (in connection with similar organizations) has demonstrated to the South that the freedmen possess good intellectual abilities and are capable of becoming good scholars. Recognizing the brotherhood of mankind and knowing that intellect does not depend upon the color of the skin nor the curl of the hair, we never doubted the Negro's ability to acquire knowledge, and distinguish himself by scholarly attainments. But the South did, or pretended to doubt it. The Southern people have been so long familiar with the degradation of the slave, that it was slow to abandon the long cherished view of the inferiority of the race." (*Board of Managers of the Freedmen's Aid Society of the M. E. Church, Annual Report*, 1873, pp. 12, 13.)

[6] "Patriotism, philanthropy and religion with united voice, urge us to consider this subject, and make provisions that this calamity which threatens us may be averted. Four millions of ignorant citizens in a national crisis may wreck the Republic. . . . This people . . . if neglected and left in ignorance will fall an easy prey to wicked and designing men, and become a terrible scourge to the nation." (Rust, R. S., *Annual Report of Freedmen's Aid Society*, 1872, p. 40.)

[7] See *Ho. Ex. Docs.*, 39th Cong., 1st Sess., No. 118, for expressions of this attitude in Congress.

upper class.[8]   Second, the better class of whites in the South realized that some kind of education should be given to the Negro, but believed that the nature of this education should be determined by the South and that the teaching should be done at the first by Southern white people and later by the Negroes themselves.[9]   Third, there was a strong feeling in the minds of the Southerners that the Northern teachers in the missionary schools were teaching the Negroes not only to aspire to social equality but to distrust and hate the white people of the South among whom they would have to live.[10]   Such influences they naturally looked upon as detrimental to the best interests of both races in that section and particularly harmful to the Negroes in their newly found freedom.

Assuming the fairness of this comparison of the attitudes of the two sections at the close of the Civil War, it is likely that if there had been no Northern philanthropy there would probably have been no Negro college in the South until a transformation had taken place in the attitude of the white South on this subject, which, without the examples furnished by the Northern religious bodies, would have required a much longer period of time than was actually the case.   For, although some Southern men of broad vision and large sympathy toward the Negro from the very first gave their efforts and their influence in offering the freedmen a chance educationally, none at that early date seems to have left a record to the effect that he favored college education for Negroes. Since it could hardly have been otherwise under the circumstances, no individual Southerner can be held blameworthy for an attitude which was the necessary result of his social and cultural environment.   The point is clear, at any rate, that however mistaken the Northern denominational bodies may have been in their educational theories, without their zeal the Negro race would have been lacking the leadership which the first generation out of slavery

[8] Frequent resorts to violence were usually ascribed to this class, and jealousy was often given as the reason. See Brown, W. W., *The Lower South*, p. 217; *Sen. Ex. Docs.*, 39th Cong., 1st Sess., No. 27, pp. 108–20; Alvord, J. W., *Report of Assistant Commissioner of the Freedmen's Bureau*, Jan. 1868, p. 8; July, 1868, pp. 13, 24, 27.

[9] *Report of Joint Committee on Reconstruction*, Pt. I, p. 112; Pt. II, pp. 74, 87, 115, 126, 130, 137, 165, 232, 290, 343.

[10] "When the combat was over and the 'Yankee' schoolma'ams followed in the train of the Northern armies, the business of educating the Negroes was a continuation of hostilities against the vanquished South, and was so regarded to a considerable extent on both sides." (Bacon, Alice M., *The Negro and the Atlanta Exposition*, Occasional Papers, Trustees of the John F. Slater Fund, No. 7, p. 6.)

furnished, the greater part of which was the product of these schools.[11]

DIFFERENT EVALUATIONS OF THE SOCIAL EFFECTS OF THE WORK OF THE DENOMINATIONAL COLLEGE

Since it is impossible at the present time to make reliable measurements of the gross social effect of an institution through a considerable period of time, it is not surprising to find that there exists, even today, a wide diversity of opinion relative to the value of the service of the Negro colleges founded and fostered by the church boards and offering orthodox classical curricula. In illustration of this diversity, several extracts are quoted from published expressions of mature students of this subject.

In the following statement, from the pen of a Negro, the schools in question are pronounced a failure:

The instruction of the freedmen was first undertaken in the fall of 1861, under the guidance of many noble, self-sacrificing white men and women from the North, who unfortunately began their labors under the false notion that their Negro pupils, with centuries of mental density behind them, should be taught by the same methods and along the same lines as Northern white children of intelligent ancestry environed with more or less cultured homes. The result has been that a series of misfortunes have ensued, all too apparent to intelligent and impartial observers. The chief blunder, however, and the one which has inflicted lasting harm upon the freedmen, was committed when religious bigotry and sectarian rivalry, casting aside all notions of the Negro's welfare, decreed his ethical and mental spoliation. This conclusion is obviously just; for when the war ended and reconstruction began, there sprang up all over the South sectarian universities, colleges, academies, institutes, and seminaries, in name, but not in efficiency, which have since proved a delusion and a snare to the cause of enlightment.

To test the correctness of the foregoing statement, we need only refer to the fact that Atlanta, Georgia, has 7 Negro institutions of learning; Nashville, Tennessee, 4; and New Orleans, Louisiana, 4; and that out of these 15 institutions, the Congregationalists control 4, the Baptists 4, and the Methodists 5 schools, with all of them constantly engaged in a factional warfare for supremacy in influence and patronage. An analysis of the latest statistics of these several institutions conclusively substantiates our contention that academic training for the Negro masses, at this state of their development, is detrimental to the best interests of the race.[12]

---

[11] A study of the leadership furnished by college trained Negroes was made by W. E. B. DuBois and published by Atlanta University in 1900. This study, in practically complete form, is reprinted under the title "The College Bred Negro" in the *Report of the United States Commissioner of Education*, 1902, I, 19–229. It forms an excellent appraisal of the effects of higher education upon the Negro up to the turn of the century.

[12] Thomas, William H., *The American Negro*, 1901, pp. 240, 241.

The figures given in the second paragraph of the above quotation were true when written and certainly point out a weakness in the management of the colleges for Negroes. The fact that there are too many schools in one place, however, hardly justifies the author in condemning wholesale the educational value of the denominational colleges for Negroes.

The next appraisal is given by a white man who is a trained scholar, and evidently very sympathetic toward the cause of the Negro. In one of his best works on the Negro he disposes of the service rendered by the Negro colleges fostered and supported by the denominational boards in these words:

The work of even the best schools conducted along sectarian and classical lines was barren of results; they contributed practically nothing to the real education of the Negroes nor to the improvement of the social and economic conditions of the race. The whole movement, particularly the bringing of Northern Negro churches into the South, widened the breach between the races, intensified race hatred, and increased the social and cultural isolation of the Negroes.[13]

The opposite view is taken by one of the leading Negro thinkers and writers of his day who himself has experienced the effect of the influence of the Negro college and, through its agency, has in turn affected the lives of thousands of students. He says:

Again, the higher education should be encouraged because of the moral impotency of all the modes of education which do not touch and stir the human spirit. It is folly to suppose that the moral nature of the child is improved because it has been taught to read and write and cast up accounts, or to practice a handicraft. Tracing the letters of the alphabet has no bearing upon the Golden Rule. The spelling of words by sound and syllable does not lead to the observance of the Ten Commandments. Drill in the multiplication table does not fascinate the learner with the Sermon on the Mount. Rules in grammar, dates in history, sums in arithmetic, and points in geography do not strengthen the grasp on moral truth. The ability to saw to a line or hit a nail aplomb with a hammer does not create a zeal for righteousness and truth. It is only when the pupil comes to feel the vitalizing power of knowledge that it begins to react upon the life and to fructify in character. This is especially true of a backward race whose acquisitive power outruns its apperceptive faculty.[14]

The opinion of another well-known Negro writer is set forth at length in a statement based upon an objective study of the Negro

---

[13] Reuter, Edward B., *The American Race Problem*, p. 266.
[14] Miller, Kelly, in *From Servitude to Service*, pp. 24–25.

college graduate made in 1901.[15]   One passage is particularly appropriate here.

All men cannot go to college, but some men must; every isolated group or nation must have its yeast, must have for the talented a few centers of training where men are not so mystified and befuddled by the hard and necessary toil of earning a living, as to have no aims higher than their bellies, and no God greater than Gold.   This is true training, and thus in the beginning were the favored sons of the freedmen trained.   Out of the colleges of the North came, after the blood of war, Ware, Cravath, Chase, Andrews, Bumstead and Spence to build the foundations of knowledge and civilization in the black South.   Where ought they to have begun to build?   At the bottom, of course, quibbles the mole with his eyes in the earth.   Aye! truly at the bottom, at the very bottom; at the bottom of knowledge, down in the very depths of knowledge there where the roots of justice strike into the lowest soil of Truth.   And so they did begin; they founded colleges, and up from the colleges shot normal schools, and out from the normal schools went teachers, and around the normal teachers clustered other teachers to teach the public schools; the college trained in Greek and Latin and mathematics, 2,000 men; and these men trained full 50,000 others in morals and manners, and they in turn taught thrift and the alphabet to nine millions of men, who today hold $300,000,000 of property.   It was a miracle—the most wonderful peace-battle of the 19th century, and yet today men smile at it, and in fine superiority tell us that it was all a strange mistake. . . .[16]

Thousands of Negroes in America today can give similar testimony, from their own experiences, in justification of the investment which has been made in the Negro college.   In the absence of an objective scale upon which to base our estimates, the judgment of those who have been affected must carry considerable weight.   It must be remembered that the value of college education in America as a whole has again and again been decried and unfavorably criticized for its futility on no better basis than a feeling or even a prejudice.   It would be too much to expect that the group of schools under consideration should escape unscathed.

The opinion of the General Education Board relative to the work of the Negro college prior to the year 1914 is of value because that organization had been definitely studying the situation with the object of giving financial assistance for its improvement. Referring to the denominational colleges its opinion was that:

These schools have, with varying degrees of success, rendered a large service, particularly in the training of teachers for the public schools and in the training of colored ministers.   In some cases they have developed colleges which will form the nucleus of a system of schools for the higher education of the Negroes.

[15] DuBois, W. E. B., "The Talented Tenth," in *The Negro Problem, A Symposium* (1903) pp. 33 ff.   [16] *Ibid.*, pp. 46, 47.

Any discussion of Negro education must recognize the disinterested motives of these organizations and the importance and value of schools maintained by them.[17]

The case of the Negro college has been tersely set forth and justified by a successful graduate of one of these colleges in the following words:

The exigencies of a peculiar social order have set apart in a world of its own one-tenth of our entire population. Although shunted off into a caste-world by itself and denied opportunities of contact with the best political, social, moral, and religious influences, this class is judged as strictly and by the same standards and responsibilities of citizenship as the more favored nine-tenths. Strangely enough, these people do not complain of the inequity of being so judged; they only demand a fair chance to prepare for the exacting test. In self-defense they say what is true, even if trite, that our American experiment in democracy is destined to become a mockery, unless we shall educate, measurably to his responsibility, every citizen of the country.

Since the World War, due to the unprecedented numbers seeking admission, all colleges of quality have proceeded on a basis of selective enrollment. The classes suggested for exclusion invariably have been those whose weakness could invite discrimination with impunity. Obviously, the Negro student was the first to be affected. For most young Negroes seeking a college education this means Negro colleges or nothing. But there is not one Negro college of real worth and standing to each million Negroes in the country. Of the half dozen Negro colleges which in recent years have emerged from "glorified high schools," scarcely one has yet reached the standards required for the full and adequate discharge of its obligations to the Negro Youth.

In spite of the continuing movement of Negro population which will result in a substantial redistribution thereof in the next decade, a very large proportion of the twelve million colored folk will remain permanently in the South. Although great strides have been made in recent years, the South as a whole has yet done very little toward providing a college education for Negroes. Therefore, the Negro college must depend chiefly upon Northern philanthropists for its support. This will be so until the colored people themselves are economically able to assist more substantially in providing for their own education. At the same time, it is worth noting that students at Talladega College, for example, pay a larger proportion of the cost of their education than do the students of Yale or Harvard.

For a long time the secondary school was the weakest link in the chain of Southern education. More recently, there has been an awakening. The movement for standard high schools, backed by nearly every Southern state, is gradually putting secondary education within the reach even of the Negro boys and girls. Unless the college at once becomes a correlated part of a whole and effective educational scheme, these increasing numbers of Negro high school graduates will find themselves in the traditional blind alley.

Shall the Negro group be led by trained or untrained leaders? Shall the

17 *The General Education Board, An Account of Its Activities, 1902–1914*, p. 191.

social, religious, and economic concerns of the Negro people be committed to competent or incompetent hands? The answers to these questions in terms of service are the high call to the Negro college. . . .[18]

We will now consider, in more detail, the work of several of the denominational boards in order to trace their origins and to note their activities in the early efforts at educating the Negro, their sources of support, and their policies relative to the whole question of the higher education of the freedmen. In the section on the American Missionary Association, which comes first, much material is included which is typical of the work of the other boards and need not be repeated. For this reason the treatment of the work of this board is more extensive than those which follow.

[18] Crawford, George W., *The Case for the Negro College.* (Circular issued by the American Missionary Association, 1930.)

CHAPTER VI

THE AMERICAN MISSIONARY ASSOCIATION

ORIGIN

THE American Missionary Association,[1] since its organization, has always been actively engaged in efforts to better the condition of the Negro race in America, first, as an anti-slavery crusader; then, as an agency of relief during the Civil War and the period immediately following; and finally, as an effective educational organization operating a chain of schools at strategic points throughout the South. Its work on behalf of Negroes, however, has not been the exclusive interest of the Association during its existence, for, in the United States, it has been active among the mountain whites in the South, the people of the far Southwest, the Indians of the Northwest, and the Negroes in Africa. The interest of this study in the activities of this organization is due chiefly to the place of paramount importance which it holds among the agencies responsible for the establishment and development of those schools in the South which have become the institutions of higher learning for Negroes.

The origin of the Association can be traced to four earlier bodies, each of which made its peculiar contribution to the merger and helped to give it character. These are The Amistad Committee, The Union Missionary Society, The Committee for the West Indian Missions, and The Western Evangelical Missionary Society for Work among the American Indians.

The Amistad case [2] was distinctly a slavery issue and served to focus the attention of an influential group of Americans upon the evils of the system.[3] In 1836 a Spanish slave vessel, *L'Amistad*, was taken in charge by Lieutenant Gedney of the brig *Washington* of the United States Navy off the coast of Long Island. On

[1] In citation the abbreviation A. M. A. will be used instead of the full name, American Missionary Association.

[2] Barless, Ellen Strong, *The Amistad Captives, An Old Conflict Between Spain and America.* (Typewritten copy in the library of the central office of the A. M. A., 287 Fourth Avenue, New York City.)   [3] Beard, A. F., *A Crusade of Brotherhood*, pp. 23–29.

board were two Spaniards and forty-two Africans. One of the Spaniards claimed the Africans as his property. The latter had mutinied, killed the captain, imprisoned the crew, taken charge of the ship, and attempted to sail back to Africa whence they had been stolen. The entire company of men, women, and children were arrested on the charge of mutiny and imprisoned at New Haven. The case, because of its unusual circumstances and conflicting claims, aroused the intense interest of a group of distinguished citizens who organized themselves in New York as The Amistad Committee for the purpose of protecting the legal interests of the accused and making provisions for their care during the trial. John Quincy Adams, former President of the United States, though advanced in age, acted as counsel for the defense in association with Roger S. Baldwin. After carrying the case through the lower courts, the freedom of the Negroes was finally won by a decision of the Supreme Court of the United States in March 1841, at the end of two years of litigation.[4] The Negroes were returned to Africa the following November under the care of three American missionaries sent by the committee. The Amistad Committee, after the conclusion of the case, was merged with the Union Missionary Society, a body formed at Hartford, Connecticut, with an anti-slavery aim. The three missionaries with the Amistad captives founded a missionary station at Kaw Mendi, West Africa.[5]

The Committee for the West Indian Missions was organized in Connecticut in 1844 for the purpose of giving support and encouragement to the efforts of the Reverend Davis S. Ingraham, of what was then known as Oberlin Collegiate Institute, in Ohio, to establish a self-supporting missionary post in Jamaica for the recently emancipated Negroes of that island.[6] The Western Evangelical Missionary Society was founded by the Western Reserve Association in 1843 for the purpose of promoting evangelical work among the Indians of Minnesota territory. This work was fostered also by Oberlin students who volunteered for this humanitarian undertaking.[7] At a meeting held in Albany, New York, in September 1847, the Union Missionary Society and the Committee for the West Indian Missions were merged under the title The

---

[4] A complete account of this case which forms such an important chapter in the history of slavery in its legal aspects is given in *6 Peters U. S. Reports*, pp. 518–98.

[5] A. M. A., *An. Rep.*, 1867, p. 10.   [6] *Ibid.*, 1847, p. 5.   [7] *Ibid.*, 1847, p. 5.

American Missionary Association.[8]   Two years later the Western
Evangelical Missionary Society completed the merger by trans-
ferring its work to the association.[9]   The following is a list of the
first officers of the new corporation: President, William Jackson,
Massachusetts; Vice-Presidents, F. D. Parish, Ohio; David
Thurston, Maine; C. D. Cleveland, Pennsylvania; J. W. C.
Pennington, Connecticut; Samuel R. Ward, New York; Corre-
sponding Secretary, George Whipple, New York; Recording
Secretary, Simeon S. Jocelyn, New York; Treasurer, Lewis Tap-
pan, New York.[10]

The effect of the merger was to launch the new organization
with more extensive interests and better direction than might
have been otherwise possible; for it not only began its work with
considerable volume but also received from its component parts a
variety of attitudes.   All elements agreed, however, upon certain
essential social and religious concepts.   These were: the demo-
cratic belief in the basic equality of human beings; the Christian
belief in the brotherhood of man; and the ethical belief in the in-
justice of human slavery.   Because of these fundamental beliefs
already incorporated in the parts that composed it, the American
Missionary Association knew its own mind from the beginning
and escaped the necessity of spending much time in the establishment of principles to determine its attitudes upon the fundamental
problems of human relationship.   Another advantage which it
held over many other benevolent organizations, one which sprang
into existence at the outbreak of the Civil War, was that it had
been in the missionary field long before that time and hence was in
possession of a well-tested machinery when the great call to service
came from the South.

As early as 1848 the executive committee had established a fund
for distributing bibles among the slaves, expressing the belief that
"no effectual opposition will be made in Kentucky to a general
distribution of the bible to our brethren in bonds." [11]   This action
indicated an interest in the welfare of the slaves at that early date.
Indeed, the organization was definitely anti-slavery [12] when that

---

[8] *Ibid.*, 1847, pp. 5, 6.   [9] *Ibid.*, 1867, p. 11.   [10] *Ibid.*, 1848, p. 3.
[11] *Ibid.*, 1846, pp. 22, 23.

[12] At its fourth annual meeting in 1850, among the resolutions adopted by the Association was
one denying the justice of the fugitive slave law and declaring the determination of the Association to disobey its provisions.   It reads as follows: "*Resolved,* that we believe the Christianity
of the nation is about to be tested, in view of the late act of Congress for recovery of fugitive
slaves, which appears equally at variance with the principles of the Association, the Constitution

movement was very unpopular and, at a time when many church-men were silent on the subject of slavery, took a very definite stand which it maintained in the face of abuse and censure.[13] For the dissemination of opinion against slavery was one of the expressly stipulated objects of the organization.[14] In its constitution it provided that active membership should be confined to those not holders of slaves or engaged in the "practice of any other im-moralities."[15] In another article it is declared that a part of its work shall be "particularly to discountenance slavery by refusing to receive the fruits of unrequited labor or to welcome to its fellow-ship those who hold their fellow beings as slaves."[16]

BEREA COLLEGE

During the twelve years intervening between the organization of the association and the beginning of the war, its activity was mainly outside the fifteen slave states. During that time it maintained itself as a general missionary association of those evangelical denominations that wished to work through its agency. In the home department in 1860, of 112 agents only fifteen were located in the slave states and Kansas.[17] The latter, however, represented the beginning of determined efforts, while slavery still existed, to organize churches and schools in the South on an anti-slavery basis and, as a result, gave rise to some of the most stirring events in the history of the association.

Berea College is the outgrowth of the work of one of the most valiant and persistent of these agents, and its story is unique in the history of American colleges. "Berea has proven the practicabil-ity of the ideal," wrote William G. Frost, its president from 1892 to 1920. "On the old soil of slavery it freely admitted white and colored students and taught them in the same classes without contamination and reproach."[18] The person most responsible for its founding was the Reverend John Gregg Fee,[19] a native of

---

of the Country, and the Law of God, and that as Christians we do solemnly covenant with each other and our colored brethren that we cannot obey it, nor any law that contravenes the higher law of our Maker, whatever persecution or penalty we may be called to suffer." (Resolution 10, Minutes of the 4th Annual Meeting of A. M. A., *An. Rep.*, 1850, pp. 10–11.)

[13] For an extended account of early anti-slavery activity of the association, see Beard, *op. cit.*, Ch. VI.   [14] A. M. A., *An. Rep.*, 1849, pp. 34, 35. "Constitution," Art. VIII.

[15] *Ibid.*, Art. III.   [16] *Ibid.*, Art. VIII.   [17] A. M. A., *An. Rep.*, 1860, p. 41.

[18] Frost, William G., "Berea College," in *From Servitude to Service*, p. 52.

[19] A most interesting sketch of Fee as a crusader in the cause of freedom is included in *Brown America*, a book by Edwin R. Embree, a grandson of Fee and president of the Julius Rosenwald Fund.

Kentucky, the son of a slaveholder, and an anti-slavery crusader of the most persistent type. He attended Lane Seminary in Cincinnati, where he became so thoroughly imbued with the anti-slavery spirit that he determined to consecrate himself to the cause of the freedom of men and the freedom of speech, whatever the cost.[20] He writes:

> In this consecration—this death to the world—I also made up my mind to accept all that should follow. Imperfect as has been my life, I do not remember that, in all my after difficulties, I had to consider anew the question of property, of comfort, of social position, of apparel, of personal safety, of giving life itself. The latter I regarded as even probable.[21]

As a result of this resolve he broke permanently with his father, who denounced him as disloyal and unfilial.[22] Failing in his attempt to build anti-slavery churches in his native county, he went to Madison County in the center of the state at the invitation of Cassius M. Clay,[23] a Southern abolitionist who had purchased a large tract of land in that mountainous region for the purpose of settlement. In 1858 we find Fee entering upon his crusade in the vicinity of Berea, founding churches and opening a school.[24]

Fee applied to the American Missionary Association for a commission as agent, which was granted in October 1848.[25] In a letter to the official organ of the association a few months after being commissioned he writes from Kentucky:

> My most sanguine expectations three years since did not anticipate such freedom of speech as we now have, nor did I expect to see such progress among the people in anti-slavery sentiment.
> Our congregations are regularly increasing in size and interest. The general impression through the community now is that an anti-slavery church can exist and prosper in a slave state. We have peace and can circulate anti-slavery documents with great readiness.[26]

The association sent other workers to aid in the enterprise, among them Dr. J. A. R. Rodgers, an Oberlin man, who became the principal of the school.[27] The little academy in the mountains soon attracted such favorable notice and became so popular that many slaveholders sent their children to it.[28] The work was not promoted, however, without great opposition. Those in

[20] Fee, John G., *Autobiography*, pp. 13, 14.   [21] *Ibid.*, p. 15.   [22] *Ibid.*, pp. 20, 26.
[23] *Ibid.*, pp. 90–93.   [24] *Ibid.*, pp. 94, 95.   [25] *Ibid.*, p. 56; A. M. A., *An. Rep.*, 1848, p. 27.
[26] See also Fee's letters in A. M. A., *An. Rep.*, 1850, p. 35; 1851, p. 43; 1854, pp. 72, 73; 1855, pp. 75, 76, 77.   [27] Fee, John G., *Autobiography*, p. 125.   [28] Frost, *op. cit.*, p. 56.

charge repeatedly were threatened and insulted by slavery advocates who opposed their program. As the South became increasingly alarmed at the boldness of the whole anti-slavery movement, threats changed into actual persecution and insults turned to physical violence, especially when Negro students were encouraged to enroll on equal terms with the whites. The school was repeatedly broken up and the teachers dispersed.[29] Fee, however, seemed undaunted and actually proposed to the Association in 1857 the founding of a College at Berea. In that year he wrote,

Free churches and free schools can be sustained. We want teachers, but Christian teachers, who shall labor to redeem their pupils from all sin.

We need a college here which shall be to Kentucky what Oberlin is to Ohio, an anti-slavery, anti-caste, anti-tobacco, anti-sectarian school—a school under Christian influence; a school that will furnish the best possible facilities for those of small means who have energy of character that will lead them to work their way through this world. I know places where improved lands and comparatively new can be bought from ten or twelve dollars per acre. . . . Three or four hundred acres would secure a village, a home for a colony. . . . The place for the college is here in the interior of Kentucky.[30]

By the end of 1858 Berea College had been organized with the motto "God has made of one blood all nations of men," and with the avowed intention of continuing the "coeducation of the races." [31] Fee became chairman of the board and Rogers, president. Some funds were received from the American Missionary Association and other sources and the unique educational experiment seemed fairly launched.[32] Fee then went North for the purpose of raising money and procuring funds for the school. The John Brown affair at Harper's Ferry, however, proved the signal for the beginning of further persecution. Fee was accused of endorsing if not actually aiding in the promotion of such schemes as Brown's.[33] As a result, Berea was threatened by a mob and the whole college community was compelled to flee for safety across the Ohio River.[34]

During the course of the war, the activities of the college were naturally suspended, but after its close in 1865 the work was re-

[29] A. M. A., *An. Rep.*, 1858, p. 48.   [30] *The American Missionary*, March 1857, pp. 65, 66. [31] The first by-law declared, "The object of this college shall be to furnish the facilities for thorough education of all persons of good moral character." The second by-law, more specific, reads as follows: "This college shall be under an influence strictly Christian, and as such opposed to sectarianism, slave-holding, caste, and every other wrong institution or practice: Opposition to caste meant the coeducation of the (so-called) 'races.'" (From Fee's *Autobiography*, pp. 138, 139.)   [32] Fee, *op. cit.*, p. 146.   [33] *Ibid.*, p. 147.   [34] *Ibid.*, pp. 148, 149.

established under the presidency of E. H. Fairchild, also a product
of Oberlin.   Relieved of the menace of mob violence, the school
moved steadily forward with Negroes and whites mingled together, practically without friction.[35]   For thirty-nine years this
fellowship of intelligence and spirit continued.   During that time
the colored students numbered from one hundred to two hundred,
scattered throughout the entire range of classes.[36]   The Legislature
of Kentucky, however, ended the bi-racial experiment abruptly in
1904, by passing a law forbidding the mingling of the races in the
same department of any institution of learning.[37]

The college authorities did not meekly acquiesce in this attack
upon the principles which they had built up through so many
years and this negation of the victories which had been won at
such sacrifice.   The case was fought in the courts by the college
but without success, the Supreme Court of the United States
handing down an adverse decision in 1904.   A dissenting opinion
made by Justice Harlan, who supported the contention of the
college that the police power of a state did not extend to the point
of separating the races in privately supported educational institutions, reads in part as follows:

In the view which I have as to my duty I feel obliged to express my opinion
as to the validity of the act as a whole.   I am of the opinion that in its essential
parts, the statute is an arbitrary invasion of the rights of liberty and property
guaranteed by the Fourteenth Amendment against hostile state action and is,
therefore, void. . . . The capacity to impart instruction to others is given

[35] Frost, *op. cit.*, p. 57.   [36] *Ibid.*, p. 62.
[37] The law as enacted reads:

1. That it shall be unlawful for any person, corporation, or association of persons, to maintain
or operate any college, school or institution where persons of the white and negro races are both
received as pupils for instruction, and any person or corporation who shall operate or maintain
any such college, school or institution, shall be fined $1,000, and any person or corporation who
may be convicted of violating the provisions of this act shall be fined $100 for each day they may
operate said college, school or institution, after such conviction.

2. That any instructor who shall teach in any school, college or institution, when members of
said two races are received as pupils for instruction, shall be guilty of operating and maintaining
same, and fined as provided in the first section hereof.

3. It shall be unlawful for any white person to attend any school or institution, where negroes
are received as pupils or receive instruction, and it shall be unlawful for any negro or colored
person to attend any school or institution where white persons are received as pupils or receive
instruction.   Any person so offending shall be fined $50 for each day he attends such institution
or school.   Provided that the provisions of this law shall not apply to any penal institution or
house of reform.

4. Nothing in this act shall be construed to prevent any private school, college or institution
of learning from maintaining a separate and distinct branch thereof, in a different locality, not
less than twenty-five miles distant, for the education of one race or color.

5. This act shall not take effect or be in operation before the fifteenth day of July 1904.
(*Acts of the General Assembly of the Commonwealth of Kentucky*, 1904, Ch. 85, pp. 181, 182.)

by the Almighty for beneficent purposes and its use may not be forbidden or interfered with by Government—certainly not, unless such instruction is in itself harmful to the public morals or imperils the public safety. . . . If pupils, of whatever race—certainly if they be citizens—choose with the consent of their parents or voluntarily to sit together in a private institution of learning while receiving instruction which is not in its nature harmful or dangerous to the public, no government, whether federal or state, can legally forbid their coming together, or being together temporarily, for such an innocent purpose. . . .[38]

Again, if the view of the highest court of Kentucky be sound, that commonwealth may, without infringing the Constitution of the United States, forbid the association in the same private school of pupils of the Anglo-Saxon and Latin races, respectively, or pupils of the Christian and Jewish faiths, respectively. Have we become so inoculated with prejudice of race that an American government, professedly based on the principle of freedom, and charged with the protection of all citizens alike, can make distinctions between such citizens in the matter of their voluntary meeting for innocent purposes simply because of their respective races? . . . Many other illustrations might be given to show the mischievous, not to say cruel, character of the statute in question and how inconsistent such legislation is with the great principle of the equality of citizens before the law.[39]

The white students of Berea, after the separation had become effective at the opening of school in 1904, addressed themselves to their former Negro college mates in a resolution expressing deep sympathy for them and condemning the law as unjust.[40]

The story of Fee and the account of Berea College are given here for the purpose of calling attention to the first opportunity of Negroes to attend college in the states where slavery existed and of presenting a typical experience of those who were pioneers in

---

[38] Dissenting opinion of Justice Harlan in Berea College *vs.* Kentucky, *U. S. Reports*, Vol. 211, p. 67.   [39] *Ibid.*, pp. 67, 69.

[40] The text of the resolution is, in part, as follows:

Friends and Fellow-students:

As we meet for the first time under new conditions to enjoy the great advantages of Berea College, we think at once of you who are now deprived of these privileges.

Our sense of justice shows us that others have the same rights as ourselves, and the teachings of Christ teach us to "remember them that are in bonds as bound with them."

We realize that you are excluded from the classrooms of Berea College, which we so highly prize, by no fault of your own, and that this hardship is a part of a long line of deprivations under which you live. Because you were born in a race long oppressed and largely untaught and undeveloped, heartless people feel more free to do you wrong, and thoughtless people meet your attempts at self-improvement with indifference or scorn. Even good people sometimes fear to recognize your worth, or take your part in a neighborly way, because of the violence of the prejudices around us. . . .

We are glad that the College is providing funds to assist you in continuing your education, and we are sure the Institution will find ways in which to do its full duty by the colored race. We know that you have as much right to its care and help as we have, and we shall cheerfully give up a part of our own advantages if necessary in order that the colored people may have their just share. (Copied from Frost, *op. cit.*, pp. 66 ff.)

fighting for the abolition of slavery and the extension of educational opportunity among Negroes. The American Missionary Association was consistently behind such movements.

FINDING ITS MISSION

It was not in such an enterprise as that at Berea, however, that the association was to find its most important task. As the strained relations between North and South approached the breaking point, it saw clearly its duty, and with it the opportunity to begin the great work which it was destined to do when the Union armies began to invade the South.[41] The human problem created by the Negro refugees has already been touched upon. Large numbers of these from the plantations of Virginia naturally drifted into the Union lines in the vicinity of Hampton, thus presenting a specific opportunity for missionary activity. Under the dictum of General Butler, as already related, such Negroes had become "Contraband of War." The first "Contraband School," as schools for Negroes were commonly called during that period, was begun by the American Missionary Association, September 17, 1861 at Hampton, not far from Fortress Monroe.[42] This school was the nucleus from which the famous Hampton Institute developed. The history of this institution and the account of the work of its real founder and guiding spirit, General Samuel C. Armstrong[43] make one of the most interesting chapters in the annals of education. A brief mention of the main facts will suffice, however, for our present purpose.

Young Armstrong was by inheritance and experience well fitted for his new task. His parents came of Massachusetts and Pennsylvania stock on his maternal and paternal sides, respectively. His father was a missionary in Hawaii, so that the son was born in an environment of service. The young man was fortunate enough to supplement his natural gifts with a good edu-

---

[41] At the outbreak of the war the association passed the following resolution:

"*Resolved*, that we recognize the overruling providence of God, in opening to the association a new field of missionary labor in the State of Virginia among the eighteen hundred bretheren rescued from slavery and now entitled to, if not fully enjoying, the advantages of compensated labor, intellectual and religious instruction and the protection of the government; and that if the means shall be furnished, it is the purpose of the association to follow the armies of the United States with faithful missionaries and teachers, until the light of knowledge and revelation shall be poured upon the darkened minds of the emancipated and they become the freemen of the Lord." (A. M. A., *An. Rep.*, 1861, pp. 7, 8.)   [42] A. M. A., *An. Rep.*, 1863, p. 37.

[43] For brief appraisals of the work of Armstrong see Washington, Booker T., *Up from Slavery*, pp. 54–58; Peabody, F. G., *Education for Life*; the series of Founder's Day Addresses delivered in successive years at Hampton Institute, and published by that institution.

cation and the personal inspiration of Mark Hopkins, president of Williams College, during his two years at that institution as a student.[44] Before graduation he entered the Union army as a captain, and before the close of the war was in command of colored troops, in which position his first deep impressions in favor of the Negro were received.[45] In 1866, having been placed in charge of the affairs of the refugees in ten counties of Eastern Virginia with headquarters at Hampton, by the Commissioner of the Freedmen's Bureau, he had an even more extensive opportunity to study the characteristics and habits as well as the deeper nature of the freedmen.[46] He found at Hampton the educational activity among the Negroes centered in the little school already described. His native qualities, reënforced by years of experience in many places and among many people, enabled him to discern at once the possibilities of the situation. At his suggestion the American Missionary Association purchased a tract of land, finally reaching one hundred and ninety acres in extent, on the shore of historic Hampton Roads.[47] It was but natural that Armstrong should be offered the principalship, and in accepting the position he took up a work whose successful issue stamps him as one of America's greatest educators.

Armstrong's ideal of the mission of the new school can best be stated in his own words. Its function should be to

train selected Negro youth who should go out to teach and lead their people, first by example, by getting land and homes; to give them not a dollar that they could earn themselves; to teach respect for labor; to replace stupid drudgery with skilled hands; and to these ends to build up an industrial system for the sake, not only of self-respect and intelligent labor but also for the sake of character.[48]

The school began work in 1868, but was not incorporated until two years later when it was placed under the control of an independent board of trustees. The charter specified that the purposes of the Institute were:

The instruction of youth in the various common-school, academic and collegiate branches, the best methods of teaching the same, and the best mode of practical industry in its application to agriculture and the mechanical arts; and for carrying out these purposes, the said trustees may establish any departments or schools in the said institution.

[44] Talbot, E. A., *Samuel Chapman Armstrong*, Ch. II.   [45] *Ibid.*, Ch. IV.
[46] *Ibid.*, pp. 136, 138.   [47] A. M. A., *An. Rep.*, 1867, p. 16; Talbot, *op. cit.*, pp. 160, 161.
[48] *Ibid.*, 1870, pp. 24, 25; Talbot, *op. cit.*, p. 157.

In the report of the executive committee of the association for 1868 there is given a description of the work at Hampton from which the following excerpts are taken:

This "Whipple Farm" lies upon Hampton Roads. The school and home buildings, valued at $20,000, occupy a beautiful site upon the shore. They are so furnished and arranged as to offer the students the helps to right living which belong to a cultivated Christian home.[49]

The aim of education as conceived by those in charge of this experiment and the method of attaining that aim are indicated by the description of the work in agriculture and home economics:

In the farm work, under the constant direction of an educated practical farmer, the graduates of this institution will have learned both the theory and practices of the most profitable methods of agriculture.

The female students do all the home-work of the boarding department. Thus, in the home, on the farm, and in the school room the students have their opportunity to learn the three great lessons of life—how to live, how to labor, and how to teach others.[50]

The curriculum, covering a three-year course, expressed the severely practical ideals of the faculty, for nothing was included that could not be used daily after graduation. The first year furnished the elementary tool subjects with geography, vocal music, rhetorical exercise, and gymnastics. In the second year these subjects were intensified with the addition of the elementary forms of business, agriculture, chemistry, soil analysis, and exercises in teaching. During the third year the study of the English language included reading, composition, orations, and bookkeeping. The other subjects were continued with the addition of practice teaching in the Butler and Lincoln Model Schools. In addition to their school work, all students worked four or five hours a day at manual labor for the first and third terms. The expenses, of course, were kept very low. Tuition was $1.00 a month; rooms 75 cents a month; board, laundry, and lights together $1.75 per week. Students could earn money for labor of from three to five hours a day at the rate of from four to twelve cents per hour.[51]

While Hampton in its early years stressed industrial education and instruction at the sub-collegiate level, yet from the very first

[49] A. M. A., *An. Rep.*, 1868, pp. 35 ff.   [50] *Ibid.*, p. 35.   [51] *Ibid.*, pp. 36 ff.

its founders saw the possibility, as expressed in its charter, of an expansion of its curriculum to include courses of collegiate grade. Its major concern, however, until recent years was the development of the industrial arts and teacher training, and its fame rests mainly upon the success which it has attained in these fields. Following the death of General Armstrong, which occurred in 1893, Dr. Hollis Burke Frissell [52] succeeded to the principalship. Under his leadership, changes in organization were effected for the purpose of improving the quality of work and raising the requirements for graduation. These improvements went steadily forward until the death of Dr. Frissell, in 1917.[53] He was succeeded by Dr. James E. Gregg, who vigorously promoted the program of his predecessor. In 1920 the Academic Normal Course was discontinued and in its place there was established a six-year course including four years of secondary work followed by two years of study at the collegiate level. At the same time a four-year course in agriculture was superimposed upon four years of secondary work. Changes in the curriculum in business and home economics lifted these subjects also to the collegiate level. In 1924 the three schools of Agriculture, Education, and Home Economics were grouped together as the Teachers College of Hampton Institute, offering diplomas at the end of the one- and two-year courses and the degree of Bachelor of Science for the four-year course. At the present time (1933) provision is made for courses in the summer session leading to the degree of Master of Arts.[54] Thus, Hampton entered the sisterhood of colleges although retaining the original designation of "Institute."

These modifications were made largely in response to the increased requirements for teacher's certificates in the Southern states, and resulted in a rapid increase in the enrollment of students of collegiate grade.[55] In his report for 1928 Principal Gregg comments upon this aspect of the situation as follows:

In 1917, there were nine hundred students in the Institute proper, of whom 44 per cent were in the elementary grades (preparatory classes, corresponding to the seventh and eighth grades) and 56 per cent in secondary classes. . . . In 1920–21 there were twenty-one students of college grade; in 1927–28 there were four hundred and seventeen.

---

[52] Frissell, Hollis Burke, see sketch in *Dictionary of American Biography*, Vol. VII.
[53] *The Hampton Bulletin*, Vol. XXVII, No. 1, p. 18.   [54] *Ibid.*, p. 42.
[55] For an extended review of the changes effected in the Hampton program see *Annual Report* of Principal George D. Phenix of Hampton for 1930.

For the school year 1931–32, 889 students were enrolled in the collegiate division, exclusive of extension courses and the summer session.[56]

That Hampton Institute has been a success from its beginning is well known in all parts of the country, and that its program has received the general endorsement of the American people is indicated by the fact that it is the best endowed institution of learning for Negroes in the world.[57] Its influence has been felt not only in the South but throughout the nation and in foreign countries. Booker T. Washington and Tuskegee Institute, which he founded, are its most famous products.[58] Its history has been presented here somewhat at length as an example of one type of development characteristic of certain institutions of higher learning among Negroes, and one worthy of careful study by students of this subject. It is probably fair to say that few ideas have been more extensively copied in modern educational practice than that conceived by Armstrong and expressed by Hampton.

The majority of institutions of learning for Negroes, even those bearing the titles of "college" and "university," introduced manual training after the popularity of the Hampton idea became manifest. The Negro land-grant colleges as a group have followed, in general, the same pattern of development, which consists in beginning with elementary studies along with strong emphasis upon agriculture, trades, and teacher training for work at the lower levels, followed by a gradual raising of standards in teacher-training courses to higher levels. This has necessitated the introduction of college courses in academic subjects, which today form an important part of the offerings of this group of schools. Hampton was itself the Negro land-grant college of Virginia, the second state to provide support for such a college under the original Morrill Act. Having received 300,000 acres of scrip from the United States Government, which it sold for $285,000, the state divided the income between Hampton and the white land-grant college of the state. Hampton was continued as the Negro land-grant college of Virginia from 1872 to

---

[56] *The Hampton Bulletin*, Catalog for 1931–32, p. 143.

[57] The Endowment of Hampton now (1933) exceeds ten million dollars (*Report of the Treasurer of Hampton Institute*, 1932).

[58] Booker T. Washington's *Up from Slavery* not only tells the story of his own life and that of Tuskegee but also reveals his philosophy of education developed largely from his life at Hampton and from his contacts with Armstrong.

1920, when the fund was transferred to the Virginia State College at Petersburg.[59]

SCHOOLS FOLLOWING THE ARMIES

At Hampton, therefore, the American Missionary Association found the real beginning of its education work among Negroes, a task undertaken along with the first movements of the invading armies and before other missionary bodies were in the field to do educational work. From this beginning, however, undaunted by the many dangers to be faced, undismayed by the appalling nature of the problem that it met on every hand, and undeterred by lack of funds, its agents rapidly extended its work. During the year 1863, schools were opened at Norfolk, Newport News, Portsmouth, Suffolk, and Yorktown, Virginia; at Newbern and Roanoke Island, North Carolina; at Beaufort, Hilton Head, Saint Helena, and Ladies' Island, South Carolina; and at St. Louis, Missouri.[60] By the end of 1864, following the opening of the Mississippi, schools were begun at New Orleans and Port Hudson, Louisiana; at Vicksburg, Corinth, and Natchez, Mississippi; at Memphis, Tennessee; at Little Rock and Helena, Arkansas; and at Cairo, Illinois.[61] At this time the missionary teachers of the Association numbered 250. As the war continued its agents were increased in number and were scattered all over those areas of the South opened up by the Union armies.

After the establishment of the Freedmen's Bureau, the activity of the association was greatly facilitated by the financial assistance given by the bureau from funds at its disposal. This aid was of the greatest importance, coming at a time when the cost of the work was rapidly exceeding the financial resources of the association. The task was somewhat eased, too, and the work became more systematic as a result of the general organization of education effected by the bureau and the protection extended to the schools through its agency, backed by the strength and authority of the Federal Government as represented by its military arm.[62]

In the report for 1870 the following four colleges are described as being under the patronage of the association: Berea College in Kentucky, Fisk University in Tennessee, Atlanta University in Georgia, and Talladega College in Alabama. Fisk operated a

[59] *U. S. Office of Ed. Bul.*, 1930, No. 9, II, p. 838.
[61] *Ibid.*, 1864, p. 20.
[60] A. M. A., *An. Rep.*, 1863, pp. 42, 43.
[62] *Ibid.*, 1866, p. 11.

preparatory department of seventeen students, a normal department of thirty students, an academic department of fifty-nine
students, and a model school and a night school with enough students to make a total enrollment of 477.   The property value was
$50,000.[63]

Atlanta University in the same year operated a normal department of thirty-three students, and announced a preparatory department in operation as well as an agricultural department in
which lectures and practical work were to be given and in which
all students were to be enrolled.   An undenominational theological school was announced for the next year to fit students for the
Christian ministry.   The following comments appearing in the
report for that year, relative to Atlanta University, indicate the
prominent part played by the association in promoting educational opportunities for Negroes in the state of Georgia, its cordial
relationship with the Freedmen's Bureau, and the progress made
or in immediate contemplation toward the physical development
of the university itself.

For six years past, various Northern aid societies have been engaged in an
educational work in Georgia.   The American Missionary Association has done
by far the largest part of this work.   It has supported schools in all the principal cities and towns of the state and has expended from its own treasury for
school work alone about $200,000.   It has been the design from the first to
establish one central institution for higher education beginning with normal
and preparatory departments and growing into a college and finally into a
university.

The Freedmen's Bureau, under the wise administration of Col. T. R. Lewis,
Superintendent for Georgia, who entered heartily into these plans, has largely
furnished means for their execution.

Atlanta, because of its central position and healthful climate, was selected as
the best place for such an institution.   A charter was obtained in October 1867
and a Board of Trustees formed.   The trustees now hold about 60 acres of land
on one of the highest elevations in the city and commanding a fine view in all
directions.   The first building was completed in September 1869.   It is a substantial, four storied brick building, neatly furnished and contains parlors,
dining-rooms, kitchen, bathrooms, and dormitories for forty lady pupils.   It
has been very much crowded during the year.   Another building, of about the
same style and dimensions, will be completed in August.   In this building are to
be temporary school rooms for the whole school and dormitories for sixty
gentlemen.

The plan of the institution for the immediate future contemplates also a
central building for chapel, school rooms, lecture-rooms, cabinet, library, etc.
Will some one furnish the necessary funds? [64]

          [63] A. M. A., *An. Rep.*, 1870, p. 40.   [64] *Ibid.*, 1870, pp. 40, 41.

Here we have the simple report of progress and plans by a group of Christian missionaries in the deep South, five years after the close of a war in which the Negro was the issue. Believing in the essential equality of human beings and knowing that for a long time the Negroes could look neither to themselves nor to their white neighbors in the South for uplift they planned to provide educational opportunities for the freedmen from the elementary school through the college. And not only did they plan, but they also executed their plans and have continued to do so, although the state and local communities have in recent years greatly eased their financial burden, and public opinion relative to their work has practically reversed itself. The quotation just given is typical of hundreds that can be gleaned from the reports of the larger denominational organizations which have promoted, in the main, higher education in the South since emancipation.

IMPROVED FINANCES

Until near the close of the war the association had been without particular denominational affiliation but had acted as the agent of individuals and groups who wished to command its service as a missionary body. Nor did it have an active organization for presenting its cause to the world, soliciting funds, and establishing a supporting constituency. Growing confidence in the worth and permanency of the body and approval of its general policy is indicated by the increase in its receipts from $47,000 in 1861–62 to $250,000 in 1865–66.[65]

In 1865 an event occurred which proved to be of the greatest importance to the association. In that year the National Conference of Congregational Churches met in Boston for the purpose of considering what action should be taken with reference to the missionary activity of that denomination in view of the conditions in the South created by the war. At that meeting the American Missionary Association was selected as the proper agency for this work. It was also recommended that $250,000 be raised and placed at the disposal of the association for carrying forward its program among the freedmen.[66] The association accepted the task, set up an organization for raising funds in the United States, and also sent a commission to England for the same purpose. The effort was successful, the sum raised during the first year falling

[65] A. M. A., *An. Rep.*, 1933, p. 94.   [66] *Ibid.*, 1867, p. 12.

short of the goal by only a small amount.[67]   Thus was the work placed on a much more stable foundation than before.   This event also marks the beginning of the relationship of the American Missionary Association and the Congregational Church.   Since that time it may fairly be considered the missionary body of that denomination, although there has been little or no denominational emphasis manifested in the work of the schools under its control.

With the united support of the Congregational Church, the financial condition of the association was greatly strengthened. And, although funds in general were raised through church collections and private donations, they were relatively dependable and reached $376,216.88 for the fiscal year 1888–89.[68]   In 1888 the permanence of the association's income was still further assured by one of those great acts of financial statesmanship which have so favorably affected education in America.   At that time, Daniel Hand of Guilford, Connecticut, established the Daniel Hand Educational Fund for Colored People, and placed in the custody of the association securities to the amount of $1,000,894.25 as a perpetual fund for the purpose indicated in its title.[69]

Although he was a New Englander, Mr. Hand had lived for a long time in the South and had made his fortune there.[70]   Hence, he knew the conditions and made his gift on the basis of this knowledge and an appreciation of the resultant need.   This gift was epoch making not only to the association and the Negro but to American education as a whole.   It was the second of the great permanent funds established exclusively for the education of the Negro, but differed from the John F. Slater Fund, which preceded it by six years, in that it has been administered ever since its establishment as part of the work of a missionary organization already in operation instead of by an independent board of trustees appointed for that specific purpose.

POLICIES OF THE ASSOCIATION

It has been pointed out that the early schools for Negroes were necessarily concerned with the rudiments of learning and that the efforts of several agencies in the field consisted largely in establishing some sort of school for the freedmen in every spot where the need was pressing, so long as funds were available. Abandoned

[67] A. M. A., *An. Rep.*, 1866, pp. 10, 11.   [68] *Ibid.*, 1889, p. 84.   [69] *Ibid.*, 1888, p. 66
[70] *Daniel Hand*, A biographical sketch issued by the A. M. A. (pamphlet).

barracks, barns, dwellings, churches, or hastily constructed shelters of almost any kind served as schoolhouses. Comforts were few, books were scarce, equipment was crude and limited, and teachers did the double duty of instructors and social workers. The situation constituted an emergency and was met by emergency methods. After the close of the war, as the fervid enthusiasm born of the actual conflict passed, a number of the benevolent societies for freedmen's aid went out of existence and left their enterprises, their equipment such as it was, and their resources, if any, in the hands of permanent organizations.[71] The American Missionary Association naturally fell heir to a large share of this responsibility, especially when the Freedmen's Bureau was discontinued in 1870. It became necessary, therefore, for its administrative authorities to take stock of the situation as it then existed, to determine the objectives of the association, and to formulate policies for determining a procedure by which the objectives might be realized. As they saw it, the problem of the American people was the preparation of the four million freedmen for effective citizenship, largely through the agency of Christian education. Dr. A. F. Beard,[72] who was prominently and intimately connected with the work of the association as secretary for many years, thus interprets the position of those who had to make decisions in that critical period in the life of the American Negro:

So far, the association had made less account of the future than it did of the fact that God was leading on, and that the association was assuredly following that leading. But now it was face to face with a long future. No transient purpose and no transient work would do. The salvation of an absolutely undeveloped race with a long heredity of ignorance, superstition, and deg-

---

[71] *U. S. Bur. of Ed. Bul.*, 1916, No. 38, pp. 268–82.

[72] No discussion of the work of the American Missionary Society would be complete without mentioning the name of Dr. Augustus F. Beard. The following excerpts are taken from a tribute to him appearing in *The American Missionary* for January 31, 1929, pp. 132, 133: "After having a leading part in the education of perhaps half a million Americans, Dr. Beard ought to know what's what in education. . . . His early faith and lifelong devotion to the 'Crusade of Brotherhood' — which he has described in a remarkable book by that title—are richly rewarded, he says, as he notes what the Negro in America is accomplishing. . . . Born when the War of 1812 was no further back than the Great War is now; graduated from Yale before the Civil War; present as a graduate student at the Cooper Union Campaign meeting of Abraham Lincoln— Dr. Beard has richly shared the development of modern America. . . . As a secretary of the American Missionary Association from 1886 on, Dr. Beard's activities have brought him into touch with the establishment and growth of many major educational institutions for colored youth. He first saw them in barracks and shacks when the only means of transportation was the mule. From time to time he still visits them—now grown famous as institutions with splendid equipment, large student bodies, high standards and thousands of Alumni." Dr. Beard reached his one hundredth birthday on May 11, 1933.

radation meant generations as to time and called for permanent institutions. This at once introduced the theory and methods of education and indicated what should be attempted.   The prophetic men who were directing the association believed that what experience had proved to be wise and efficient influences for Christianizing and civilizing white people ought to be equally good for black people.   Indeed, the evidence already before them seemed to be sufficient to justify this judgment.   The association had gone far enough to confirm the opinion that the black people could be enlarged in thought and mind by the same influences and methods of discipline which had proved their power in other peoples; this much against the opinions of the Southern people, who held for the most part to the essential incapacity of their former slaves for anything beyond elementary improvement.   At all events, said these men in the direction of the association, we must work toward the possibilities.   No race can be permanently dependent upon another race for its ultimate development.   This Negro race must be taught to save itself and how to do it; to work out its own future with its own teachers and educators.   Therefore, reliance must be placed on permanent institutions and permanent teachers for them, and for the steady and determined consecration of those ready to take up the work with this high conception of it.[73]

Nor was there doubt in the minds of these pioneers what should be the nature of these permanent schools.   First, the schools under white teachers must prepare Negroes as rapidly as possible to take over the task of teaching in the elementary schools.   This was accomplished by introducing teacher training instruction in the advanced grades of elementary schools and gradually raising the grade of some of these schools to the secondary level, designating them as normal schools.   These secondary schools, however, immediately implied higher education for those exceptional pupils who should be prepared for higher teaching and the other professions.   Beard continues:

The fathers of forty years ago anticipated the criticism of later years as to the wisdom of colleges for the development of a backward race.   So, they said, let it be granted that other lines of education are imperative; colleges also certainly are needed, and we must set the standards for the education of the race now!   Thorough training, large knowledge, and the best culture possible are needed to invigorate, direct, purify, and broaden life; needed for the wise administration of citizenship, the duties of which are as sure to come as the sun is to shine, though today or tomorrow may be cloudy; needed to overcome narrowness, one-sidedness, and incompleteness.

They took their theories of education from their estimates of men.   If what is possible was to be demonstrated, there must be institutions for those whose gifts, attainments, character, and example should make them a constant and large uplifting hope for others; a steadying power and a wise guidance for

[73] Beard, A. F., *A Crusade of Brotherhood*, pp. 146, 147.

those not equally privileged or endowed, and which should give opportunity for the youth of the future, whose intellectual capacity might justify the largest mental furnishing. Therefore, they said, educate, educate, educate, in all ways, from the lowest to the highest, for whatever is possible for a full-orbed manhood and womanhood. This, of course, predicated the education of the highest part of one's nature. Their theory was right. If education does not make for spiritual life and spiritual power, it is lamentably insufficient.[74]

During the entire period since the Civil War, the association has been promoting education among Negroes in accordance with the broad basic policy as enunciated by the pioneers in the association and repeated in the preceding quotation, including the permanency of the institutions established, especially those of collegiate grade.

This must not be interpreted to mean that the association desired to control the schools permanently. While it has performed its task with consecration and high idealism, it has constantly kept in mind the American principle that education is primarily the function of the states and the local communities. Realizing this ultimate obligation, its work at the elementary level was undertaken as an emergency measure to be promoted for the purpose of assisting in the task only so long as outside aid was needed, and of setting worthy examples in educational procedure. Therefore, its part in educational work at that level has gradually declined from a major to a minor activity as the burden has been assumed by those primarily responsible for its promotion. The same policy has held with reference to secondary education, although the slower development of public high schools throughout the South has delayed the retirement of the association from that field. The colleges under the control of the association have developed from schools of lower grade and are now in the process of eliminating elementary and secondary work except such as is needed to provide practice facilities for the large number of college students preparing for the teaching profession. The constant aim has been to improve the quality of the college work under its control by limiting its efforts at this level to a few selected schools. That this aim is being realized is indicated by the fact that Talladega College has received the highest rating granted by the Association of Colleges and Secondary Schools of the Southern States.

Even in the collegiate field, however, the association is willing for the sake of increasing educational efficiency either to merge its

[74] Beard, A. F., *A Crusade of Brotherhood*, pp. 149, 150.

colleges with others or to release them entirely to independent boards of trustees.   The first course is seen in the recent merger of Straight College in New Orleans, one of the oldest and best of the schools under the association, with New Orleans University of the Methodist Episcopal Church to form the new Dillard University.   The second procedure is illustrated by Hampton, Atlanta, and Fisk, all of which had their beginnings under the fostering care of the association but now operate under independent boards.

The following extracts from a bulletin released by the association in 1932 state clearly the present policies of the association.

It is the policy of the American Missionary Association wherever it is duplicating work which is being or might be done by local boards of education to transfer the work either bodily or gradually to the local authorities.   In some cases this is done outright as in Mobile, Alabama, where a few years ago the Board of Education assumed full responsibility for Emerson Institute, and purchased the association's property.   The same was true of Gregory Institute of Wilmington, N. C.   In this case the School Board assumes the responsibility, and the A. M. A. makes a decreasing annual appropriation towards the maintenance of the school.   Examples of this method may be found in Greenwood, S. C., and Troy, N. C.

Wherever the A. M. A. continues full responsibility for elementary and secondary schools it seeks the coöperation of local boards of education.   In a number of schools thus operated there are from one to six teachers who are employed by the public school authorities but assigned to teach in the A. M. A. schools.   The A. M. A. in turn coöperates with other agencies both in financial support and active service.   This is true of the Committee on Interracial Coöperation and the Commission on the Church and Race Relations.

Furthermore, wherever the A. M. A. can advance the effectiveness of an educational institution, either by assisting it to complete independence or by uniting one institution to another, it has been ready to do so.   Examples of this policy are Hampton Institute, Atlanta University, Fisk University and the present merger of Straight and New Orleans Universities to form the New Dillard University.

The general tendency of the A. M. A.'s work is toward concentration in a limited number of institutions of higher learning like Talladega, Straight, Tillotson, Tougaloo, LeMoyne, and Brick.   In these institutions buildings and equipment are being perfected, better prepared teachers are being employed, academic requirements and tuition fees are being advanced.[75]

TALLADEGA COLLEGE

A brief account has been given of Berea College in connection with the work of the American Missionary Association because,

[75] Brownlee, Fred L., "Policies of the American Missionary Association." *A. M. A. Bulletin*, 1932.

through one of its agents, it gave the initial impetus to the project which first gave Negroes the chance to attend college in slave territory even though at that time the work was not of college grade. Hampton, which the association also sponsored, has been described not only because of its evolution from an industrial school to a college, offering both undergraduate and graduate degrees, but also because of its profound influence upon educational thought in America. But neither of these schools grew into an effective college in the modern sense while connected with the association. The story of Talladega, however, is that of a college of high standing, founded, developed, and maintained under the auspices of the association and finally brought to such a point of excellence as to receive the highest rating granted by the recognized regional association covering the Southern states. A brief sketch of its development as fairly typical of many of the strongest Negro colleges of today seems appropriate at this point.

The school was founded at Talladega, a small town in Eastern Alabama, in November 1867 with three teachers and 140 students, and received its charter February 17, 1869.[76] The Freedmen's Bureau assisted in purchasing a tract of thirty-four acres upon which a large brick building had been erected,[77] the location being in the midst of the "black belt" and surrounded by nine counties which had no school of any kind which colored children could attend. The people of these counties asked the principal of the school for teachers. In response to this appeal an arrangement was made by which each of the several localities was asked to send its most promising young man to the school to study and to send along with him enough corn, bacon, and other supplies to feed him while in school. Those selected came to the school mostly on foot, bearing their rations with them. Their sleeping quarters consisted of the bare floors of the cabin homes of neighbors who would receive them since the school had no living accommodations.[78] The curriculum began with the alphabet and extended through the third reader. When, after a few months of intensive effort, the students had advanced that far they "practiced" on other pupils so as to learn how to teach reading. When summer came they returned home to ply their newly acquired art on their less fortunate comrades who had not been away to school.[79]

[76] A. M. A., *An. Rep.*, 1871, p. 45.
[78] *The American Missionary*, Oct. 1868, pp. 217, 218.
[77] *Ibid.*, 1869, p. 42.
[79] Beard, *op. cit.*, p. 174.

It was in such crude surroundings and under such unpromising conditions that the missionary teachers from the North performed a labor of love which only devotion to a cause can inspire. Talladega was not an exception but a type of all the educational effort for the Negro in those critical years during and immediately following the Civil War. The teachers had to be persons possessing great faith in the possibilities of humanity and willing to lose themselves in their task and to endure hardships, social isolation, insult, and often personal danger. They lived with their students and taught them lessons in living outside of school hours often more valuable than the lessons learned in the classrooms.[80]

The original building at Talladega had been erected by slaves. It was used as a boys' school for the upper social classes. During the war it had served as a prison in which Union soldiers were confined. It is said that a slave carpenter who helped to erect the building as a school for the children of the master class lived to see three of his own children receive diplomas from the Negro college using the same property.[81]

The year after the school was established a church was opened and courses were inaugurated for the training of ministers. Eighteen students were enrolled. From this beginning there developed a department of biblical study which was formally organized in 1873.[82] By 1875 the work of Talladega had so impressed the white people of the community that a local newspaper commenting upon its work said:

> The eighth annual session of this institution came to a close on the 30th day of June. We were not so fortunate as to be able to attend during the final examination; but from what we saw and have learned from many of our best citizens who did attend, we have no hesitation in saying that Talladega College is not only one of the most successfully conducted of the many institutions of learning established in the South by Northern philanthropists, but is, in every feature that constitutes a good school, the equal of any school of its grade in the state.

The development of college work at Talladega is a typical refutation of the criticism that the denominational schools offered college work to Negroes before they were ready for it. At Talladega, from the crude beginnings described, the grade of work was raised only in accordance with the demand as indicated by

[80] The pages of the monthly issues of the *American Missionary*, the official organ of the A. M. A. for the years 1861 to 1875, are rich with accounts of the personal experiences of these pioneer teachers.   [81] *Ibid.*, p. 176.   [82] Beard, *op. cit.*, p. 177.

the progress of the pupils. Not until 1879 did the association begin planning for work of collegiate grade. In that year, Reverend Henry Lee DeForest, a Yale man, became president.[83] During his term of office, covering seventeen years, the grade of the institution was gradually advanced and the quality of the work improved. No outline of a college course appeared in the catalog until 1890, and the first college degree was granted in 1895. The enrollment figures at intervals of five years shown in Table III illustrate the slow growth of college work and the proportion of students enrolled below college grade.

TABLE III

ENROLLMENT IN COLLEGE AND TOTAL ENROLLMENT, TALLADEGA COLLEGE, AT FIVE-YEAR INTERVALS FROM 1892 TO 1932 *

Year	Enrollment	
	College	Total
1892...............................	2	510
1897...............................	10	693
1902...............................	23	534
1907...............................	32	613
1912...............................	30	722
1917...............................	57	628
1922...............................	123	511
1927...............................	187	563
1932...............................	221	443

* Data taken from the annual reports of the A. M. A. for the years indicated.

These figures show that in 1892, twenty-five years after the establishment of the school, only two students out of a total of 510 were enrolled in college; and in 1912, twenty years later, only thirty out of a total of 722, or 4 per cent of the total student body, were of college grade. In 1922, after the college had been in operation for fifty-five years, only 123 students out of a total of 511, or about 24 per cent of the total, were enrolled in college classes. Not until 1932 did the college enrollment reach one-half the total enrollment of students in the institution. Several deductions may fairly be made from these figures: First, that the absence of public school facilities in Alabama during the early years of Talladega's existence and the total absence of public schools of secondary grade threw the burden of such training

[83] A. M. A., *An. Rep.*, 1880, p. 41.

upon the private schools.   Second, that during these years there were practically no students prepared for college work.   Third, that the persons administering the institution were content to perform the task at hand rather than to enroll students in college before they could meet such entrance requirements as were considered respectable at the time in question.

These facts, and the deductions growing out of them, are typical of all the better colleges for Negroes.   That Talladega waited twenty-five years to enroll two college students seems fair evidence that she did not take illiterate Negroes from the cotton fields and offer them at once the curriculum of the New England college.

Like nearly all the schools for Negroes, Talladega has had to pursue a hand-to-mouth existence in matters of financial support. Until recent years, when the great educational foundations turned their attention to that field, the Negro colleges have had to struggle along practically without endowment.   A later section of this study is devoted to that topic.   At this point it is appropriate to say that the work of Talladega has been placed upon a much more substantial basis because of the establishment of an endowment fund of $1,000,000.   On June 1, 1931 President Sumner reported that he had completed the conditions which would make possible an endowment fund of that amount.   The General Education Board agreed to match a fund of $500,000 raised by the college with a similar amount, with the understanding that the total amount be pledged by June 1, 1931 and paid by June 1, 1933.[84] Since the first condition was duly met the General Education Board has matched dollar for dollar the subscriptions paid in. The total amount thus realized by June 1933 was approximately $700,000.

PRESENT ACTIVITY IN HIGHER EDUCATION

In accordance with the policies of the association discussed above, its work has been readjusted from time to time until its educational activities among Negroes in 1932 were confined to five degree-granting colleges, one junior college, and twelve schools of lower grade.   Table IV gives the names and locations of the colleges, with other data for the year ending September 30, 1932.[85] The table shows that more than one-half the students enrolled

[84] *The American Missionary*, March 5, 1931, p. 309.
[85] Data taken from A. M. A., *An. Rep.*, 1932, pp. 57, 59.

TABLE IV

STATISTICS FOR COLLEGES UNDER THE AMERICAN MISSIONARY ASSOCIATION
FOR 1931–32

Name and Location	Total Enroll-ment	Number College Stu-dents	Number College Grad-uates	Num-ber on Fac-ulty	Income Excluding Boarding Department	Amount Received from A. M. A.
Four-year Colleges:						
LeMoyne, Memphis, Tenn....	278	233	18	13	$47,888.20	$26,093.71
Straight, New Orleans, La....	240	121	17	26	61,611.06	46,982.29
Talladega, Talladega, Ala.....	443	221	41	47	202,508.53	85,394.84
Tougaloo, Tougaloo, Miss.....	328	98	18	29	81,959.61	51,256.74
Tillotson, Austin, Tex........	183	140	12	14	33,227.96	25,605.86
Total.....................	1,472	813	106	129	$427,195.36	$235,333.44
Junior College:						
Bricks, Bricks, N. C.........	189	95	0	20	43,540.51	36,377.95
Grand Total..............	1,661	908	106	149	$470,735.87	$271,711.39

were of college grade; that the ratio of students to teachers was about 11 to 1; that the per capita cost, based upon current income, was approximately $284; and that the American Missionary Association contributed approximately $164 for the education of each student in these schools. Were it possible to distribute this cost between college students and those in lower grades, the per capita for the college students would naturally be higher, owing to the smaller size of the classes.

The figures given are typical of similar institutions in the South, both public and private. They indicate that the education of Negro college students is promoted with great economy, to say the least, when compared with the cost of educating college students in the United States as a whole.

CHAPTER VII

THE FREEDMEN'S AID SOCIETY OF THE METHODIST EPISCOPAL CHURCH

THE Methodist Episcopal Church suffered division on the question of slavery when the conferences in the South found themselves at variance with their Northern brethren on the moral issues involved. As a result, the Methodist Episcopal Church, South, came into being in 1845.[1] After the separation, the members of the parent body, no longer restrained by a regard for the sentiments of their former associates, became even more militant and outspoken in their condemnation of slavery. This sentiment took definite form at Cincinnati in August 1866 in the organization of the Freedmen's Aid Society. The activities of the denomination before that date had been in coöperation with other organizations engaged in the work of elevating the freedmen, to which it contributed generously during the Civil War.[2]

At the cessation of hostilities it was decided by the leaders of the church that its work in the uplift of the recently emancipated millions through Christian education could best be promoted by a separate body, organized for that purpose, a procedure which was already being followed by several other denominations. The missionary society of the church performed the function of supplying preachers, and the Church Extension Society was diligently applying itself to the task of erecting churches. Thus, together the two societies were performing the purely religious tasks for which the denomination considered itself responsible. These bodies, however, did not and could not meet the educational need of the freedmen—a service which was looked upon as necessary if the freedmen were to become self-directing persons and good citizens.[3] The Freedmen's Aid Society was the agency of the church through which this work was to be accomplished.

---

[1] For a detailed report of the controversy leading to the separation, see Buckley, J. M.. *A History of Methodists in the United States*, Ch. XVII, pp. 417 ff.

[2] Freedmen's Aid Society of the Methodist Episcopal Church, *Annual Report*, 1868, p. 3. (Cited hereafter as F. A. S., *An. Rep.*)   [3] *Ibid.*, p. 4.

The idea of forming a distinct denominational agency was stimulated by similar action on the part of the United Presbyterians, the Reformed Presbyterians, the United Brethren, the Baptists, the Congregationalists, and the Protestant Episcopal churches, each of which made plans to care for the interests of its own followers through separate organizations while aiding in the general uplift movement.[4] Only one of these denominations, the Baptists, exceeded the Methodists in the number of communicants among the Southern Negroes at the close of the Civil War. There came to Methodism, therefore, a call not only from humanity but from her own children.

During slavery the religion of the Negroes was largely the religion of their masters, who interpreted its teachings as justifying slavery. "Servants be obedient unto your masters," was looked upon as a divine injunction to the slaves to continue in their state of involuntary servitude. The Methodist Church in the North took the opposite attitude and looked upon the war and its results as the working of the Divine will. At the General Conference of 1864 this view was expressed in a resolution which was adopted and which reads as follows:

The grave problem in regard to this people, which has long baffled both statesmen and Christians, is being wrought out in our own day. While the Government is investing the neglected and despised bondmen with freedom, the way opens for Christian benevolence to throw around them those elevating influences of civilization by which they may be prepared for the higher achievements of man. The way opens for the Church of Christ to carry to them a Gospel which, instead of countenancing their servitude, sanctions their liberty and recognizes their manhood.[5]

That the entire power of the Methodist Church was to be placed behind its chosen agent in the field of Negro education is indicated by the message to the denomination issued by the Board of Bishops in session in New York City on November 8, 1866. The message states clearly the conception of the responsibility not only of the Methodist Church but of all other Christian denominations which emancipation and its aftermath had created. It is quoted here, in part, as indicating the fervid zeal and high purpose which animated Christian philanthropy relative to its duty toward the Negroes:

[4] Freedmen's Aid Society of the Methodist Episcopal Church, *Annual Report*, 1868, p. 5.
[5] *Journal of the General Conference of the Methodist Episcopal Church*, 1864, p. 441.

Dear Brethren,—The emancipation of four millions of slaves has opened at our very door a wide field calling alike for mission and educational work. It has devolved upon the Church a fearful responsibility. Religion and education alone can make freedom a blessing to them. The school must be planted by the side of the Church; the teacher must go along with the missionary. In no other way can our work reach its highest success among the Freedmen of the South. They claim this culture as immortal beings, at our hands. Without it their true position as members of society can never be attained. It is needful that they may sustain proper domestic relations among themselves, and that their children may be saved from the blighting effects entailed by the system of slavery. It is indispensable to the highest and most permanent success of our mission work among them. And then, too, a consideration of vital importance to the Christian world is the fact that from among themselves the ministers are to be raised up who shall conserve, carry forward, and make permanent the work of Christianizing and educating the race.

The time may come when the States in the South will make some provision for the education of the colored children now growing up in utter ignorance in their midst. But thus far they have made none, nor perhaps can it soon be expected of them. Christian philanthropy must supply this lack. While other Churches, North and South, are entering this broad field, we have our own work and our own duty to perform. We cannot turn away from the appeal that comes home to our consciences and hearts. Nor can we delay. *The emergency is upon us and we must begin the work now.*

As a suitable channel through which the benefactions of our Church to this object may best reach their design, the Freedmen's Aid Society of the Methodist Episcopal Church has been organized. It is designed to coöperate with our missionary work in the South, and, in fact, to supplement that work. There are openings for hundreds of teachers at this moment. Hundreds of teachers are ready to go. The means to send them are only wanting.

In view of the great emergency of the case, and the certainty that the benefactions of our people can better reach their end through our own channels than through any other, we commend to you the Freedmen's Aid Society of the Methodist Episcopal Church. And especially would we urge upon all pastors and congregations, in view of the present great and pressing wants, to make for this object a collection as soon as practicable.

We also recommend that the Churches in the East contribute with special reference to the establishment of schools in the Southern States bordering upon the Atlantic, and that the Churches in the West direct their effort especially to the states lying south of them in the great Mississippi Valley. We further recommend to the Executive Committee of the Freedmen's Aid Society, to distribute the schools established by them in the South, so as to cover the whole territory of the South as far as practicable, so that the fruits of this blessed work may be most widely diffused.

Done by order of the Board of Bishops, at New York City, November 8, 1866.[6]

⁶ F. A. S., *An. Rep.*, 1867, p. 4.

In the early reports of the society there occur from time to time remarks which indicate that the rivalry between the Protestants and Roman Catholics was one of the strongest incentives to denominational zeal and one of the important reasons why each Protestant denomination felt that it must provide schools of its own to ward off what it looked upon as the menace of Romanism. The report of the secretary of the board of the Freedmen's Aid Society in 1871 contains an example of such expressions, and illustrates the bitterness of feeling on this subject that existed at that time.[7]

The policy of the society, as of the denominations, was to meet the educational need where it was found by promoting elementary education, and as soon as possible, to train teachers and preachers with the minimum equipment necessary to take up the task of educating and evangelizing the masses. The schools were located where they were most needed and in accordance with the desires of the Freedmen's Bureau, which gave timely aid to these early ventures. By 1869 schools of elementary grade had been established as follows: Tennessee, seven; Georgia, twenty; Alabama, four; Kentucky, two; Louisiana, four; Virginia, three; South Carolina, nine; North Carolina, one; Mississippi, eight. These schools employed 105 teachers and enrolled 2,000 pupils.[8]

In addition to these lower schools, the society had established six colleges and normal schools, two biblical institutes, and one orphans' asylum. The schools designated as colleges included Central Tennessee College at Nashville, Tennessee (later Walden University), Clark University at Atlanta, Georgia, Claflin University at Orangeburg, South Carolina, and Shaw University at Holly Springs, Mississippi (now Rust College).

That the Negroes eagerly gave of their scanty funds to aid in the promotion of these schools is indicated by the following statement from the report of 1870.

They have aided liberally in building churches, erecting school-houses, sustaining teachers, supporting the aged and infirm, and providing homes. It is wonderful with what clearness they recognize the importance of schools and churches to their highest usefulness and happiness. The colored people during the past year have contributed fourteen thousand dollars to the schools under our care, and the next year they will, without doubt, double the amount.

[7] F. A. S., *An. Rep.*, 1871, pp. 9, 10.   [8] *Ibid.*, 1869, pp. 6, 7.

They board the teacher and meet the incidental expenses of the school, while the Society pays the salary and traveling expenses; so that nearly one-half of the cost is sustained by them, and in some instances nearly two-thirds of it.[9]

The report for 1871 showed a distinct reduction in the income of the society, which caused some alarm on the part of those primarily interested in carrying forward the educational work so well begun.   The receipts for the first five years were as follows:

First year........................	$37,139.89
Second year.......................	50,167.24
Third year........................	93,513.50
Fourth year.......................	82,719.49
Fifth year........................	51,568.43
Total.............................	$315,108.55 [10]

The marked decline in income from the third to the fifth year was due to the loss of contributions by the Freedmen's Bureau. Those in charge of the work, however, realizing that unless the income increased the expansion of their educational program would be hampered, decided to seek a closer relationship with the church organization with which it was somewhat loosely joined. They believed that the whole situation would be improved if the Freedmen's Aid Society became one of the recognized units of the church organization and was placed under the jurisdiction of the General Conference instead of being allowed to remain a semi-independent body, operating with the good will and endorsement of the denomination.   In order to establish the desired relationship and thus create an obligation on the part of the church adequately to support the educational work among Negroes, the board of directors of the Freedmen's Aid Society sent to the General Conference a memorial setting forth the justifications for the request that the society be received into full connection. The reasons given for such action were:

1. The Society has performed a great and good work with a small amount of money.   2. The Society was called into existence for the performance of a work essential to the success of our Church enterprise in the South, and which did not legitimately come within the province of any of our benevolent enterprises. 3. The efficiency of this Society would be greatly increased by its recognition. 4. The Government, which, at the beginning, gave liberal appropriations to the educational work among the freedmen, does not now furnish any assistance

<hr>

[9] F. A. S., *An. Rep.*, 1870, p. 12.   [10] *Ibid.*, 1871, p. 28.

in the support of our schools. 5. Permanence and stability would be secured to our educational interests. 6. The liberality and exertion of other churches in this cause, should incite us to greater diligence and enlarged benevolence. In conclusion, the memorialists say, in a work like this, which is manifestly similar to that to which Methodism was originally called by providential agency, it is not enough that our missionary appropriations equal those of other denominations. It becomes us, in view of our history, numbers, wealth, professions, and facilities, to lead the hosts of God's people in establishing schools and colleges, erecting churches, and in doing all that is needed for the evangelization of this impoverished people.[11]

The General Conference of 1872, in response to the request of the society, constituted it one of the benevolent societies of the Methodist Episcopal Church, endorsed its constitution, and inserted in the church discipline certain articles referring directly to the society and calling attention to its work as one of the definite obligations of the entire church.[12] Following this action, the income of the society rose in ten years from $51,568, in 1872,[13] to $157,003 in 1882–83.[14]

THE PERMANENT NATURE OF THE SCHOOLS

During the seventies, the society was handicapped, in common with all other benevolent organizations similarly engaged, by at least three opposing factors acting simultaneously. First, the active resistance of certain elements of the population of the South to the promotion of education for Negroes, already discussed in other sections of this study, had to be met and endured until a change in sentiment removed this difficulty.[15] Second, the general economic depression of the country, resulting from the reaction following the war, interfered seriously with the collection of funds for benevolent purposes so that the costs of the necessary projects constantly exceeded the income of the society, thus creating a deficit. Hence, the constant plea during those years was for greater liberality by the church for this cause.[16] Third, the unsettled political situation in the South due to the conflicting theories of reconstruction constantly furnished a disturbing factor in the educational equation.[17]

[11] F. A. S., *An. Rep.*, 1872, p. 36.
[12] *Ibid.*, pp. 37, 40; Stowell, Jay S., *Methodist Adventures in Negro Education*, p. 189.
[13] F. A. S., *An. Rep.*, 1871, p. 28.   [14] *Ibid.*, 1888, p. 10 (table).
[15] See letters from the field in F. A. S., *An. Rep.*, 1883, pp. 8–14; also footnotes, pp. 86, 87, 88 of *Report* for 1874.   [16] F. A. S., *An. Rep.*, 1874, pp. 42 ff.
[17] The *Ninth Annual Report* of the Board of Managers of the society opens with these words: "Our work during the past year has been embarrassed by the reduction of incomes, the deprecia-

The society recognized these difficulties but persevered in its assigned task, meeting the difficulties with tact, patience, and a limitless faith in the help of God in overcoming all obstacles.[18] Those in charge of the work saw clearly that it would be many years before either the South or the Negroes themselves could provide the educational opportunities necessary to meet the needs of the freedmen and to avert social calamity. They built, therefore, for the future, feeling that theirs was no emergency measure but a permanent investment.

The way was left open, however, to place the responsibility for the schools upon the several conferences, if and when such action seemed necessary or desirable. The general policy in this regard is expressed as follows:

It may be deemed hereafter expedient to transfer these schools to the several conferences within whose limits they are located, so that, under the fostering care of the Church, they may continue to prosecute the good work for which they were established. The grounds have been selected, the buildings erected, and the institutions chartered, and some of them partially endowed, with the distinct idea that they are to be permanent, and continued in operation so long as Christian education is demanded for the preservation of our liberties and the salvation of the world. No one should hesitate to make a bequest to this society in behalf of any of these colleges, or to endow a professorship in any of them, for fear they may be broken up or discontinued, for no provision has been made for their termination; but it is the settled policy of their friends that they shall live as long as similar institutions in this country continue to exist and only be broken up in the general ruin that shall destroy them all.[19]

PROGRESS DURING THE FIRST DECADE

In the eleventh annual report of the society, 1878, the schools under its control are listed and classified as follows:

---

tion of property, and the disturbed state of the public mind, in regard to political affairs. It is difficult to persuade people to sustain their benevolent enterprises with a liberal hand in the general depression of business, or during a heated political canvass. Strange as it may seem, retrenchment, even among the followers of Christ, too often begins with their charities, rather than with their luxuries and extravagances."

[18] The Reverend E. W. S. Hammond in an address at the thirteenth anniversary celebration of the society fervently expressed this faith as follows: "The Almighty Father of us all, by a chain of mysterious providence, has decreed that here, upon this continent, in this great republic, and under this best type of human government upon earth, should be enacted its greatest drama—the emancipation of four millions of slaves. The great Methodist Episcopal Church is providentially destined to be the instrument of events that will startle the civilized world. It is the great missionary Church to the colored man whom the nation has emancipated, qualified in a preëminent degree with the means of preparing the late slaves for the enjoyment of the rights of citizenship, and inspiring them with a high and noble ambition to save from superstition and thralldom their greater fatherland."

[19] F. A. S., *An. Rep.*, 1878, p. 6.

Chartered Institutions

Central Tennessee College, Nashville, Tenn.
Clark University, Atlanta, Ga.
Claflin University, Orangeburg, S. C.
New Orleans University, New Orleans, La.
Shaw University, Holly Springs, Miss.

Theological Schools

Baker Institute, Orangeburg, S. C.
Centenary Biblical Institute, Baltimore, Md.
Thomson Biblical Institute, New Orleans, La.

Medical Colleges

Meharry Medical College, Nashville, Tenn.
New Orleans Medical College, New Orleans, La.

Institutions Not Chartered

Bennett Seminary, Greensboro, N. C.
Cookman Institute, Jacksonville, Fla.
Haven Normal School, Waynesboro, Ga.
La Grange Seminary, La Grange, Ga.
La Teche Seminary and Orphans' Home, La Teche, La.
Meridian Academy, Meridian, Miss.
Rust Normal School, Huntsville, Ala.
Wiley University, Marshall, Tex.
Walden Seminary, Little Rock, Ark.
West Tennessee Seminary, Mason, Tenn.

In the schools listed, the numbers of students taught in the several departments were:

Biblical	400
Law	25
Medical	50
Collegiate	75
Academic	275
Normal	1,000
Intermediate	510
Primary	605
Total	2,940 [20]

Several explanatory comments relative to this list are appropriate here. Central Tennessee College later became Walden University and worked in close affiliation with Meharry Medical College for a number of years before it was discontinued. Meharry continued as an independent institution and is now one of

[20] F. A. S., *An. Rep.*, 1878, p. 7.

the two medical schools in the United States for Negroes.[21] Centenary Biblical Institute is now Morgan College, an independent school under the Washington and Delaware Conferences of the Methodist Episcopal Church. New Orleans University lost its identity in the merger which created Dillard University. New Orleans Medical School remains only as Flint Goodrich Hospital, also part of the Dillard University merger.[22]   The name of Shaw University has been changed to Rust College to avoid confusion with Shaw University in Raleigh, North Carolina. Bennett Seminary has become Bennett College and confines its instruction to women.   Cookman Institute has been merged into what is now known as Bethune-Cookman College at Daytona Beach, Florida.

It should be noted in the tabulation of enrollment: first, that the emphasis at that time was definitely placed upon the preparation of teachers and preachers; second, that the number of college students is only seventy-five, which allows an average enrollment of less than thirteen college students to each of the institutions designated as colleges and universities; third, that counting the law, medical, and college enrollment as representing the work in higher education, about five per cent of the effort of these schools was spent upon students working at the higher levels.   By 1882, out of 3,506 students reported, 225 were of college and professional grade, showing a doubling of the percentage of college students in less than five years.[23]

ENLARGED FUNCTIONS

The growing feeling of good will in the white South after the reconstruction crisis had passed and the restoration of "home rule" had been accomplished was quite manifest by 1880, and leaders of thought and action often took occasion to praise the work that the Christian missionaries had done for the uplift of their former slaves.   One such occasion is thus described by Bishop Warren:

On the 16th of October, 1880, Ex-Governor Brown, of Georgia, now United States Senator, stood on the platform of the new building for Clark University in Atlanta, and publicly gave thanks to the representatives of the North for the aid given the South in the matter of education.   Before him was a throng of colored people.   They were sons and daughters of a race that for the first

[21] Referred to again in this study in the chapter on "Organized Philanthropy."
[22] To be treated in a later section of this study.   [23] F. A. S., *An. Rep.*, 1882, p. 28.

time stood facing the sunrise. Their countenances glowed with the light of a new morning. The sun that was about to rise lighted the sky with an Aurora of hope soon to brighten into an immortal day. Beside him were three other governors of Georgia, the School Commissioner of the State, and representatives of the enterprise and intelligence of that swiftly rising commonwealth. On the same platform were the professors, who had gone forth in the true missionary spirit from pleasant homes and friends beloved to take up a work genial only to those who were filled with the spirit of Him who left the glory of heaven for the shame of earth, who, though rich, became poor that we through his poverty might become rich. Behind him were four bishops, one of the blood of the race to be benefited, and three representatives of a great Church of Christ, that had been pouring out its men and its money to aid in bringing light to those who sat in darkness and the shadow of intellectual and moral death. They were there in a moment of victory to lift up the banner, to raise the shout, and then hasten on to the achievement of new victories. It was in such a presence that Senator Brown said in effect: I want to publicly thank you men of the North for doing what we were not able to do. We are too poor. But it needed to be done. You have done it. Its results are apparent today. I thank you, and pray you to continue your help.[24]

In 1882 the property value of the colleges under the Society was as follows:

Clark University......................	$100,000
Central Tennessee College.............	80,000
Claflin University....................	40,000
New Orleans University...............	20,000
Rust University......................	40,000
Wiley University.....................	20,000 [25]

During the same year, by act of the General Conference, the supervision of all educational work in the South was committed to the society, and the Board of Managers was instructed to aid schools for white people as far as it could without embarrassing the work among Negroes. This enlargement of the work brought under the direction of the society three chartered colleges and twelve institutions of lower grade with 2,300 students and seventy-five teachers.[26]

In 1888, as a result of the enlarged duties assigned to the society, the name of the organization was changed to The Freedmen's Aid and Southern Education Society of the Methodist Episcopal Church, by act of the Court of Common Pleas of Hamilton County, Ohio. The act reads, in part, as follows:

And thereupon this cause came on to be heard upon the petition and notice, and upon good cause shown it is ordered that the name of said The Freedmen's

[24] F. A. S., *An. Rep.*, 1880, p. 51.   [25] *Ibid.*, 1882, pp. 29, 30.   [26] *Ibid.*, 1882, p. 39.

Aid Society of the Methodist Episcopal Church be, and the same is hereby, changed to "The Freedmen's Aid and Southern Education Society of the Methodist Episcopal Church," according to law and the prayer of the Petition, and the Petitioners are ordered to file a copy of this order with the recorder of Hamilton County, Ohio, and to publish a copy hereof in some newspaper of general circulation in said county, as required by law, and to pay the costs of this proceeding taxed at ...... dollars.[27]

Up to the time when the name was changed, the society had spent for education in the South the sum of $2,291,903.66 including $200,000 set aside as an endowment fund.[28]

INDUSTRIAL EDUCATION

Although the colleges under the control of the society followed the practice of offering classical curricula to college students, yet a changing emphasis appeared after 1880 in the introduction of industrial work where it had not found a place before and by strengthening such courses where a beginning had already been made. This feeling was doubtless encouraged partly by the success of industrial schools in attracting support and partly by the conviction that industrial training should form one of the essential elements in the education of a people conditioned as were the Negroes. This work was particularly stressed at Central Tennessee College, Clark University, and Claflin University, three of the leading institutions of higher learning under the society. Shops were erected and equipped with the latest tools and machinery for tailoring, plumbing, iron and wood working, painting, wagon building, harness making, shoemaking, and printing—all courses for men. In coöperation with the Woman's Home Missionary Society of the Methodist Episcopal Church courses for girls were developed in sewing, cooking, nursing, and laundry work and homes were erected in which these arts could be practiced.

Various values for such activities were claimed by those promoting the idea of industrial training in colleges for Negroes. The one most often referred to was the utilitarian. One president, thinking of the skilled wage-earner, said:

In teaching the colored people trades, we make skilled wage-workers; we help them take standing among mechanics; but it is not best to push those trades

---

[27] Book No. 6, p. 261, Hamilton County, Ohio, Records.
[28] Freedmen's Aid and Southern Education Society of the Methodist Episcopal Church, *Annual Report*, 1888, p. 9.

most that require great capital to run, or those that usually take the form of a corporation. In the first place, the wage-worker can not have the independence and free determination of the man who is the owner of his own shop; and in the second place, the colored man can not often get the capital and the other advantages out of which to start for himself. There is more independence and greater thrift and inspiration toward manhood in the man who starts out with his own "kit" of tools to set up for himself in some one of the manual trades, than there is in any ordinary skilled wage-worker.[29]

Another president emphasized the value of student labor both to the school and to the pupil thus:

The students, with the aid of their teachers, have built several neat cottages, one good-size blacksmith-shop, added to the carpenter-shop about twenty feet, built various other small buildings, made book-cases and clothes-presses, tables and bedsteads, and other articles of furniture; have done a great deal of repairing during the last year; have aided largely in building a machine-shop for this department, which is an excellent building, forty-eight by ninety feet, with fifteen-foot posts, and is considered a model machine-shop by all who have seen it.[30]

A third president praised its moral value as discipline in these words:

The moral influence has been very favorable. The young men who have worked in the Industrial Departments have been kept employed, and have no doubt been saved to a great degree from the foolishness, so common among college students, of finding their highest enjoyment in tormenting others, and thinking that performing mischievous pranks without being detected is a mark of intellectual shrewdness. The value of this opportunity afforded the students of forming habits of industry while learning a trade is very great. The power to earn a living in various ways gives a consciousness of strength of independence, that is very helpful in the formation of true manliness. Giving this education to the colored youth will help to give them right views of life, and to make good use of the opportunity they may have of being good citizens, and of securing for themselves the results of intelligent industry.[31]

Toward the end of the century there began a decline in the esteem in which industrial work was held by the colleges which became quite evident by the end of the first decade of the twentieth century. Those in charge of the colleges began to feel that the combination of industrial and college work was too expensive and unnecessary. Besides, such work could be better done at Hampton, Tuskegee, and the rising land-grant colleges. A third factor was doubtless the changing character of industry resulting

[29] Freedmen's Aid and Southern Education Society of the Methodist Episcopal Church, *Annual Report*, 1890, p. 177.   [30] *Ibid.*, p. 162.   [31] *Ibid.*, p. 164.

from the development of automatic machinery and mass production. A fourth may have been the new psychology which denied such disciplinary values as were claimed for manual training. Whatever the cause, the colleges operated by the society today place little emphasis upon trade-training but confine their efforts to orthodox curricula in liberal arts and teacher training instead.

REORGANIZATION OF 1908

The General Conference of 1908 reversed its action of 1882 and separated the supervision of the educational work of the schools for the two races in the South and again assigned the Negro schools to the care of the society under its original title, The Freedmen's Aid Society of the Methodist Episcopal Church. An amended charter was granted October 14, 1908.[32]

Between the years 1907–08 and 1914–15 the group of schools under the society classed as "collegiate" declined in enrollment and in size of faculty, although one school, Sam Houston College, was added to the list. By including that school in the list for 1907, comparisons can be made as shown in the following table.

Table V reveals at least two interesting facts. First, during the seven-year period covered, the enrollment declined by 2,037 students, or 40 per cent. Since the reports do not show the distribution of students by academic levels, it is impossible to determine whether the number of college students increased or diminished. Even in 1914–15, however, the students of collegiate grade probably numbered less than two hundred in the ten colleges here listed. The Survey of Negro Education in 1916 reports only 196 college students in the schools under the society.[33] Another important fact revealed by the comparison is the sharp drop in enrollment of George R. Smith College and Walden University. Both of these colleges were closed within a few years, thus indicating the policy of the society to discontinue an institution when it is no longer a justifiable investment.

INSPECTION AND RECOMMENDATIONS

In 1912 it was thought advisable to request that a thorough inspection be made of all the schools under the society, in order to determine upon a policy of future development in view of the

---

[32] Stowell, *op. cit.*, p. 190.   [33] *U. S. Bur. of Ed. Bul.*, 1916, No. 30, p. 303.

TABLE V

COLLEGES UNDER THE FREEDMEN'S AID SOCIETY OF THE METHODIST EPISCOPAL
CHURCH 1907–08 AND 1914–15 [34]

Name and Location	Teachers		Students		Value of Property	
	1907–1908	1914–1915	1907–1908	1914–1915	1907–1908	1914–1915
Bennett College Greensboro, N. C........	10	14	266	368	$36,000	$44,500
Claflin University Orangeburg, S. C........	59	37	538	542	230,950	265,000
Clark University Atlanta, Ga............	30	15	576	273	240,033	338,300
George R. Smith College Sedalia, Mo............	13	11	174	76	52,175	40,200
New Orleans University New Orleans, La........	20	21	649	502	110,975	138,000
Philander Smith College Little Rock, Ark........	35	25	677	423	53,885	50,000
Rust University Holly Springs, Miss......	47	19	458	223	111,200	78,000
Sam Houston College Austin, Tex............	20	23	375	314	40,716	78,000
Walden University Nashville, Tenn.........	70	12	925	144	75,000	72,500
Wiley University Marshall, Tex..........	43	24	650	386	66,041	198,000
Total.................	347	201	5,288	3,251	$1,016,975	$1,302,500

growth in public school systems in the South, the distribution of
the institutions under the Methodist Episcopal Church, and the
development of schools under other boards and denominations.
It was very desirable also to discover, at first hand, what the
modern survey finds out relative to the quality of the work being
done in a school in view of generally accepted standards. The
board of managers, therefore, requested the appointment of a
group of educators to make such an inspection, with the result
that in 1913 the following commission was appointed to carry out
the purpose indicated:

W. H. Crawford, president of Allegheny College, Meadville, Pennsylvania;
Herbert Welch, president of Ohio Wesleyan University, Delaware, Ohio; Samuel Plantz, president of Lawrence College, Appleton, Wisconsin; C. A. Fulmer,

[34] Figures for 1907–08 from *The Christian Educator*, Nov. 1908, p. 3; those for 1914–15 from
F. A. S., *An. Rep.*, 1915, p. 5.

president of Nebraska Wesleyan University, Lincoln, Nebraska; and T. F. Holgate, dean of Northwestern University, Evanston, Illinois.[35]

In 1914 the commission made a report whose most important conclusions and recommendations are given here as an unbiased summary statement showing the condition of higher education among Negroes as promoted by one of the most active and earnest of the denominational boards engaged in this important work. The report says in part:

We are persuaded that in spite of the better rural schools now being provided for the Negroes and in spite of some growth in normal school and high school accommodations, the work of the Freedmen's Aid Society is still an urgent need of the South. So far from sounding any retreat, we of the church should make a great advance, provide a large endowment, give more adequate facilities, pay better salaries, and, in general, strengthen the institutions we have established. They are needed to train a Christian leadership for the colored race, and while they can touch but a few out of the Negro millions, they can do, as they have already done, great things through these selected leaders.

The election of an educational secretary of experience and training who shall be responsible directly to the board, and who, under the board, shall have immediate supervision of the schools and their work.

That the powers of the president in each school be larger and be more clearly defined. Having been chosen to carry out for the institution a particular policy determined by the board, he should be intrusted with responsibility and authority for the effective accomplishment of that purpose.

That the board prepare and adopt a uniform system of keeping accounts, and that local bursars and treasurers be furnished with books and complete sets of blanks for the same. We believe it would be advisable at least once in two years to send an expert accountant to each school to audit the accounts and to give any needed instruction in keeping the accounts and records in correct form.

A uniform system of keeping school records should also be adopted, and necessary cards or books provided for the same by the board.

In view of some grave mistakes which have been made in the construction of buildings, we recommend that a competent school architect be named, to whom all plans for new buildings or the remodeling of existing buildings shall be submitted, and who shall make recommendations to the board concerning them before they are adopted.

That a constructive policy be adopted for the future development of our schools. It is evident to the commission that we have too many colleges (11 now offering college work, with only 250 college students in all, in some places as few as 8 or 9), and that some of our institutions should undertake particular lines of work, looking to local adaptation and needs. We question the wide use of the word "university," and also the effort of so many institutions to do college work for which they have neither the equipment nor the teaching force.

[35] F. A. S., *An. Rep.*, 1913, p. 14.

We suggest the advisability of conferring with the governing boards of other denominations and educational agencies, with a view to securing uniform action in finding appropriate names for the southern schools.

That everything below the ninth grade be classed as grammar school, and that such work, particularly of the lower grades, be discontinued as soon as local conditions will warrant, except as may be required for practice teaching.

That when college and secondary work are given in the same institution, they should be kept as distinct, as regards the work of instruction and the mingling of students in classes, as circumstances will permit.

That some instructors are teaching more hours each week than can be done efficiently, and that recitation periods should not be less than forty-five minutes in work above the grades; also that a larger proportion of men teachers is desirable.

That more flexibility be given to the courses of study, so that schools can be better adapted to local needs and conditions, and to the particular kinds of work the students propose to do.

There is a constantly increasing demand for well-trained Negro teachers. We therefore recommend that, where college work is to be continued, some courses in education more advanced than secondary work be offered.

We would emphasize the necessity for exactness in thought and speech, for accuracy and thoroughness in action, for regularity of habit, and would urge special attention to these in the work of classrooms and in the life of the schools everywhere.

We note that laboratories are generally inadequate and that work in science is generally poor. We therefore recommend that a more generous equipment be sought and larger provision for science be made in the curriculum, whenever the facilities are available.

That thorough instruction be given in all grades in personal and public hygiene.

We are so impressed with the importance of industrial work for both boys and girls that we recommend that a place be made in the curricula in all academies and academic departments of colleges for such work, and that at several points a larger development of training for domestic arts and various trades be carried on. The addition of garden and farm work is everywhere greatly to be desired.

We approve of the "duty system" and recommend the extension of the plan for the care and improvement of the grounds and buildings. This work should be done under supervision, and in some cases payment might be allowed.

We suggest that high ideals govern the construction and maintenance of dormitories and other buildings, especially those relating to light, ventilation, cleanliness, toilet and bathing facilities, the provision of single beds, and the construction of bedroom closets. Special emphasis should be placed upon cleanliness of person and upon neatness of buildings and grounds, in order to teach the colored people how to live. The respectability of manual labor should be taught by precept and example.

We suggest the introduction into the schools of savings plans to encourage thrift, and of any practicable forms of community extension and service.

Libraries with few exceptions are composed of almost worthless books donated by ministers and others, unclassified and unused.   We recommend that libraries be classified and built up by the addition of modern, usable books as rapidly as possible.[36]

RECENT DEVELOPMENTS

In 1920 the General Conference of the church once more changed the name of the society to "Board of Education for Negroes of the Methodist Episcopal Church." Under the new board, the work went forward on the flood tide of the postwar enthusiasm for education, so that enrollments mounted and threatened to outrun the capacity of the schools. At the same time, because of increasing costs, it became necessary to study means of using most wisely the resources available. A third noticeable influence, after 1920, was the general movement toward standardization which placed every school doing college work upon the defensive unless it could be designated "accredited."

Some notable evidences of adjustment by the board to the new demands are seen in changes in the presidencies of five of the ten colleges under the board from 1920 to 1922;[37] the reorganization of Meharry Medical School by the creation of a $550,000 endowment in 1921;[38] the rapid improvement in physical plants by the erection of modern buildings and the extension of properties;[39] the appointment of a permanent educational director for all the schools under the board; the improvement of faculties by raising the standards of appointment and increasing salaries;[40] and the merger of Cookman Institute of Jacksonville with the Daytona Normal and Industrial Institute at Daytona Beach, Florida, to form the Daytona-Cookman Junior College.[41]

In 1924 the Board of Education for Negroes was merged with the Board of Education of the Methodist Episcopal Church, for greater unity and efficiency. The justification for the merger is found in the first paragraph of the report of the Committee on Financial Relief and Promotion of Educational Interests, which reads as follows:

In the combination of interests represented in this amalgamated Board it is of utmost importance that each of the major causes involved shall find voice and expression such as will duly emphasize its importance in the thought

[36] Quoted in *U. S. Bur. of Ed. Bul.*, 1916, No. 38, pp. 141, 142.
[37] Board of Education for Negroes, Methodist Episcopal Church, *An. Rep.*, 1922, p. 2.
[38] *Ibid.*, pp. 3, 4.   [39] *Ibid.*, pp. 2–8, *passim.*   [40] *Ibid.*, p. 9.   [41] *Ibid.*, p. 7.

of the Church. In accordance with this principle we consider it vital that the interests of our colleges, universities, theological schools, secondary schools, and the organizations for whose promotion the Board of Education was organized at the General Conference of 1908, shall be adequately presented to all our congregations and to our total constituency.[42]

At the same meeting the commission on the Survey of Negro Schools made a number of recommendations relative to the individual colleges which indicated a definite intention to strengthen a few schools so that they could do creditable college work; to restrict others to the junior college field; and to discontinue others altogether, or to merge them for greater efficiency with other schools.[43] A significant feature of at least two of these recommendations is that they give evidence that mergers are not impossible even though denominational lines must be crossed to effect them. One recommendation is to the effect that

Efforts should be made, perhaps through the General Education Board, to unite New Orleans College and Straight College as one strong well-equipped Protestant college in a different location from that which either now occupies.

This merger has been accomplished in Dillard University, an institution which will be discussed later in this study.[44]

A similar gesture toward a merger of colleges under different boards is seen in the recommendation "that negotiations be begun, perhaps through the General Education Board, looking toward the possible consolidation of Samuel Houston College and Tillotson College in Austin, Texas." By promoting such mergers the Methodist Church is performing a distinct service to the higher education of the Negro by setting an example in coöperative effort untrammeled by denominational partisanship.

[42] Board of Education, Methodist Episcopal Church, *Proceedings*, Feb. 3 and 4, 1926, p. 49.
[43] *Ibid.*, pp. 51–53.
[44] See also Board of Education, Methodist Episcopal Church, *Proceedings*, Feb. 4–6, 1930, pp. 200–02.

CHAPTER VIII

THE AMERICAN BAPTIST HOME MISSION SOCIETY

EARLY ACTIVITY

MORE Negroes in America belong to the Baptist Church than to any other denomination. This was as true before the Civil War as it is today. It is not surprising, therefore, to find that the Northern Baptists have been among the leaders in promoting the education of Negroes since their emancipation. For they were not only taking part in a great humanitarian movement but were ministering to a group, a large number of whom were bound to them by the ties of denominational kinship.

The American Baptist Home Mission Society, organized in 1832, united all branches of the Baptist denomination in an effort to evangelize the West where the tide of migration was steadily flowing, thus offering a fertile field for militant Christian effort. At that time such work among the Negroes of the South was evidently not considered a special venture but, by implication at least, was not excluded from the general program. There is no record of missionary work among the Negroes of the South during the three decades between 1832 and 1862, although one of the workers of the denomination, Benjamin M. Hill, as early as 1843 mentioned the fact that missionaries in the states of Florida, Georgia, Mississippi, and Texas "found spiritual fruitage" among the people of color.[1]

Within a year after the outbreak of the Civil War, an agent of the society visited Fortress Monroe and the adjacent area, studied the conditions of the Negroes there, and reported his findings. The crisis brought about by the political and social upheaval, which resulted in freeing the Negroes in the District of Columbia and the proposed gradual abolition of slavery, was the most important matter before the annual meeting of the society held in Providence, Rhode Island, May 29, 1862. At that meeting

---

[1] American Baptist Home Mission Society, *Annual Report*, 1843, p. 17. (Cited hereafter as A. B. H. M. S., *An. Rep.*)

resolutions were adopted that preparations be made at once to send missionaries and teachers into the South and all other accessible areas as rapidly as possible.[2]   In accordance with this action missionaries were sent at once to St. Helena and Beaufort, South Carolina, and to the District of Columbia.[3]   In September 1863 the society, as the result of a thorough canvass of the situation, adopted the following resolutions:

WHEREAS, Communications have been addressed to this Board, requesting us to make some provision for the sending of assistants to our missionaries in the South and our missionaries themselves represent the desirableness of having assistants to engage in such instruction of the colored people as will enable them to read the bible and to become self-supporting and self-directing Christians,

Resolved, That this Board will gladly receive all moneys contributed and designated for this purpose and appropriate the same agreeably to the wishes of the donors.

Resolved, That in accordance with the above resolution, this board will receive applications, with proper recommendations for appointments as assistants.

Resolved, That the moneys designated for the above purpose be termed the Freedmen's Fund.[4]

As a result of these efforts, sixty-eight missionaries of the Baptist Church saw service in twelve Southern states by the close of the war in 1865.[5]

After the close of the war the society met in St. Louis, Missouri, and considered the policy to be followed in carrying forward the educational work of the denomination among the Negroes of the South.   Two considerations stood against further activity in that direction.   The first was that the denomination in the Washington, D. C., area had already established a body known as the "National Theological Institute," which had received a charter from Congress and had actually started schools at several places in the South.   The second was the establishment of the Freedmen's Bureau, which caused some of the leaders of the denomination to have the impression that the Federal Government, through the agency of the bureau, would generously provide for the Negro schools.   On the report, however, that $5,000 had been collected for the Freedmen's Fund and that eighty-six missionaries were already in twelve Southern states, the society

[2] *Ibid.,* 1862, pp. 9, 50.

[3] White, Charles L., *A Century of Faith,* p. 103.

[4] "Preamble and Resolutions Relative to the Freedmen's Fund," A. B. H. M. S., *An. Rep.,* 1864, p. 14.   [5] White, *op. cit.,* pp. 103, 104.

resolved to go forward with the work so well begun in the evangelization and education of the freedmen.   The resolutions follow:

Resolved, That, in the heaving to the surface of American Society four millions of people formerly slaves, we recognize a Providence as august and a responsibility as vast as ever felt by a single generation of men.

Resolved, That, as Christians, we know of but one method for the speedy and certain elevation of this race, and turn with confidence to the religion of Christ as comprising all the elements of their future prosperity and usefulness.

Resolved, That in the development of a ministry of their own race, we find the chief instrumentality for their religious advancement.

Resolved, That, while we recommend the continuance of efforts under the direction of the Board for the instruction of colored preachers by resident missionaries of this society, we recommend also the establishment of a school for the Christian education of teachers and preachers upon the place set forth in the circular of Dr. Binney.

Resolved, That the Board be instructed to place in trust, under the management of this supervisory committee, any property which may be procured for each school, and that the supervisory committee be appointed at the meeting, and empowered to raise funds for the enterprise.

The first, second, and third resolutions were adopted but instead of the fourth and fifth the following was substituted.

Resolved, That the Board of this Society be instructed to continue their work among the freedmen, with such increased efficiency as the means placed at their disposal will allow: giving special attention to the religious education of the colored preachers as in their discretion the circumstances of the case demand and their means will permit.[6]

As the result of a number of conferences between representatives of the society and the National Theological Institute, the latter withdrew from the field and the society thus assumed the entire responsibility for missionary work among the Negroes.[7]

By 1870 the society had under instruction 3,720 students in its schools.[8]   Gifts of money from many sources made possible the purchase of sites and the erection of buildings at many points throughout the South.   Prominent among the schools in operation at that time were Wayland Seminary at Washington, D. C.; a school at Nashville, Tennessee (later Roger Williams University); one at Raleigh, North Carolina (later Shaw University); one at New Orleans, Louisiana (later Leland College); and others at Richmond, Virginia, St. Helena, South Carolina, and Augusta,

[6] A. B. H. M. S., *An. Rep.*, 1866, pp. 31, 32.
[7] *Ibid.*, 1867, pp. 10 and 67; 1869, pp. 35 ff.; 1870, pp. 6–10.   *Ibid.*, 1870, p. 20.

Georgia.[9] Since the movement was primarily one not of mere education but of Christian education, the early reports constantly stress the training of ministers of the gospel to act as Christian leaders of their own people.   It is not strange, therefore, that all the schools mentioned included a theological seminary as part of the organization.

From 1870 to 1880 the following sums were spent in establishing plants for the schools which were destined to be rated among the best of the colleges for Negroes:

Shaw University, Raleigh, N. C., site and building	$61,000
Benedict Institute, Columbia, S. C., site	16,000
Wayland Seminary, Washington, D. C., site and building	33,375
Leland University, New Orleans, La., site and buildings	70,000
Nashville Institute, Nashville, Tenn., site and building	75,000
School at Natchez, Miss., site	17,000

The story of the schools under the Baptist denomination during their formation period, which covered roughly the decade from 1870 to 1880, parallels in nearly every particular the histories of the schools under the Congregational and the Methodist boards already described.   The same crude beginnings, the same opposition, the same eagerness on the part of the students, the same devotion on the part of teachers, the same hand-to-mouth existence—these characteristics recur frequently in the reports of all the schools and were common to the work of all the denominations.   Hence a repetition of conditions already described is unnecessary.

In 1880 a new site was purchased for Richmond Institute for $15,000; Benedict College erected a dormitory and dining hall costing $7,500; Bishop College, at Marshall, Texas, received a building and property at a cost of $25,000; and Shaw University was given a dormitory for medical students which cost $5,000.[10]

The same year the society removed the Augusta Institute from Augusta to Atlanta, Georgia, and changed its name to Atlanta Baptist Seminary.   In 1879 the name of the school was changed to Atlanta Baptist College.   In 1913 the name of the school was again changed to Morehouse College in honor of Dr. Henry Lyman Morehouse, who served from 1879 to 1902 as secretary of the society.[11]   This college, now a college for men, has had a distin-

[9] A. B. H. M. S., *An. Rep.*, 1870, pp. 21–23.   [10] White, *op. cit.*, pp. 105–06.

[11] For the story of this school to 1917 see Brawley, Benjamin, *History of Morehouse College* (Atlanta, Georgia, 1917).

guished history, has met the requirements for the highest rating by the regional association covering the Southern area, and is one of the three schools involved in the Atlanta-Morehouse-Spelman affiliation, to be referred to in a later section of this study.

SPELMAN COLLEGE

Although Spelman College does not belong to the list of colleges directly under the society, yet its relationships to the society have been so close that it seems appropriate to refer here to that remarkable institution.   Starting from the most humble beginnings in 1881, it has developed into a school for women which has received not only the commendation of the public but also an "A" rating by the Association of Colleges and Secondary Schools of the Southern states.   The school was begun in the basement of a Negro church in Atlanta by two New England white women, Miss Sophia B. Packard and Miss Harriet E. Giles. Encouraged by the interest of the Woman's American Baptist Home Mission Society of New England, they went to Atlanta and opened a school for girls in Friendship Baptist Church with eleven pupils, mainly grown women.   During the following summer, Miss Packard met Mr. John D. Rockefeller at a church in Cleveland where she was soliciting funds for her school. Favorably impressed, Mr. Rockefeller contributed something immediately, promising more should the enterprise prove permanent.

A permanent location was procured for the school in 1883 by the purchase, for $5,000, of property formerly used as a barrack and drill ground for the Union soldiers during the Civil War.   The Negro Baptists of Georgia subscribed $3,000 and other Negroes $1,300 toward liquidating the debt incurred, but by 1884 half the amount was still owed on the property although several extensions of the payment had been made.   In April of that year Mr. Rockefeller and his family visited the school.   He was so deeply impressed with what he saw that he paid off the debt. About that time, at Miss Packard's suggestion, the name of the school was changed to Spelman Seminary from the name of Mrs. Rockefeller's family.   This manifestation of interest by such an important person proved to be a valuable endorsement of the work and the beginning of a relationship of the school with the Rockefeller family that continues to the present time.   Favorable actions from Northern church organizations and individuals made it possible for the school to keep up with its growth in enrollment. The John F. Slater Fund began its contributions to the school in 1883 for industrial work, and supplied funds the next year for a printing department. In 1884 Mr. Rockefeller gave $40,000 for the erection of a brick building, a gift that was followed through the years by others from the same source.[12]

The school has been under excellent management, both business and educational, from the beginning. As a result, its growth from an elementary school to a college has been slow and carefully directed, hence substantial. The physical plant shows the result of wise planning, good management, and generous support. It has developed with the needs of the college, both in quantity and in character. This means that the curriculum has never outrun the physical capacity of the plant. A four-year college was organized only when the school possessed the faculty, the laboratories, and the library facilities to do creditable four-year college work.

The reports of the treasurers of the American Baptist Home Mission Society show that between 1883 and 1932 that body contributed $330,052.27 to Spelman.[13]

FINANCES

About 1900 the society found that the proper development of the work which it had undertaken among Negroes was straining its resources in view of the heavy responsibilities which it felt obliged to carry in other fields of missionary endeavor. Mayo, referring to this phase of the work in 1901, says:

In the fifteen years of the service of Dr. McVicker as corresponding secretary the schools had increased from 8 to 34, from 38 teachers to 200, from an attendance of 1,191 to 5,000 or 6,000 pupils. Thirty-five substantial buildings had been reared and a school property of $1,000,000 placed on the grounds. The schools had greatly improved in quality and the cost of their maintenance had accordingly increased. At least 7 of the larger schools put in an immediate demand for a stronger corps of instruction. In five years $150,000 would be needed for the annual expenditure. The powerful competition of the schools of other churches would leave the schools of this sect in the background when left to the test of respective merits. The Home Mission Society has already found it impossible to meet this demand except by the sacrifice of important missionary and educational enterprises.

[12] *Spelman College Bulletin*, Vol. V, No. 1, April 1932, pp. 7–9.   [13] White, *op. cit.*, p. 107.

The society is steadily falling behind in pecuniary affairs. A reduction of 40 or 50 per cent in missionary appropriations should be made, if the schools in the South are kept up. It is safe only to appropriate $50,000 a year for this important work. A permanent fund of $1,000,000 is imperatively needed, as the present expenditure requires the income of $2,000,000 at 5 per cent interest.[14]

It was quite evident to this able educator and informed student of Negro education even at that time that some careful planning must be done with reference to the allocation of work and the selection of students, in order to escape serious embarrassment. He continues:

The training of leaders should be the chief, if not the only, work of the schools of the society. The graduates should be not only prepared as teachers and ministers, but trained for leadership in every department of life, social, civil, private, and public. All theological work should be confined to the school at Richmond, Va. Only a limited number of schools should be allowed to do proper college work, seven at the most, and not more than two schools be permitted to give a full professional training for which a normal diploma should be granted. A careful system of examination and inspection should be inaugurated in all the schools and the quality as well as quantity of the teaching force should be strictly considered. A large portion of the report deals with a bad condition of affairs in one of the institutions in Texas, and the burning by incendiary fires of several of their school buildings in Arkansas, Texas and South Carolina.

In 1895 the Baptist church had made a hopeful advance toward the improvement of the school work in the appointment of an advisory committee in connection with the schools for colored people in the South supported by the Home Mission Society. The committee was to be only advisory, with no general or educational authority, but to have access to all schools and invited to present the results of their investigation to the two Home Mission Boards and the acting authorities of the institutions. This was a favorable movement toward what must inevitably come, and practical union and coöperation for all general purposes of the great educational missionary bodies, especially of the Protestant evangelical churches in both sections of the Union. Indeed, the practical beginning of this outward advancement toward some union of the sort is today evident to all observers competent to hold in one view the past experience and the inevitable burden that will fall upon these denominations if they continue the purely sectarian policy of expansion that has already brought the richest and most zealous of them to the brink of a financial crisis.[15]

Very definite efforts have been made since 1900 to avert disaster by making some of the adjustments suggested and with considerable success although the society has been compelled to

---

[14] Mayo, A. D., "The Northern Churches and the Freedmen," in *U. S. Com. of Ed., An. Rep.,* 1902, p. 313. [15] *Ibid.,* pp. 313, 314.

make drastic readjustments to meet the economic depression following 1929.

It must constantly be borne in mind that this society, in common with all the others working in the field of Negro education, contributes only a part, and sometimes a small part, of the income required to operate a school under its patronage. For example, in 1916–17, the report indicates that the society appropriated $100,000 to schools whose total cash transactions were $500,000. This means that for each dollar spent by the society the Negroes spend four. The report goes on to say:

At an expense of $100,000 we are training over 6,000 young people and fitting them for Christian service at a cost to the society of $17.00 each.[16]

In the report of the Board of Managers for 1929, attention was called to the rapidly increasing cost of maintaining the Negro schools as a result of the rise in the level of instruction. It was noted that "thirty years ago $10,000 a year would maintain a school of 400 children below the twelfth grade. Now $40,000 will not maintain a school of 300 college students." Yet the appropriations of the society for the Negro schools had hardly changed in these years.[17] In spite of an increased amount paid in by students as fees, the society found it necessary gradually to withdraw its aid from some schools in order to carry out its plan of maintaining at least one good school in each Southern state. This, however, was found impossible even in the years of economic prosperity which ended in the year of the report quoted. The report urged an increase in annual appropriations of $100,000 or new endowments of $2,000,000 so that the Baptist schools might be put "on a par with other Negro colleges."[18]

In order to meet the pressing financial difficulties the society has been generously aided by the General Education Board. From 1908 to 1917 it gave the society for its work in Negro education the sum of $84,413.75. From 1917 to 1928 it gave for current expenses, $463,072; for new buildings and additional land, $476,700 and for endowment $1,200,000, a total of $2,139,772. For the twenty years from 1908 to 1928 the total is $2,224,185.75.[19]

[16] A. B. H. M. S., *An. Rep.*, 1916–17, p. 47.

[17] The inability to increase income in proportion to the rising cost of education may fairly be considered a common characteristic of the Negro colleges under denominational boards and the basic reason for the need of increasing support from sources outside the church.

[18] A. B. H. M. S., *An. Rep.*, 1929, p. 31   [19] White, *op. cit.*, p. 110.

POLICIES

In 1932 the society issued a volume in commemoration of its one hundredth birthday. The volume is by Dr. Charles L. White and is entitled *A Century of Faith*. It is fair to assume that the policies of the society with reference to the Negro colleges under its direction and patronage can be justly derived from material given in this volume which presumably has the endorsement of the society. In the section entitled "Prophetic Trends," the author says:

The Society has never chosen lines of least resistance and has often gone forward in the face of serious difficulties. In 1870 public schools in the South began to give instruction to Negro children, and the leaders of the churches needed a higher training. High schools, therefore, were added to the Society's primary schools in certain localities and others were discontinued or released to public-school authorities.

In 1894 Secretary Thomas J. Morgan asserted in his annual report that the same education should be given to Negroes that the white young people received, and especially to leaders through whom the masses must be reached. At this time, public high schools began to be provided for colored children and the Society gradually developed colleges for the training of Christian teachers and preachers and largely discontinued the primary work which had not already been given into other hands. In 1903 the annual report reiterated the view "that the paramount purpose in the establishment of these schools was the training of Christian ministers and teachers."

The constant extension of Negro high schools through the South also led to the general lessening of aid to twenty-one secondary institutions and, in 1930 the Society confined the appropriations to nine colleges. All but three of these have Negro faculties: Benedict College, Columbia, South Carolina; Bishop College, Marshall, Texas; Jackson College, Jackson, Mississippi; Leland College, Baker, Louisiana; Morehouse College, Atlanta, Georgia; Roger Williams College, Memphis, Tennessee; Shaw University, Raleigh, North Carolina; Spelman College, Atlanta, Georgia; Virginia Union University, Richmond, Virginia.

In 1931 the Board voted that one or more members of the Society's Board should be nominated to fill vacancies in the boards of the Negro schools, while they are under the control of the Society.

For the last twenty-five years the Board has been generally unable to increase its appropriations to the schools, except as it has administered enlarged endowments, but the actual income and expenditures have increased three to fourfold. This has been derived from additional endowments, greater contributions from Negroes and higher charges for board and tuition.

The Society has always adjusted its educational work to changing conditions, has concentrated its efforts at strategic points and in schools of higher grades and has primarily trained preachers, teachers, and other leaders. It has always endeavored to develop the self-respect of the Negro to prepare him to cope with the vital questions of social, educational, and religious life, with a breadth of view comparable to that given the white young men and women in their Christian colleges. It is the policy of the Society to complete the steps already taken, to advise that ultimately the Boards of Trustees shall consist entirely of Negroes, with the Society giving counsel and directing only the expenditure of money that it receives. The Board also desires to turn over the support of the schools as soon as possible, administering only the numerous trust funds that it holds for them. While the Society generally confines its support to one institution in each State, it has favored the merging of institutions wherever feasible, and the coördination of colleges as in Atlanta University.

The Society also in most cases has been forced to maintain colleges without adequate equipment, although the advance in educational standards has rapidly increased. In ten years the attendance in college classes has grown from 318 to 1,474, calling for greatly increased expenditure; but the approved denominational budget has required the diminishing of appropriations. Tuition and other charges have been raised and Negroes are bearing a larger part of the cost of their education. But even so, the income has not kept the schools up to the desired standards. The requirements of the State Education Boards in the South are constantly being raised, and some colleges have been in imminent danger of losing their rating.

The strain upon the Society to maintain the colleges has been very great. To meet the need in part, the General Education Board for several years gave annually over sixty thousand dollars and provided three practise-school buildings and three science halls. The financial and equipment needs of Spelman College, which the Society strongly assisted in former years, have been generously met by the General Education Board and by the Laura Spelman Rockefeller Foundation.[20]

In 1932 the society controlled the following colleges: Benedict College, Columbia, South Carolina; Bishop College, Marshall, Texas; Jackson College, Jackson, Mississippi; Leland College, Baker, Louisiana; Morehouse College, Atlanta, Georgia; Virginia Union University, Richmond, Virginia.[21]

[20] White, *op. cit.*, p. 113–15.   [21] A. B. H. M. S., *An. Rep.*, pp. 50–53.

CHAPTER IX

THE BOARDS UNDER OTHER NORTHERN DENOMINATIONS

WHILE the three denominational organizations discussed above have been the most active in the education of the Negro since 1865, other religious bodies have assisted in the task and have succeeded in developing several very creditable institutions of higher learning.

THE PRESBYTERIANS

The Committee of Missions for Freedmen of the Presbyterian Church, North, entered the educational field in behalf of the Negro as early as 1865, following, in general, the parochial system of relating their schools closely with individual churches. In 1871 the board was operating forty-five schools with fifty-eight teachers and 4,530 pupils. According to the report of the board of that year, the churches of the denomination throughout the country had not responded with contributions as generously as had been expected. As a result the board was heavily in debt.[1] Among the schools operating during that period, which later gave college work, were Biddle Memorial Institute at Charlotte, North Carolina, and Scotia Seminary at Concord in the same state.

In 1883 the general assembly of the Presbyterian Church, North, voted to establish "The Presbyterian Board of Missions for Freedmen of the Presbyterian Church in the United States of America," thus changing the name of the missionary agency. The body was incorporated the same year. By that time the annual income had increased to $108,120.85.[2]

Little advance was made in the work during the following decade. By 1896 a debt had accumulated and the board reported that a number of schools had been suspended. In 1897 the general receipts declined to the lowest point in nine years. Commenting upon this situation Mayo says:

[1] Mayo, A. D., p. 301.   [2] *Ibid.*, p. 302.

It is not easy to understand why the powerful and wealthy Presbyterian Church of the Northern States has fallen so far behind the Congregational and Methodist bodies in the support of its schools for the freedmen. It will be remembered that at an early date this religious sect had formed the backbone of the educational work for the white people of the Southern States, and has always been distinguished for the cultivation, ability, and Christian zeal of its ministry. Perhaps an explanation will be found in the fact that in this church the central purpose of training teachers for the common schools of the colored people of the South has been almost ignored, there being only five schools of this sort, none of them of the first class in numbers and importance, engaged in this work. Their day schools have been "strictly parochial," and, of course, out of touch with the general work of the American common school. The financial depression of several years previous to 1897 told on all these missionary school agencies, and those that were exclusively ecclesiastical were the first to suffer.[3]

The survey of Negro education in 1917 shows that the board in 1916 had under its control eighty-five schools whose total value was $2,151,321. Thirty-two of these schools were classed as large and fifty-three as small.[4] Of these only five are of particular interest in the present study. These are Biddle University, Charlotte, North Carolina, Barber Memorial Seminary, Anniston, Alabama, Scotia Seminary, Concord, North Carolina, Mary Allen Seminary, Crockett, Texas, and Swift Memorial College, Rogersville, Tennessee.

Biddle Memorial Institute, now Johnson C. Smith University, a school for men, was founded in 1867 by the Presbytery of Catawaba, at Charlotte, North Carolina, largely as the result of a determination of the Reverend S. C. Alexander and the Reverend W. L. Miller to found there a school to train teachers and preachers of the Negro race who would go forth in turn and minister to the needs of their people. Alexander undertook to administer the affairs of the infant school at home while Miller presented its claims to the country in the capacity of financial agent.[5]

The name of the school was chosen in honor of Major H. Biddle, whose widow, hearing of the new project, gave $1,400 toward its promotion. The first eight acres of land for a site for the institution were given by Colonel W. R. Mears, a wealthy white citizen of Charlotte.[6]

With funds received from the Freedmen's Bureau in 1867, the

[3] Mayo, A. D., p. 302.   [4] *U. S. Bur. of Ed. Bul.*, 1916, No. 38, p. 342.

[5] McCrory, Henry L., "History of Johnson C. Smith University," *Quarterly Review of Higher Education Among Negroes*, April 1933, pp. 29, 30.

[6] *Johnson C. Smith University Bulletin*, April 1933, p. 17.

first buildings were erected and the school began its work at its permanent site in 1869 with two departments of study—one for students of secondary grade and the other for those ready to pursue advanced preparation as teachers and preachers.[7] The first building of importance erected on the campus for general purposes was named Logan Hall in honor of Dr. S. C. Logan, who was corresponding secretary of the Freedmen's Committee of the denomination during the formative years of the institution. The first large building to house the students was erected in 1895, twenty-eight years after the establishment of the school, and named Carter Hall in honor of Miss Mary A. Carter of Geneva, New York, who donated the necessary funds.[8]

The first president of the institution was Doctor Stephen Matton, whose administration extended from 1870 to 1883. During these thirteen years, the permanency of the school was assured and local prejudice was overcome. At the close of his administration the charter was amended and the name of the institution changed to Biddle University.[9] The second president was the Reverend W. A. Halliday, whose administration extended over one year. He was succeeded in 1885 by Dr. W. F. Johnson, whose term of office extended over a period of six years to 1891.

At that time the experiment of placing a Negro at the head of the school, in the person of Dr. Daniel J. Sanders, was favorably considered by the board. Although many persons thought that the experiment was premature and many church publications condemned it, the board believed that the time was ripe to test the ability of the race in the management of such an institution. Dr. Sanders justified this faith and gave Biddle a most successful administration until his death in 1907. With this brilliant example of Negro leadership before them, the trustees naturally appointed as his successor a Negro member of the faculty, Dr. Henry L. McCrory, who has administered the affairs of the college with marked success during the past twenty-six years.[11]

Under the McCrory administration the institution has changed from a small struggling school to one of the most notable colleges among the higher institutions for Negroes. Dr. McCrory real-

---

[7] McCrory, *op. cit.*, p. 31. [8] *Ibid.*, p. 32.
[9] *Ibid.*, p. 32. (The catalog of the school for 1932 gives this date as 1877. *Johnson C. Smith University Bulletin*, April 1932, p. 17.) [11] McCrory, *op. cit.*

ized from the beginning that the most pressing immediate needs of the school in order to lay the foundations for effective college work were increased financial support and a more extensive plant. During the first decade of his administration he erected a library building for $15,000, of which sum Mr. Andrew Carnegie contributed $12,500, and raised an endowment of $12,500 for its support. He also persuaded friends of the school to extend the area of the grounds from sixty to seventy-five acres.

In 1921 the school was fortunate in winning the friendship of Mrs. Johnson C. Smith of Pittsburgh, Pennsylvania, who, between that date and 1929, gave to the school $400,000 for buildings and equipment and $302,500 for endowment. These gifts amounting to $702,500, in addition to the Duke endowment mentioned below, enabled the administration to improve the character of the work very greatly and to go forward with a feeling of financial security before unknown. In 1929 the high school department was abolished and the school left free to concentrate upon the work of its liberal arts college and its theological seminary.[12] In recognition of the generosity of Mrs. Smith, the trustees, in 1923, changed the name of the institution to Johnson C. Smith University, and an amended charter was procured from the legislature of North Carolina.[13]

In 1924 by the will of Mr. James B. Duke of Charlotte, North Carolina, an endowment trust was set up, a part of which was designated for the benefit of Johnson C. Smith University. By the terms of the will:

Four per cent of said net amount not retained as aforesaid for addition to the corpus of the trust shall be paid to the Johnson C. Smith University (by whatever name it may be known) an institution of learning for colored people, now located at Charlotte, in said State of North Carolina, so long as it shall not be operated for private gain, to be utilized by said institution for any and all of the purposes thereof.[14]

This legacy, estimated at from $1,000,000 to $1,500,000,[15] is the largest single gift for endowment for a Negro college that has been made public.

In 1932 Barber-Scotia College of Concord, North Carolina,

---

[12] McCrory, *op. cit.,* p. 34.   [13] *Johnson C. Smith University Bulletin, op. cit.,* p. 18.
[14] *The Duke Endowment Yearbook,* No. 1, Dec. 11, 1924, p. xi, Indenture.
[15] President McCrory, in his statement to the trustees of the Duke Endowment in 1924, estimated the value at $1,000,000 (*ibid.,* p. 49); in his article in *Quarterly Review of Higher Education Among Negroes,* April 1933, p. 34, he places it at $1,500,000.

was affiliated with Johnson C. Smith University as one of the undergraduate junior college divisions of that institution, thus furnishing a commendable example of concentration and co-operation.   This affiliation places in one institution all the collegiate work directly under the board now under discussion and gives to Johnson C. Smith University the status of a co-educational college above the sophomore year.[16]

Scotia Seminary was founded as a school for women in 1870. In 1916 the name was changed to Scotia Women's College. Barber Memorial College was founded in 1896 at Anniston, Alabama, also as a school for women.   In 1930 these two schools were merged to become Barber-Scotia College,[17] the work of the merged institutions being carried on at Concord, North Carolina, until 1932 when the affiliation with Johnson C. Smith was consummated.   The Barber-Scotia Junior College remains at Concord, under the direction of a dean.

Mary Allen Seminary (located at Crockett, Texas), now of junior college grade, had in 1932 an enrollment of 125 students of college grade.   Swift Memorial College at Rogersville, Tennessee, is also of junior college grade with a college enrollment of twenty-eight.

While Lincoln University (in Pennsylvania) is not as a whole controlled by the board now under consideration, the Theological Seminary of that institution is controlled by that body.   The university is governed by an independent board of trustees, but is generally looked upon as very closely related to the Presbyterian Church.   The institution was founded by the Presbyterians as Ashmun Institute in 1854, thus antedating in its establishment any other institution in America which later became a college for Negroes.   In 1866 it received its charter under the name of Lincoln University.[18]

THE BOARD OF FREEDMEN'S MISSIONS OF THE UNITED PRESBYTERIAN CHURCH

The United Presbyterian Church was one of the first to engage in work among the freedmen.   The Reverend J. G. McKee was sent, in 1863, as the first missionary from the Second Synod of the

---

[16] *Johnson C. Smith University Bulletin*, April 1932, p. 18.
[17] *Barber-Scotia Bulletin*, Catalog Number, 1932–33, p.11.
[18] *Lincoln University Herald*, Jan. 1932, p. 13.

West, to take up the work among the Negroes at Nashville, Tennessee.[19] During the later years of the war and following that time, other schools were opened in the states of North Carolina, Alabama, Tennessee, and Virginia.

In 1916 fifteen of these schools were in existence, of which eleven were classed as large and four as small.[20] Only one has attained rank above the secondary level. In 1872 the board, after surveying the whole area available for a mission school of high grade which the denomination might develop into an institution of higher learning, founded Knoxville College in the city of that name in central Tennessee as a coeducational school. The institution slowly developed until in 1932 it was given "B" rating by the Southern Association of Colleges and Secondary Schools. The plant, including ninety acres of land and twelve buildings, is valued at $600,000.[21] In 1926–27 its income was $68,687, of which $49,342.19 came from church appropriations.[22] The college enrollment for 1931–32 was 300.

THE AMERICAN CHURCH INSTITUTE FOR NEGROES OF THE PROTESTANT EPISCOPAL CHURCH

The American Church Institute for Negroes was organized by the Protestant Episcopal Church and incorporated in 1906 as the body to take care of the interests of the church in its promotion of education for the Negro. The 1917 survey of Negro education lists ten large and fourteen small schools under this board.[23] One of these has developed into a four-year college while three others have developed into junior colleges. The schools under the board doing college work at the present time, with dates of establishment, are:

College	*Date*
Four-year college	
Saint Augustine's College, Raleigh, North Carolina.............	1867
Junior colleges	
Fort Valley, Normal & Industrial Institute, Fort Valley, Georgia....	1893
Saint Phillip's Junior College, San Antonio, Texas..............	
Saint Paul Normal & Industrial Institute, Lawrenceville, Virginia...	1888[24]

[19] *Historical Sketch of the Freedmen's Missions of the United Presbyterian Church,* 1862–1904, p. 1.   [20] *U. S. Bur. of Ed. Bul.,* 1916, No. 38, p. 344.
[21] *Knoxville College Bulletin,* April 1932, p. 10.
[22] *U. S. Bur. of Ed. Bul.,* 1928, No. 7, p. 758. (*Survey of Negro Colleges and Universities.*)
[23] *U. S. Bur. of Ed. Bul.,* 1916, No. 38, pp. 146, 147.
[24] McCuistion, Fred, *Higher Education Among Negroes,* pp. 9, 10.

THE UNITED CHRISTIAN MISSIONARY SOCIETY OF THE DISCIPLES OF CHRIST

This body founded the Southern Christian Institute at Hemingway, Mississippi, and obtained a charter in 1875. In 1882 it was moved to a new site at Edwards, Mississippi, its present location. In 1926–27 the school received an income of $43,800.72, of which $19,000 came from the society.[25] In 1932 it had progressed far enough in its curriculum to be classed as a junior college with an enrollment of nineteen college students.[26]

The society operates one other school of collegiate rank— Jarvis Christian Institute, located at Hawkins, Texas. This school was founded in 1914. By 1928–29 it was receiving an income of $33,320, of which $21,000 came from the society.[27] In 1932 it was ranked as a junior college, enrolling 38 students of college grade.[28]

SISTERS OF THE BLESSED SACRAMENT OF PENNSYLVANIA OF THE ROMAN CATHOLIC CHURCH

While the Roman Catholic Church has promoted educational activities in nearly every state in the South since the emancipation of the Negro, all of them were below collegiate grade until recent years. In 1917 Jones reported 112 schools under the Catholic Board of Missions, seven of which were classed as large and 105 as small.[29]

The one school for Negroes under the auspices of the Catholic Church that has developed into a college is Xavier College in New Orleans, Louisiana, which was established as a high school in 1915. In 1917 a normal school was begun which eight years later was developed into a teachers college. During the same year a two-year course in premedical work was offered in a college of liberal arts. A school of pharmacy was added in 1927. In 1918 the school was incorporated by the State of Louisiana under the title "Xavier University," although Xavier College is the name used by those in charge. The Sisters of the Blessed Sacrament, incorporated in the State of Pennsylvania, have charge of both the educational and the financial affairs of the institution.[30]

---

[25] *Survey of Negro Colleges and Universities*, p. 441.
[27] *Survey of Negro Colleges and Universities*, p. 866.
[29] *U. S. Bur. of Ed. Bul.*, 1916, No. 38, p. 339.

[26] McCuistion, *op. cit.*, p. 9.
[28] McCuistion, *op. cit.*, p. 10.
[30] *Ibid.*, 1928, No. 7, p. 381.

In June 1929 a new site was obtained as part of a plan of expansion, and in October 1931 the construction of three buildings was begun. These are the faculty building, the science building, and the main college building.[31] The school enrolled 192 students in college classes in 1931–32.[32]

[31] *Xavier College Bulletin*, 1932–33, p. 4.   [32] McCuistion, *op. cit.*, p. 9.

CHAPTER X

THE NEGRO DENOMINATIONS

THE history of the Negro religious denominations in America is a story of a struggle against terrible odds, resulting from poverty, ignorance, and economic discrimination, by groups who desired to direct themselves by establishing and maintaining organizations independent of the great parent bodies from which they sprang. Bishop Tanner thus tersely expresses the basic impulses that led to the separation of the African Methodists from the parent body:

The great crime committed by the Founders of the African Methodist Episcopal Church, against the prejudiced white American, and the timid black —the crime which seems unpardonable, was that they dared to organize a Church of men; men to think for themselves; men to talk for themselves; men to act for themselves: a Church of men who support from their own substance, however scanty, the ministrations of the Word which they receive; men who spurn to have their churches built for them, and their pastors supported from the coffers of some charitable organization; men who prefer to live by the sweat of their own brow and be free. Not that the members of this communion are filled with evil pride, for they exhibit a spirit no more haughty nor overbearing than Paul, who never neglected to remind the world that he was a man and a Roman citizen. Slavery and prejudice stood up like demons before Allen and his compeers, and forbade them to use the talents which God had given. Slavery bellowed in one ear, "You may obey but you shall not rule." Prejudice thundered in the other, "You may hear but you shall not speak." And to utterly break their spirits, they both took up the damning refrain, "God may permit you to be Levites, but not Priests." [1]

It was mainly this desire for independence and self-control as opposed to what the founders considered unfair treatment by the parent bodies that accounts for the existence of the Negro denominations as we find them in America today. Because of their independence, these denominations, for the most part, have been compelled to finance their various enterprises, such as churches, missions, and schools, from incomes derived from a constituency whose economic status is the lowest of any group in the United States. Those who furnish the funds include in their number no

[1] Tanner, Benjamin T., *An Apology for African Methodism*, pp. 16, 17.

individuals of wealth who can be called upon to meet emergencies but people who, in general, labor with their hands. Of course, no legacies of any size have been available nor have millionaires established foundations for the support of the various educational enterprises of these denominations. These schools represent the sacrifices of a group economically handicapped.

In spite of the serious disadvantage under which this group of schools must secure support, they have rendered splendid service to the education of the race and, in comparison with the other colleges for Negroes supported by denominational boards, have been as well supported. As a result of the survey of Negro colleges made in 1926 and 1927 by the United States Bureau of Education, the Negro denominations were found to have done so well in the support of their institutions of higher learning as to be rated, in this respect, above the Northern white denominations maintaining colleges for Negroes. According to the figures presented in the report of this survey, the average annual income of sixteen colleges owned, controlled, and supported by the Negro denominations was $66,977 as compared with the corresponding figure of $61,075 for the thirty-one colleges under Northern white denominational boards.[2] Commenting upon this fact, the report says:

Colleges having the third largest average annual income per institution comprise the group under the supervision of State negro church organizations or conferences, an impressive ranking in view of the lack of wealth existing generally among the Negroes of the South. That the Negro church organizations have been able to provide an average annual income for their colleges in excess of that of institutions operated by the Northern white denominational boards is a high tribute to their sacrificial and unselfish devotion to Negro higher education.[3]

THE AFRICAN METHODIST EPISCOPAL CHURCH

As a result of dissatisfaction at their treatment by the Methodist Episcopal Church, sixteen delegates from Pennsylvania, Delaware, and New Jersey, at a convention held in Baltimore, Maryland, in 1816, organized an independent denomination of Negroes with the title the African Methodist Episcopal Church.[4] The Reverend Richard Allen was the first bishop

[2] *U. S. Bur. of Ed. Bul.*, 1928, No. 7, p. 7.   [3] *Ibid.*, pp. 7, 8.
[4] Woodson, Carter G., *The History of the Negro Church*, pp. 72–78; Payne, Daniel A., *History of the A. M. E. Church*, Chap. IV.

elected, and until his death he was one of the leading spirits of the denomination.   Before the Civil War the denomination grew slowly, confining its activities mainly to the Northern states. During its first forty years it increased to ten conferences and 20,000 members.   By 1866, after the close of the Civil War, there were ten conferences and 75,000 members,[5] the increase being due to the extension of the denomination into the Southern states. Since that date the denomination has spread to every state in the Union.

As a group the founders of the church were ignorant men, most of them illiterate.   During the early years of the organization nothing seems to have been done with reference to the establishment of educational institutions [6] in marked distinction to the educational activities of the parent body of Methodism from which schools and churches were inseparable.[7]   Not until 1833 does there appear in the record any specific reference to the need of educational agencies for the promotion of the good of the people.   In that year the following resolutions were adopted at the annual meeting of the Ohio Conference:

Resolved, 1st.   As the sense of this house, that common schools, Sunday-schools and temperance societies are of the highest importance to all people, but more especially to our people.

Resolved, 2d.   That it shall be the duty of every member of this Conference to do all in his power to promote and establish these useful institutions among our people.[8]

In 1843, at the annual conference in Philadelphia, resolutions were adopted containing the outline of a course of study for traveling and local preachers.   This resolution by vote was ordered to be presented at the next general conference of the denomination for adoption so that it would apply to the entire convention. There was actual opposition to the movement toward an educated ministry, based upon a fear that "if the measure proposed be adopted by the General Conference, discord and dissolution will necessarily take place in the church between the ignorant and intelligent portions of it." [9]

At the first education convention of the church, held in Philadelphia, two rival schemes were presented for the purpose of in-

[5] DuBois, W. E. B., *The Negro Church*, p. 42.   [6] Payne, *op. cit.*, pp. 393, 394.

[7] Simpson, Matthew, *A Hundred Years of Methodism*, pp. 31, 32, 252; Tewksbury, Donald G., *The Founding of American Colleges and Universities Before the Civil War*, pp. 103 ff.

[8] Payne, *op. cit.*, p. 394.   [9] *Ibid.*, p. 396.

suring an educated ministry. The first was the organization of
an educational association to raise funds to defray the expenses of
promising young men who would attend any of the several schools
which at that time would admit Negro students. The second was
to found and maintain a collegiate institution for the education of
youth, owned and controlled by the church. Both plans were
adopted, but neither was brought to fruition by the conferences of
the East which composed the convention.[10]

It was the Ohio Annual Conference which first set up an educational institution on a tract of land about fourteen miles from
Columbus, Ohio. In describing this school the historian says:

> The institution was called Union Seminary. It did not succeed. Much
> time was spent in collecting funds to buy the land (one hundred and eighty
> acres, more or less), and to erect a comparatively small frame building upon it.
> A primary school was kept up for several years, but it was such a school as no
> intelligent parent would send a child from Columbus, Ohio, fourteen miles
> away, to attend, because better schools supported by state funds, were at their
> command and at their threshold in all the large towns of Ohio.[11]

This reason given for the failure of this school indicates the difference between conditions in Ohio in 1856 and in the Southern
states immediately following the close of the Civil War. In Ohio
a poor school for Negroes could not succeed because of the competition of public schools which Negroes could attend. In the
South, almost any kind of school for Negroes would be eagerly
attended and considered successful in the absence of anything
better.

Meanwhile the Cincinnati Conference of the Methodist Episcopal Church had been working out a plan for the establishment
of an educational institution for the Negroes of Ohio which resulted in the establishment, in 1856, of Wilberforce University at
Tawawa Springs, a few miles from Xenia, Ohio. This school was
named in honor of William Wilberforce, the English abolitionist
and philanthropist. It did work of elementary grade until 1863,
when it was offered to the African Methodist Episcopal Church
for $10,000, a sum which covered its indebtedness, and accepted
for the church by Bishop Daniel A. Payne, who served for thirteen
years as the first president of the school.[12] A summary of the
founding and early history of Wilberforce can best be told in
Bishop Payne's own words written in 1876.

[10] Payne, *op. cit.*, pp. 398, 399.   [11] *Ibid.*, p. 399.
[12] Payne, Daniel A., *Recollections of Seventy Years*, pp. 152, 153.

Fully to appreciate the results of our efforts, it is necessary to remember:

First. That the 10th of March, 1876, will be just thirteen years since we purchased the real estate of Wilberforce University at a cost of $10,000, and the end of July, 1876 will be thirteen years since the school opened.

Second. That we had not a dollar when we made the bid for the property.

Third. That we opened the school with but six pupils in primary English studies, having but one teacher, and that we were burnt out about two years after we made the purchase of the property. Our dormitories, recitation rooms, library and chapel were all consumed, and our school almost broken up. We had to begin anew. Now we have so far completed our new building that we shall be able to dedicate it this summer. The burnt edifice was made of wood, erected on a light brick foundation—it was beautiful, but a light, airy thing. Our present edifice is of heavy brick on a massive stone foundation. The cost, when completed and furnished, will be about $45,000.

Within thirteen years from the time we opened our primary English school we shall have graduated thirteen young ladies and sixteen young men—total, twenty-nine. All our graduates have been engaged in the honorable and useful employment of the pulpit and the school-room. Three have been elected to full professorships in their *Alma Mater*, and one is principal of Lincoln Institute, a high and normal school in the state of Missouri for the secondary education of colored youth. In addition to these, scores of undergraduates have received partial education within the past twelve years, who are now employed, or have been, as teachers and preachers in the western and southern states, but chiefly in the latter.

Concerning the election of trustees and faculty. Inasmuch as Wilberforce is under denominational auspices, it was deemed prudent at the time of its organization to have each Annual Conference represented by two laymen and three clergymen, and therefore, inasmuch as there are twenty-three Annual Conferences, there are one hundred and fifteen denominational trustees. To these add nine honorary trustees and the six Bishops, who are *ex officio* trustees, and we have the enormous board of one hundred and thirty; but practically we have not more than twenty-four, the largest number ever present at an annual meeting. The lesson taught us at the end of twelve years is, that there is no need of having more than one clergyman and one layman to represent an Annual Conference, who may have alternates. These, with ten or twelve honorary members, and the *ex officio*, from whom a quorum can be convened within three hours' ride of the University, would be sufficient for all practical purposes. . . .[13]

Financial aid from white friends played an important part in the early history of the school. In 1867–68 the Society for the Promotion of Collegiate and Theological Education in the West made a grant of $1,800 and voted the same amount the next year, which was paid in part. Between 1868 and 1875 the American Unitarian Association gave approximately $4,000. The Hon-

[13] Payne, Daniel A., *History of the A. M. E. Church*, pp. 437, 438.

orable Gerrit Smith gave $500 in 1868, and the same year Chief Justice Salmon P. Chase procured for the school $300 from an English friend, and he himself left the institution $10,000 in his will. The Freedmen's Bureau granted to Wilberforce $3,000 in 1869 and $25,000 the following year—the latter by special congressional action. The principal support for the school, however, came from collections raised by the several conferences of the church and allocated to education.[14]

In the beginning the instruction was naturally on the elementary and secondary levels. In 1865 the Payne Theological Seminary was organized on the campus but under a separate board of trustees. Two years later a college of liberal arts was established, although the enrollment in this department remained small for a considerable period. The state of Ohio in 1889 entered into an arrangement with Wilberforce University under which the legislature established a normal and industrial department at the university providing for its support from public taxes. As a result of this development Wilberforce University is governed by three different bodies. The liberal arts college and the high school are under a board of one hundred persons elected by the annual conferences of the African Methodist Episcopal Church, which elects twenty-one from its membership to administer the work of the college directly. The Payne Theological Seminary is controlled by a board of seven members, three of whom must be bishops and the remainder ministers of the denomination. The Combined Normal and Industrial Department is governed by a board of nine persons, including the president of the university. Five members are appointed by the governor of the state of Ohio, and three by the Ohio Conference of the African Methodist Episcopal Church.[15]

The statement given in Table VI relative to the income of the university for a period of five years shows a decided increase from 1922–23 to 1926–27, and also indicates the important part played by state appropriations in its support.

The physical plant of Wilberforce University is valued at $2,001,248. This evaluation includes the eighteen buildings owned by the state and by the university which are used for educational purposes: 347 acres of land, 234 acres of which are owned

---

[14] Payne, Daniel A., *Recollections of Seventy Years*, pp. 229, 230.
[15] *U. S. Bur. of Ed. Bul.*, 1928, No. 7, pp. 602, 603.

TABLE VI

Sources of Income of Wilberforce University from 1922–23 to 1926–27 *

Source	1922–23	1923–24	1924–25	1925–26	1926–27
State appropriations......	$126,883.00	$187,135.50	$187,135.50	$279,160.00	$279,160.00
Church appropriations....	58,613.04	65,527.13	76,739.91	78,241.27	84,136.53
Interest on endowment....	5,794.67	5,794.67	5,794.67	5,794.67	5,794.67
Interest on investments...	203.75	203.75	203.75	203.75	203.75
Gifts for current expenses..	50.00	1,971.00	591.25	50.00	......
Student fees.............	27,476.34	26,294.43	28,072.89	32,598.36	35,544.21
Net income from sales and services..............	509.91	1,077.88	560.25	122.64	478.66
Other sources...........	3,167.46	3,226.95	6,170.75	3,882.65	4,884.94
Total................	$222,698.17	$291,231.31	$305,268.87	$400,053.34	$409,202.76

* *U. S. Bur. of Ed. Bul.*, 1928, No. 7, p. 604.

by the state and the remainder by the university, and equipment valued at $146,333.[16]

The enrollment of students doing four-year college work shows a sharp loss from 1922–23 to 1930–31 in the liberal arts college and a sharp gain in the college of education. The figures for 1922–23 are: liberal arts 218, education 30, total 248; and for 1930–31: liberal arts 162, education 371, total 533. The total enrollment of college students more than doubled in the eight-year period considered, with a decided shift of students into the teacher-training curriculum.[17]

The general plan of the denomination has evidently been to place its institutions of higher learning at strategic points in as many of the states of the South as possible, consistent with reasonable possibilities. In accordance with this idea, institutions doing work of college grade were established in six of these states at the places and times shown below:

Allen University, Columbia, S. C..................... 1870
Paul Quinn College, Waco, Tex...................... 1881
Edward Waters College, Jacksonville, Fla............. 1883
Morris Brown College, Atlanta, Ga.................. 1885
Kittrell College, Kittrell, N. C...................... 1885
Shorter College, Little Rock, Ark................... 1886

Of these, in 1931–32, Allen University with 263 students and Morris Brown with 264 were four-year colleges, while Paul Quinn

[16] *U. S. Bur. of Ed. Bul.*, 1928, No. 7, p. 606.
[17] *Ibid.*, p. 612; *Wilberforce Bulletin*, Vol. XVI, No. 4, pp. 180–89.

with 90 college students, Kittrell with 58, and Edward Waters with 49 were listed as junior colleges. These, together with Wilberforce University, constitute the institutions of higher learning supported by the largest of the Negro denominations, the African Methodist Episcopal Church. Together they enrolled, in 1931–32, 1277 students of college grade.[18]

THE AFRICAN METHODIST EPISCOPAL ZION CHURCH

The history of the origin of this branch of Methodism is similar to that of the denominations just discussed. It was the outcome of the dissatisfaction of the Negro Methodists at the treatment accorded by their white brethren. It was a revolt against the spirit of segregation and discrimination which began to manifest itself in the Methodist Church toward the latter part of the eighteenth century.

This denomination was formed in New York City in 1796, its original title being the African Methodist Episcopal Church. The word "Zion" was later added to the title in honor of the church by that name which was the first member congregation of the new denomination.

The difficulty, in this case, developed in St. John's Methodist Episcopal Church, New York, which bears the honor of being the first Methodist Church founded in the present area of the United States. At first the Negro communicants of the church enjoyed the same privileges as the white. As the denomination spread the color question became acute until, at the meeting of the Methodist Conference, held in Baltimore in 1880, the twenty-fifth question propounded in the conference was:[19]

Ought not the assistant (Mr. Asbury) to meet the colored people himself and appoint as keepers in his absence proper white persons and not suffer them to stay late and meet by themselves?[20]

St. John's Church adopted the attitude implied by the question just quoted, although a number of Negroes were granted licenses to preach. Whenever a Negro preached, however, his audience must be made up of Negroes and some white man must be present.[21] The resentment of the Negroes grew after this formal ac-

[18] McCuistion, Fred, *Higher Education of Negroes*, pp. 9, 10.
[19] Hood, J. W., *One Hundred Years of the African Methodist Episcopal Zion Church*, pp. 3, 4.
[20] Quoted by Hood, *op. cit.*, p. 4.
[21] Moore, J. J., *History of the African Methodist Episcopal Zion Church*, p. 15.

tion was taken, and resulted first in the formation of a separate church and finally in a separate denomination.

While the denomination has promoted a number of educational institutions since the Civil War, most of them have been on the elementary and secondary levels.[22]   The college work fostered by the church has been confined to one school, Livingstone College, Salisbury, North Carolina, named in honor of David Livingstone, the missionary and explorer.

The school was founded as Zion Wesley Institute at Concord, North Carolina, in 1879, and opened in 1880 with eleven pupils. The home of the principal served for holding classes, as no property for the school had been purchased.   The next year Bishop J. W. Hood and Mr. J. C. Price raised $10,000 for the school while on a tour of England.   A site consisting of forty acres of land and purchased at a cost of $4,600 was selected at Salisbury, North Carolina.   Toward this amount the white people of the city contributed $1,000.   Zion Wesley Institute was moved to Salisbury in 1885 and chartered under the name of Livingstone College, with Price as president.[23]

Livingstone has developed until today it is organized into a four-year college, a theological seminary, and a high school.   Its plant consists of 314 acres of land, valued at $116,000, on which have been erected eight brick buildings, valued at $293,100 and containing equipment worth $100,000.[24]

THE COLORED METHODIST EPISCOPAL CHURCH

As related above, the Methodist Episcopal Church split in 1845 over the question of slavery.   When the Methodist Episcopal Church, South, was formed as a result of this action the Negro membership of the church in the South had no alternative but to go with their masters.   This relationship continued until the close of the Civil War.   In 1866 the General Conference of the Methodist Episcopal Church, South, meeting in New Orleans, organized its Negro members into separate congregations and conferences whenever the Negroes desired this arrangement.   It also agreed to the formation of a new denomination, should the

---

[22] For an account of the educational activity of the denomination, see Clement, R. E., *The Educational Work of the African Methodist Episcopal Church.* (Unpublished Master's thesis, Northwestern University, 1922.)

[23] Clement, *op. cit.*, p. 88.

[24] *U. S. Bur. of Ed. Bul.*, 1928, No. 7, p. 546; Livingstone College, *Annual Catalog*, 1931–32.

desire for it be expressed.[25] At the General Conference held in Memphis, Tennessee, in 1870, the new denomination was set up with the name the Colored Methodist Episcopal Church in America. The separation was not in the form of a revolt and left no ill feelings. It was believed by some of the most thoughtful members of both groups that the separation was best in that it relieved the white people from embarrassment and gave the Negroes an opportunity to manage their own religious affairs. Because of the cordial relationship between the two bodies as a result of this mutually agreeable separation, the Methodist Episcopal Church, South, has maintained fraternal relationships with her offspring, especially in its educational work.

The four colleges under the auspices of the Colored Methodist Episcopal Church, with location and date of founding, are as follows: Lane College, Jackson, Tennessee, 1878; Paine College, Augusta, Georgia, 1882; Texas College, Tyler, Texas, 1894; Miles Memorial College, Birmingham, Alabama, 1902. In 1932 Lane College enrolled 236 college students; Paine College, 154; Texas College, 264; and Miles Memorial College, 91—making a total of 745 for the four colleges.

The interest of the Methodist Episcopal Church, South, in the affairs of these colleges is noteworthy. After Lane College had operated as the Colored Methodist Episcopal Institute and Lane Institute, the officers decided in 1887 to ask the Methodist Episcopal Church, South, to select from its membership a president for the school. As a result, the Reverend T. F. Saunders, a member of the Memphis Conference, was appointed and served for fifteen years. During his presidency the name of the school was changed to Lane College.[26]

Paine College was founded as the result of the deliberation of a joint committee of three members representing each of the two denominations. This committee, in coöperation with the members of the parent church, established the school as Paine Institute on November 1, 1882, the name selected being in honor of the Right Reverend Robert Paine, at that time Senior Bishop of the Methodist Episcopal Church, South. One of the purposes of the school has been to stress the interracial character of the enterprise. Negroes and native Southern white people have worked

[25] Woodson, Carter G., *The History of the Negro Church*, p. 195.
[26] *Lane College Reporter*, Aug. 17, 1932, p. 12.

together on the faculty from the beginning, and all the presidents have been white men.[27]

Miles Memorial College, at Birmingham, Alabama, offers a striking example of the possibilities of coöperative effort. It was organized by the Colored Methodist Episcopal Church as an expression of its desire for a school of collegiate rank. It is generally looked upon as a merger of a school organized in Thomasville, Alabama, in 1898 with one at Booker City, Alabama. The college was organized at Booker City, October 1, 1902. In 1907 the school was moved to Birmingham and the next year it was chartered as Miles Memorial College. It operated with fair success until 1930–31, at which time it found itself seriously embarrassed financially. To save the situation, the trustees decided to entrust the management of the school to a Committee of Management which should be composed of all the Negro Methodist Churches and the Methodist Episcopal Church, South.[28] The results of this unique experiment, so far, seem encouraging. At least it is an example of the possibility of breaking down denominational lines and racial barriers in handling to the best advantage such critical enterprises as the Negro colleges in the South.

THE NEGRO BAPTIST CONVENTIONS

The bulk of the educational work on the college level promoted by the Baptist denomination has been carried on in schools under the control of the American Baptist Home Mission Society. Other schools under independent boards have been aided by this society. Still others, maintained and controlled by the society for many years, have been released to independent boards of trustees. For example, Arkansas Baptist College at Little Rock, Arkansas, and more recently Shaw University at Raleigh, North Carolina, have been thus released from the control of the society, which no longer assumes any obligation for their support.

Meanwhile, beginning about 1870, the several state conventions of Negro Baptists undertook to provide educational facilities for their youth in such areas as seemed in most pressing need of them, but which the American Baptist Home Mission Society could not include in its program. In most cases these schools were small and, being supported out of the poverty of the Negro

[27] *Paine Bulletin*, Sept. 1931, pp. 9, 10.
[28] *Bulletin of Miles Memorial College*, 1931–32, pp. 9, 10.

people, were necessarily inadequately equipped and housed. In these schools, with all their crudity, we have an example of the efforts of the Negro to educate himself in the absence of public educational facilities.

By 1916 the Negro Baptist Conventions maintained 110 schools with 474 teachers. Dr. Thomas Jesse Jones, in the survey of Negro education made in 1915–16, described thirty-one of these schools as "large or important" and seventy-nine as "small or less important." These schools were distributed among thirteen states of the South and the District of Columbia.[29]

In Chapter XV of this study Table XV lists all the colleges for Negroes, based upon the best information available, which were in operation in the school year 1931–32. In this list ten are accredited to the Negro Baptist Conventions, and eight of these are among those listed by Dr. Jones in 1916 as being under the same auspices at that time. The other two are Arkansas Baptist College, Little Rock, Arkansas, and Selma University, Selma, Alabama—both of which were formerly listed in the reports of the American Baptist Home Mission Society. Usually when the society withdraws from the support of colleges, the Negro Baptist conventions naturally assume the major responsibility for them. To this list, therefore, should be added Shaw University, which was listed as "Supported Largely by the A. B. H. M. S." in 1929–30 but was omitted in 1931–32.[30]

With this revision, then, the colleges now supported and controlled by the Negro Baptist conventions with the dates of founding are as follows:

Four-Year Colleges	*Date of Founding*
Arkansas Baptist College, Little Rock, Ark.	1885
Selma University, Selma, Ala.	1878
Natchez College, Natchez, Miss.	1885
Shaw University, Raleigh, N. C.	1865
Virginia College and Seminary, Lynchburg, Va.	1888

Junior Colleges	
Central City College, Macon, Ga.	1899
Coleman College, Gibsland, La.	1890
Friendship College, Rock Hill, S. C.	
Morris College, Sumter, S. C.	1905
Guadalupe College, Seguin, Tex.	1887

[29] "Negro Education," *U. S. Bur. of Ed. Bul.*, 1916, No. 30, p. 347.
[30] See A. B. H. M. S., *An. Rep.*, 1930, p. 177; *op. cit.*, 1932, p. 154.

CHAPTER XI

THE LAND-GRANT COLLEGES

ALTHOUGH the privately supported institutions bore the major burden of educating the Negro immediately after the emancipation and still constitute the most important group for higher education, yet during the past twenty-five years the state-supported schools have constantly assumed a larger and larger share of this function. The growth of the public high school has relieved the private institutions of the necessity of providing secondary education to as great an extent as formerly, and the state-supported colleges have assumed a slowly increasing part of the task of providing facilities for higher education.

There are seventeen land-grant colleges for Negroes at the present time, one in each of the states that maintain a dual system of schools. They came into existence as a result of the first and second Morrill Acts, just as did the corresponding institutions for white people, but not at the same time. The first Morrill Act (passed July 2, 1862),[1] providing for agricultural and mechanical colleges in all the states, unfortunately did not provide for a division of federal funds on racial lines. As a result of this omission the funds received were, in most cases, used for the development of those colleges from which Negroes were excluded.

Three states, however, shortly after the Civil War and before the second Morrill Act was passed, set aside a portion of the funds for the support of land-grant colleges to serve their Negro population. In 1871 the state of Mississippi received $188,928 for its script under the Morrill Act. It gave three-fifths of this amount to what was then called Alcorn University and the remaining two-fifths to the University of Mississippi, which was designated as the white land-grant college. Finding that with the regular state appropriations added to the land-grant fund Alcorn's income was greater than its needs, the legislature, in 1874, transferred the federal fund to Oxford University, another Negro

---

[1] *U. S. Statutes at Large,* XII, 503.

school in Mississippi. In 1878 the grant was returned to Alcorn University with its name changed to Alcorn Agricultural and Mechanical College.[2]

In 1872 Virginia sold its script for $285,000. After much debate the legislature decided to grant one-half the yield of the income from this fund to Hampton Institute, which was designated as the Negro land-grant college of the state. Hampton continued this relationship with the state for forty-eight years. In 1920 the legislature transferred the federal fund to the Virginia Normal and Industrial Institute at Petersburg, which was later named The Virginia State College for Negroes.[3]

The third state to establish a Negro land-grant college was South Carolina. In 1872 the script granted to that state by the Federal Government was sold for $191,800. The reconstruction legislature, controlled by Negroes, granted the income of this fund to Claflin University, a school established and maintained by the Freedmen's Aid Society of the Methodist Episcopal Church. For some reason the fund was used for other than educational purposes, thus depriving Claflin of the expected income. In 1879 the state restored the land-grant endowment by money received from taxation, and organized a white land-grant college to receive one-half the income while Claflin received the other half. In 1896 the state established the Colored Normal, Industrial and Mechanical College as a state institution in Orangeburg, where Claflin is located, and transferred the land-grant money to the state school.[4]

While Kentucky assigned a part of its land-grant fund under the Morrill Act of 1862 to a Negro school, without compulsion of law, it delayed this action until 1879, when it granted one-twelfth of the income from the fund to the Kentucky State Industrial School at Frankfort, later called the Kentucky State Industrial College.[5]

The Morrill Act of August 30, 1890 [6] specifically provided that the land-grant funds be equitably divided where separate schools for the two races were maintained. The text of the act making this provision is as follows:

---

[2] *U. S. Office of Ed. Bul.*, 1930, No. 9, II, pp. 837 ff.
[3] *Ibid.; The Hampton Bulletin*, March 1932, p. 19.
[4] *State Agricultural and Mechanical College Bulletin*, Vol. XXI, No. 3, p. 14, July 1932; *U. S. Office of Ed. Bul.*, 1930, No. 9, II, p. 839.
[5] *Ibid.*, p. 839.   [6] *U. S. Statutes at Large*, Vol. 26, p. 417.

That no money shall be paid out under this act to any State or Territory for the support and maintenance of a college where a distinction of race or color is made in the admission of students, but the establishment and maintenance of such colleges separately for white and colored students will be held to be in compliance with the provisions of this act if the funds received in such State or Territory be equitably divided as hereinafter set forth.

That in any State in which there has been one college established in pursuance of the act of July 2, 1862 (first Morrill Act), and also in which an educational institution of like character has been established, or may be hereafter established, and is now aided by such States from its own revenues, for the education of colored students in agriculture and the mechanic arts, however named or styled, or whether or not it has received money heretofore under the act to which this act is an amendment, the legislature of such State may propose and report to the Secretary of the Interior a just and equitable division of the fund to be received under this act, between one college for white students and one institution for colored students, established as aforesaid, which shall be divided into two parts and paid accordingly, and thereupon such institution for colored students shall be entitled to the benefits of this act and subject to its provisions, as much as it would have been if it had been included under the act of 1862, and the fulfillment of the foregoing provisions shall be taken as a compliance with the provision in reference to separate colleges for white and colored students.

Within a decade of the passage of this act all the states where separate schools are legally required had agreed to establish land-grant colleges for Negroes. Table VII lists these schools and gives other appropriate data.

It is clear from Table VII that a large majority of these colleges, ten to be exact, were privately supported institutions before the passage of the second Morrill Act, and became state schools by their being selected to receive the share of the land-grant funds allocated to the education of Negroes. Three were established the same year that their respective states accepted the terms of the act and three were established later.

It should be noted here that, until the year 1916, none of the schools given in this list offered work of collegiate grade. The carefully made survey of Negro education,[7] published that year and discussed in more detail later in this study, reveals the fact that the only college education offered to Negroes before that date had been made available in privately supported schools. The development of these schools as degree-granting institutions, therefore, extends over a period of about fifteen years. During that period, however, gratifying progress in enrollment has been

[7] *U. S. Bur. of Ed. Bul.*, 1916, Nos. 38, 39.

TABLE VII

PRESENT NAMES,* LOCATION, DATE OF STATE ACCEPTANCE OF TERMS UNDER MORRILL ACT OF 1890, AND DATE OF ESTABLISHMENT OF LAND-GRANT COLLEGES FOR NEGROES

(Adapted from Table I of article by John W. Davis, "The Negro Land-Grant College," *Journal of Negro Education*, II, 3, p. 316, July 1933.)

Name	City	State	Date When State Accepted Terms for College under Morrill Act of 1890	Date of Establishment
State Agricultural and Mechanical Institute	Normal	Alabama	Feb. 13, 1891	1875
Agricultural, Mechanical and Normal College	Pine Bluff	Arkansas	April 9, 1891	1872
State College for Colored Students	Dover	Delaware	Feb. 12, 1891	1891
Florida Agricultural and Mechanical College for Negroes	Tallahassee	Florida	June 8, 1891	1887
Georgia State Industrial College	Industrial College	Georgia		1890
Kentucky State Industrial College	Frankfort	Kentucky	Jan. 13, 1893	1887
Southern University and Agricultural and Mechanical College	Scotlandville	Louisiana	Jan. 23, 1893	1880
Princess Anne Academy	Princess Anne	Maryland	1892	1887
Alcorn Agricultural and Mechanical College	Alcorn	Mississippi	1890	1871
Lincoln University	Jefferson City	Missouri	March 13, 1891	1866
The Negro Agricultural and Technical College	Greensboro	North Carolina	March 6, 1891	1894
Colored Agricultural and Normal University	Langston	Oklahoma	March 10, 1899	1897
State Colored Normal, Industrial, Agricultural, and Mechanical College of South Carolina	Orangeburg	South Carolina	1896	1896
Tennessee Agricultural and Industrial State Teachers College	Nashville	Tennessee	Feb. 26, 1891	1913
Prairie View State Normal and Industrial College	Prairie View	Texas	March 14, 1891	1879
Virginia State College for Negroes	Ettrick	Virginia	1891	1920 † 1883
West Virginia State College	Institute	West Virginia	March 17, 1891	1892

* A number of the colleges listed have changed their names since establishment.

† In 1920 Virginia State College began receiving federal funds.

made; for in 1932 the publicly supported colleges in fifteen Southern states enrolled 7,294 college students as against 10,118 for the private schools in the same area.[8]

Information relative to the source of support of the group of schools under discussion is given in the report of the Survey of Land-Grant Colleges, issued by the United States Office of Education. Table VIII is adapted from that report.

TABLE VIII

RECEIPTS OF THE 17 NEGRO LAND-GRANT COLLEGES, EXCLUDING
CAPITAL OUTLAYS FOR FISCAL YEAR 1928 *

	Amount	Per Cent
Federal Funds:		
Land-grant acts...........................	$260,928	8.5
Smith-Hughes Act.........................	77,461	2.8
State funds:		
Operation and maintenance.................	1,379,484	45.2
Private gifts................................	126,115	4.2
Institutional funds:		
Student fees..............................	173,388	5.6
Board and lodging........................	688,240	22.5
Departmental earnings.....................	127,933	4.2
Miscellaneous and other sources..............	219,090	7.2
Total.....................................	$3,052,639	100.0

* *U. S. Office of Ed. Bul.*, 1930, No. 9, II, p. 856.

This table shows clearly the extent to which the Southern states have contributed to these schools. The figures indicate that the sum of $1,379,484 or 45.2 per cent of the total current income in 1927–28 was derived from the states and only 11 per cent from the Federal Government. While this amount shows a gratifying advance in this regard and signifies a great change in sentiment since the early days described in the foregoing sections of this study, yet it must constantly be borne in mind that the actual sum spent by the states for the higher education of Negroes is still very small, inadequate, and inequitable when compared with the amount spent for the higher education of the white people in the same area. The survey reveals several significant facts.

In the first place, the Negro land-grant colleges enrolled in 1928

[8] McCuistion, Fred, *Higher Education of Negroes*, p. 18.

a total of 9,823 students, of whom 3,691 were counted as in college and 6,132 as of sub-collegiate grade.[9] This means that these schools are doing much of the work that should be taken over by the public high schools and the cost should be charged to that account rather than to Negro higher education.

In the second place, these appropriations represent the only expenditure for four-year college education offered by the Southern states to Negroes with the exception of North Carolina and West Virginia. In North Carolina a liberal arts college and a four-year teachers college are maintained, and in West Virginia a four-year teachers college is provided. In both cases these are in addition to the land-grant colleges for Negroes.[10] For the white students every state maintains a state university. In a number of cases the state universities and the land-grant colleges are identical.

In the third place, $1,379,484,[11] the total amount of the state appropriations for the seventeen land-grant colleges in 1928 was nearly equalled or exceeded by the state appropriations for white students in the case of several individual land-grant colleges. Selected instances for the year 1928 are:

Florida	$1,298,637	Tennessee	$1,327,684
Kentucky	1,309,450	West Virginia	1,419,732
North Carolina	996,450	Louisiana	927,009 [12]

In the fourth place, the white land-grant colleges are not burdened with students of sub-collegiate grade, since all of them require for admission graduation from a four-year high school, with at least fifteen units of secondary credit.[13]

The land-grant colleges for Negroes, then, suffer in these four items, as shown by the survey. But they also suffer from being expected to perform too many functions at the same time. They are supposed to be first of all schools of agriculture and the mechanic arts. The function of training teachers not only for these but for other fields has been forced upon them. As a necessary concomitant of these functions, liberal arts courses have been included and adapted to the curricula of technical departments. The question naturally arises whether or not this is a fair requirement to place upon the Negro land-grant colleges or, for that

---

[9] *U. S. Office of Ed. Bul.*, 1930, No. 9, II, pp. 896, 897. [10] McCuistion, *op. cit.*, pp. 9, 10.
[11] *U. S. Office of Ed. Bul.*, 1930, No. 9, II, p. 856. [12] *Ibid.*, I, p. 94. [13] *Ibid.*, p. 264.

matter, upon any land-grant college.   While economy may dictate the inclusion of these varied and somewhat discrete functions in the same institution for a limited period, it is to be expected that the problem of different kinds of college work for different in-dividuals will be solved for the Negroes in the same way that it is being solved for the white people of the United States—by offering technical education and liberal education in different institutions. It is possible, of course, that the American scheme of higher edu-cation is undergoing a modification at the present time that will justify the combination of technical and liberal education.   Until the problems involved have been settled, however, it would seem to the best interests of the Negro to follow, where possible, the accepted American practice.[14]

It is fair to say, therefore, that, although the progress has been gratifying considering historical conditions, yet the states still have a long way to go in providing for the higher education of their Negro citizens.   For, in the future, the state school must be expected to play an ever-increasing part in providing educational facilities on the higher levels.

[14] For detailed information concerning the colleges in the group see, "Survey of Land-Grant Colleges and Universities," *U. S. Office of Ed. Bul.*, 1930, No. 9, II, Part X, pp. 837 ff; also see Davis, John W., "The Negro Land-Grant Colleges," *Journal of Negro Education*, II, 312 ff.

CHAPTER XII

THE SITUATION IN 1916

THE picture presented thus far in our study of the work of the denominational boards in promoting the higher education of the Negro has been a story of pioneering in an area hitherto largely unexplored. The constant appeal to the benevolent impulse of humanity to aid the lowly and downtrodden had been sounded throughout the country from thousands of pulpits, as well as by the regular authorized agents of the several educational bodies promoting the work of Negro education, until there were few communities which did not make some contribution to this cause in partial discharge of their obligation to the Negro.

Several changes had occurred since the stormy years following emancipation when the movement was rushing forward on the flood tide of sentiment and religious zeal. In the first place, the antagonism between the white people of the North and South had been rapidly dying out and they were able to confer calmly and without bias on the common problems of the country, than which none was more pertinent to any discussion of the South than that concerning the Negro. As a result of this change of attitude, Northern men and Southern men met in conferences to determine the best procedure for promoting the educational interests of the poverty-stricken South, struggling to emerge from its late ruin. A series of such conferences resulted in the creation of the Southern Education Board, out of which, indirectly, the General Education Board developed. These movements will be dealt with more fully in the following chapter.

In the second place, the cost of maintaining schools was mounting and, as a result, it was necessary for those in charge of the schools to carry on a constant campaign for funds. Many presidents and principals spent the greater part of their time soliciting funds—often by door to door visitations to persons of means who seemed susceptible to appeals for gifts for Negro education. As a result of the brilliant example of the Fisk Jubilee Singers, who raised large sums of money in the early history of Fisk University, many schools kept quartettes or musical bodies of some kind on the road to sing their way into the hearts of Northern philanthropy and thus induce a benevolent attitude toward the particular school represented. As a result of such constant activities by so many agencies, the Northern philanthropists were often perplexed as to the most worth-while objects of their material assistance.

In the third place, the development of scientific procedures in the business world resulted in the development of the survey technique, on the basis of which business men could wisely proceed in their enterprises as a result of a body of factual knowledge upon which to rely. Furthermore, such men began to realize that in amassing their fortunes they had worked on the basis of facts, whereas in giving them away they relied upon sentiment.

During the first decade of the twentieth century, therefore, it became increasingly evident that there was a distinct need of investigation of the whole field of Negro education, so that those interested, both from within and without, might have available as a basis for action the kind of information that only a carefully made survey could give. Through a coöperative effort of the United States Bureau of Education and the Phelps-Stokes Fund, such a survey was made possible during the years 1915 and 1916, and the findings were published in 1917 in two volumes, issued as Bulletins 38 and 39 of the bureau for that year. In explaining the object of the survey the director said:

It was believed, and the results of the examination have confirmed the belief, that there can be no more important agency to bring about the improvement of education than dignified publicity regarding educational conditions. It brings good institutions and good methods to the favorable attention of patrons, voters, and teachers everywhere, and similarly, by disclosing the actual facts, shows what institutions and methods are unworthy of general support.[1]

The survey was made by experts who conducted it with care and deliberation, checking all data through personal visitation, and was sponsored by the Federal Bureau of Education. Its findings, therefore, so far as factual material is concerned, must be considered the most reliable body of source material on Negro education as a whole available up to that time. Many adverse criticisms followed the report but these, when followed up, were

[1] *U. S. Bur. of Ed. Bul.*, 1916, No. 38.

found in most cases to apply to the expressions of opinion and the recommendations relative to the several schools rather than to the accuracy of the actual information presented. In spite of these criticisms it is evident that the survey had the most salutary effect upon the entire field of Negro education. This is particularly true of the field of higher education, which the survey showed to be in a deplorable condition. Section IV of the report on "College and Professional Education" is thus introduced:

No type of education is so eagerly sought by the colored people as college education. Yet no educational institutions for colored people are so poorly equipped and so ineffectively organized and administered as the majority of those claiming to give college education. Howard University is an institution of university proportions but its endowment is negligible. Fisk University is genuinely a college according to most of the standards, but its endowment is insufficient. Atlanta University, Meharry Medical College, Virginia Union University, Morehouse College, Bishop College, Lincoln University, Benedict College, Talladega College, Tougaloo College, Knoxville College, Shaw University, Claflin College and a few others are offering instruction of college grade, but the number of college students in most of these institutions is not more than 10 per cent of the total enrollment and they are therefore compelled to devote the major portion of their resources to secondary education.[2]

Tables IX and X show the situation at the time of the survey. Table IX is taken directly from the report, while Table X is an adaptation of the findings to emphasize certain facts with special reference to higher education.

It should be noted that Table IX includes all private and higher schools. For our present purposes the items "City High Schools" and "County Training Schools" may best be omitted since neither group in 1916 enrolled students of college grade.

Certain of the deductions relative to higher education, based upon the data presented, are startling even today as we take a retrospective view of the situation as it was in 1916. The effect was even more startling to those immediately concerned, and awakened them into immediate and energetic action looking toward improvement and reform.

Table X shows, for example, that of the 92,593 students enrolled only 2,641, or less than 3 per cent, were of college grade. Generously calling this number 3 per cent of the whole, and assuming that the per capita cost of educating the college students was twice that of educating the others, we may say that 6 per cent

[2] *U. S. Bur. of Ed. Bul.*, 1916, I, 55.

TABLE IX

SCHOOLS FOR NEGROES, CLASSIFIED ON THE BASIS OF OWNERSHIP AND CONTROL, 1916 *

Ownership and Control	Number of Schools			Counted Attendance				Teachers and Workers			Income for Current Expenses	Value of Property
	Total	Large or Important	Small or Less Important	Total	Elementary	Secondary	College	Total	White	Negro		
ALL PRIVATE AND HIGHER SCHOOLS	747	388	359	107,206	80,376	24,186	2,641	5,851	1,358	4,493	4,241,572	35,870,125
1. Schools under Public Control	122	122	…	23,527	9,812	12,662	1,053	1,317	38	1,279	1,215,112	7,373,179
Federal Schools	1	1	…	1,401		400	1,001	103	33	73	172,257	1,756,920
Land-Grant Schools	16	16	…	4,875	2,595	2,268	12	400		400	544,520	2,576,142
State Schools	11	11	…	2,638	1,466	1,132	40	188	2	186	246,834	1,394,547
City High Schools	67	67	…	8,707		8,707		484	3	481	200,000	1,500,000
County Training Schools	27	27	…	5,906	5,751	155		139		139	51,501	145,570
2. Schools under Private Control	625	266	359	83,679	70,564	11,527	1,588	4,534	1,320	3,214	3,026,460	28,496,946
Independent Schools	118	46	72	14,851	12,273	1,841	737	1,144	249	895	1,099,224	12,369,441
Denominational Schools	507	220	287	68,828	58,291	9,686	851	3,390	1,071	2,319	1,927,236	16,127,505
Under White Boards	354	160	194	51,529	43,605	7,188	736	2,562	1,069	1,493	1,546,303	13,822,451
Under Negro Boards	153	60	93	17,299	14,868	2,498	115	828	2	826	380,933	2,302,054

* U. S. Bur. of Ed. Bul., 1916, No. 38, Pt. I, p. 115.

TABLE X

ABBREVIATED AND MODIFIED TABLE OF NEGRO INSTITUTIONS DOING
COLLEGE WORK, 1916

	Schools Under		Total
	Public Control	Private Control	
Number of Schools...............	28	625	653
Counted Attendance			
Elementary....................	4,061	70,564	74,625
Secondary....................	3,800	11,527	15,327
Collegiate and Professional......	1,053	1,588	2,641
Total.......................	8,914	83,679	92,593
Teachers and Workers............	694	4,534	5,228
Income for Current Expenses......	$963,611	$3,026,460	$3,990,071
Value of Property...............	$5,727,609	$28,496,946	$34,224,555

is a fair estimate of the percentage of total income of these schools
spent upon students of college grade. Since the students at all
levels were usually taught by the same teachers and since costly
laboratory and library equipment which would increase the cost of
college work were practically nonexistent in these schools at that
time, it is a fair assumption that there was little difference in the
per capita costs for the different levels. Allowing twice as much,
therefore, for the per capita cost of college students as for those of
the secondary and the elementary levels, we have 6 per cent of the
total income of $3,990,071, or $239,404, for the support of 2,641
college students for a year, or a per capita expenditure of less than
one hundred dollars, a sum entirely inadequate even in 1916.
The reports of the separate schools, in Volume II of the survey,
give vivid accounts of the conditions which resulted from such
meager support. On the basis of these findings no Negro college
with the inadequate physical facilities and the poorly trained
faculties which could be provided out of such restricted income
was or could be considered at that time as even approaching the
academic standards of the colleges of the North. There were, of
course, exceptional schools, exceptional students, and exceptional
teachers. It was quite evident, however, that the situation as a
whole was deplorable and that the institutions of higher learning
for Negroes needed immediate and serious attention.

After the first expressions of pique and disappointment had given way to the sober business of self-examination which this report suggested to every board of trustees, state board, church board, and philanthropic body, all groups concerned turned their attention to improvements all along the line.

Commenting upon the report fifteen years after it was issued, Dr. Anson Phelps-Stokes, president of the Fund, says:

1. Its thorough statistical material regarding all Negro schools above elementary grades and regarding the relative per capita expenditures for white and colored children in each state on the basis of teachers' salaries.   The maps which accompanied these statements made it clear to every impartial student that the Negro schools were receiving only a fraction as much as the white schools.   These facts were the basis of helpful discussion in every Southern legislature.

2. Its clear recognition of the differentiation between, and the importance of both the elementary training of the rank and file of Negro youth in a way to fit them for self-support and useful living in their own communities, and the need of adequate training for Negro leadership in all honorable occupations and professions through colleges and universities.

3. Its description of every important school and college for Negroes with recommendations as to improvements, not only in curricula, but in financial methods, teaching standards, adaptation to community needs, etc.

The statistical facts in the study have never been seriously questioned.   As to the criticisms of the Report because of its emphasis on the vocational and social elements of education, it may be said that Dr. Jones has strenuously advocated the same type of education for the white man, the Indian and all other groups.   As to the criticism of the administration of certain schools, it may be stated that there has been considerable improvement since the Report was published, and that now the number of schools in the South under Negro direction conducted on the best possible basis, has greatly increased.

Perhaps the best evidence of the standing of the Report is that its author was awarded the Grant Squires Prize by Columbia University, given every fifth year by the University for "original investigations of a sociological character carried on during the five years preceding the award."   A more recent authoritative estimate of the permanent significance of the Report is given by the United States Commissioner of Education, Hon. John J. Tigert, in his letter of transmittal in 1928 of the "Survey of Negro Colleges and Universities": "It is generally acknowledged that a Report on Negro Education in the United States, published by the Bureau of Education in 1917, has contributed greatly to the tremendous reconstruction of schools for Negroes which has taken place during the past ten years."   Dr. Jones' reports are still in much use for reference purposes by government officials, church boards of education, philanthropic organizations, and students of education and race relations.[3]

[3] *Twenty Years of the Phelps-Stokes Fund, 1911–1931*, pp. 13, 14.

CHAPTER XIII

ORGANIZED PHILANTHROPY

In a broad sense all the money and effort expended for the education of the Negro by those who have not expected to receive direct benefits from the expenditure may be described as philanthropic. Since the activities that have been carried on by the religious denominations have been directed by boards established for that purpose they fall under the description implied in the word "organized." As used in this chapter, however, the term "organized philanthropy" refers to those educational foundations established outside the church whose purpose has been to promote education without sectarian motives or even denominational interest. The foundations referred to came into existence largely as the result of the deplorable social and economic conditions existing in the South as the aftermath of slavery and the war. They were established by persons who, having attained great fortunes, considered it a patriotic duty to share their wealth with the nation by the promotion of education where the need seemed greatest.[1]

The foundations which have been exclusively devoted to the education of the Negro are the John F. Slater Fund, the Daniel Hand Fund, the Julius Rosenwald Fund, and the Anna T. Jeanes Fund. The principal foundations established for education in general and shared by the Negro are the Peabody Education Fund, the Duke Endowment, and the General Education Board.

The Daniel Hand Fund has been referred to in the section of this study dealing with the work of the American Missionary Association. It was unique in its management in that it was never administered by a separate board; nor was its income, in general, specifically allocated to stated projects but was used for the general promotion of the work of the association in the field of Negro education. Since the American Missionary Association has been so actively engaged in the field of higher education, the

---

[1] For more extended treatment of this subject see Leavell, Ullin W., *Philanthropy in Negro Education*, Chs. III–VI.

importance of the Daniel Hand Fund to the Negro college is obvious.

The Anna T. Jeanes Fund, which was created in 1907 for the assistance of rural schools for Negroes in the South, while most important to Negro education as a whole, has been of no direct benefit to higher education,[2] although its indirect benefits to Negro education at all levels, through its effect upon morale, have doubtless been very great.

THE PEABODY EDUCATION FUND

The first of the great foundations for education in the South, the Peabody Education Fund, was that established by Mr. George Peabody in 1867.   At that time he gave the sum of $1,000,000, later increased to $2,384,000, for that purpose.   The fund was placed under the administration of a carefully selected board with large discretionary powers, including the right to dispose of forty per cent of the principal.   The purpose of the donor is expressed in his letter establishing the fund, addressed to the trustees, which says, in part, that the income of the fund is to be

. . . used and applied in your discretion for the promotion and encouragement of intellectual, moral, or industrial education among the young of the more destitute portions of the Southern and Southwestern states of our Union; my purpose being that the benefits intended shall be distributed among the entire population, without other distinctions than their needs and the opportunities of usefulness to them.[3]

It was the desire of Mr. Peabody that at first the fund should be used in aiding the South to establish a public school system as the surest and most speedy means of social reform.   The board of trustees, composed of men of wisdom and integrity, faithfully carried out the will of the donor [4] in spirit as well as in letter and thereby gave an impetus to public education in the South which hastened the forward movement of all educational activities in that area.   In this way it brought nearer the possibility of the Negro college as an actuality.   No donations were made from this fund directly to Negro colleges; hence whatever benefit was derived from the Peabody Fund by higher education for the Negro was indirect.   However, when the fund was finally dis-

---

[2] See Dillard, James H., *Fourteen Years of the Jeanes Fund* (pamphlet).

[3] Quoted by Leavell, *op. cit.*, pp. 59, 60.

[4] The names of the board as originally appointed by Mr. Peabody, together with those who filled vacancies created by death or resignation, are given in an article by A. D. Mayo in *U. S. Com. of Ed., An. Rep.*, 1901, Vol. 1, pp. 454–55.

solved in 1914, the sum of $350,000 was given to the John F. Slater Fund,[5] whose income was devoted entirely to Negro education, including that at the collegiate level.

THE JOHN F. SLATER FUND

During the decade following the Civil War there existed considerable apprehension as to the effect upon the nation if the four million liberated slaves and their progeny remained without the benefits of schooling over a considerable period of time. This fear was one of the chief bases of appeal for funds by the religious denominations. The education of the Negro was looked upon by most thoughtful people not only as an act of humanity but as a patriotic duty that could not well be shirked without disaster.[6] It was doubtless such a conviction, reinforced by great piety and a Christian sense of duty, that was influential in causing Mr. John F. Slater, a merchant of Norwich, Connecticut, to establish the fund which bears his name. In 1882 he set aside, under the direction of a board of trustees, the sum of $1,000,000, the income of which was to be used in the promotion of education among the Negroes in the Southern states. The opening paragraphs of the donor's first letter to the board of trustees which he had selected states clearly his reasons for the establishment of such a fund:

To Messrs. Rutherford B. Hayes, of Ohio; Morrison R. Waite, of the District of Columbia; William E. Dodge, of New York; Phillips Brooks, of Massachusetts; Daniel C. Gilman, of Maryland; John A. Stewart, of New York; Alfred H. Colquitt, of Georgia; Morris K. Jesup, of New York; James P. Boyce, of Kentucky, and William A. Slater, of Connecticut:

Gentlemen:

It has pleased God to grant me prosperity in my business, and to put into my power to apply to charitable uses a sum of money so considerable as to require the counsel of wise men for the administration of it.

It is my desire at this time to appropriate to such uses the sum of one million dollars ($1,000,000.00); and I hereby invite you to procure a charter of incorporation under which a charitable fund may be held exempt from taxation, and under which you shall organize; but I intend that the corporation, as soon as formed, shall receive this sum in trust to apply the income of it according to the instructions contained in this letter.

The general object which I desire to have exclusively pursued, is the uplifting of the lately emancipated population of the Southern States, and their posterity, by conferring on them the blessings of Christian education. The disabilities formerly suffered by these people, and their singular patience and

[5] *U. S. Bur. of Ed. Bul.*, 1922, No. 26, p. 90.
[6] See note 6, Ch. V, of this study for an expression of this conviction.

fidelity in the great crisis of the nation, establish a just claim on the sympathy and good will of humane and patriotic men.   I cannot but feel the compassion that is due in view of their prevailing ignorance which exists by no fault of their own.

But it is not only for their own sake, but also for the safety of our common country, in which they have been invested with equal political rights, that I am desirous to aid in providing them with the means of such education as shall tend to make them good men and good citizens—education in which the instruction of the mind in the common branches of secular learning shall be associated with training in just notions of duty toward God and man, in the light of the Holy Scriptures.

The means to be used in the prosecution of the general object above described, I leave to the discretion of the corporation; only indicating as lines of operation adapted to the present condition of things, the training of teachers from among the people requiring to be taught, if, in the opinion of the corporation, by such limited selection the purposes of the trust can be best accomplished; and the encouragement of such institutions as are most effectually useful in promoting this training of teachers.[7]

The trustees, in administering the fund through a period of fifty years, have contributed to Negro schools at all levels and to those engaged in work of all kinds.   The stress has been placed upon different classes of schools at different periods, usually in accordance with the attitude of the general agent or the president, who was charged with the active direction of the affairs of the fund.[8]   For the donor made only one important restriction upon the freedom of the board to change its mind at any time as to the wisest use of the fund.   He insisted that it be applied to aid those who were financially unable to help themselves.   The section of his original letter making clear his wishes in this regard is as follows:

I purposely leave to the corporation the largest liberty of making such changes in the methods of applying the income of the fund as shall seem from time to time best adapted to accomplish the general object herein defined. But being warned by the history of such endowments that they sometimes tend to discourage rather than to promote effort and self-reliance on the part of beneficiaries; or to inure to the advancement of learning instead of the dissemination of it; or to become a convenience to the rich instead of a help to those who need help; I solemnly charge my trustees to use their best wisdom in preventing any such defeat of the spirit of this trust; so that my gift may continue to future generations to be a blessing to the poor.

[7] *A Letter of Fifty Years Ago.*   (Published in pamphlet form by the John F. Slater Fund, 1932.)

[8] For an extended study of this fund see Butler, John H., *An Historical Account of the John F. Slater Fund and the Anna T. Jeanes Foundation.*   (Unpublished Doctor's dissertation, University of Southern California, 1932.)

It is my wish that this trust be administered in no partisan, sectional, or sectarian spirit, but in the interest of a generous patriotism and an enlightened Christian faith; and that the corporation about to be formed, may continue to be constituted of men distinguished either by honorable success in business, or by services to literature, education, religion or the State.[9]

The list of the officers of the fund since its organization is as follows:

President

1882–1893	Rutherford B. Hayes
1893–1908	Daniel Coit Gilman
1908–1917	William A. Slater
1917–1931	James Hardy Dillard
1931–	Arthur Davis Wright

Vice-president

1882–1888	Morris R. Waite
1888–1890	(Office not filled)
1890–1910	Melville W. Fuller
1910–1921	Richard H. Williams
1921–1923	Wickliffe Rose
1923–1924	Charles Scribner
	(Office discontinued in 1924)

Chairman of the Board

1924–1927	Charles Scribner
1927–	Albert Shaw

Treasurer

1882–1908	Morris K. Jesup
1908–1909	Benjamin Strong (acting)
1909–1925	Metropolitan Trust Company of New York
1925–	Chatham Phenix National Bank and Trust Company of New York

Secretary

1882–1893	Daniel Coit Gilman
1893–1903	J. L. M. Curry
1903–1905	(Office not filled)
1905–1910	Benjamin Strong
1910–1917	James Hardy Dillard
1917–1931	Miss Gertrude C. Mann
1931–	C. P. Donnelly

Assistant Secretary

1920–	Miss Alice M. McGee

General Agent

1882–1891	Atticus G. Haygood
1891–1903	J. L. M. Curry [10]
1903–1907	Wallace Buttrick
1907–1917	James Hardy Dillard [11]

Field Agent

1906–	W. T. B. Williams [12]
1907–1910	G. S. Dickerman
1910–1931	B. C. Caldwell [13]

The first general agent was Dr. Atticus G. Haygood of Georgia, who left the presidency of Emory College to take up this larger task. He served the fund from 1882 to 1891, a period during which beginnings had to be made and policies formulated. Dr. Haygood believed strongly in the inclusion of industrial training in the curricula of the schools for Negroes. As a result of this attitude on the part of the general agent it became the policy of the fund to aid only those schools which offered industrial training. Because of the financial strain under which all schools for

[9] *A Letter of Fifty Years Ago.*   [10] Title was "Chairman of Education Committee."
[11] Title from 1911 to 1917 was "Director."   [12] Title in 1906–07 was "School Visitor."
[13] *A Letter of Fifty Years Ago.*

Negroes were working, many of them adjusted their curricula to qualify for aid from the fund, among the number being most of the Negro colleges.

During the administration of Dr. Haygood, extending through nine years, twenty-five institutions of higher learning were aided by appropriations from the Slater Fund. Table XI gives the

TABLE XI

Negro Colleges Aided by the Slater Fund, 1882 to 1891 *

Name	Year Ending								
	1883	1884	1885	1886	1887	1888	1889	1890	1891
Atlanta University............	x	x	x	x	x	x	x	x	x
Benedict College.............									x
Biddle University............						x	x	x	x
Central Tennessee College....		x	x	x	x	x	x	x	x
Claflin University............	x		x	x	x	x	x	x	x
Clark University.............	x		x	x	x	x	x	x	x
Fisk University..............		x	x	x	x	x	x	x	x
Howard University...........		x	x	x	x	x	x	x	x
Jackson College..............					x	x	x	x	x
Kentucky University.........		x	x	x	x	x			
Leland University............	x	x	x	x	x	x	x		
Leonard Medical School......		x	x	x	x	x	x	x	x
Livingstone College..........					x	x	x	x	x
Meharry Medical College.....			x	x	x	x	x	x	x
New Orleans University......					x	x	x	x	x
Paul Quinn College..........					x	x	x	x	x
Philander Smith College......					x	x	x	x	x
Roger Williams University....		x	x	x	x	x	x	x	x
Rust University..............		x			x	x	x	x	x
Shaw University..............	x		x	x	x	x	x	x	x
Spelman Seminary............			x	x	x	x	x	x	x
Straight University..........					x	x			
Talladega College............	x		x	x	x	x	x	x	x
Tougaloo University..........	x	x	x	x	x	x	x	x	x
Zion Wesleyan College.......				x					
Total for Each Year.......	7	10	15	16	22	23	21	20	21

* John F. Slater Fund, *Proceedings of the Trustees*, as follows: 1883, pp. 19–20; 1884, pp. 10–11; 1885, p. 7; 1886, pp. 7–8; 1887, pp. 8–9; 1888, pp. 7–8; 1889, pp. 11–12; 1890, pp. 8–9; 1891, pp. 40–41; also, Butler, *op. cit.*, p. 467.

names of the colleges aided during this period, with the years for which grants were made. The number rose from seven schools in 1882 to twenty-three in 1891.

The second general agent of the fund was Dr. J. L. M. Curry, a Southern man, who, after a distinguished career as a soldier, statesman, and diplomat was elected in 1891 to the position, which he filled with distinction until 1903. Under Dr. Curry's administration as general agent the policy of the board changed with reference to favoring, in the appropriations, the colleges and universities as contrasted with the other schools for Negroes. During this period the number of institutions of higher learning aided by the fund dropped from twenty in 1891–92 [14] to seven in 1902–03,[15] while the percentage of the total appropriations of the board that went to colleges dropped from 62.4 under Haygood [16] to 51.5 under Curry.[17] Even with this difference in percentages the actual amount granted to institutions of higher learning under Curry was $272,498 as contrasted with $200,860.76 [18] for the Haygood administration. Dr. Curry was highly impressed with the educational ideals of Hampton and Tuskegee Institutes and therefore influenced the board to give generous assistance to these two schools. During the Haygood administration less than 10 per cent of the total appropriations went to these schools. This figure rose to 50.3 per cent during the last three-year period of the Curry administration, ending with 1903.[19] These institutions at that time offered no work at the collegiate level and hence were not counted in the list of colleges.

Table XII shows the disbursements of the Slater Fund not only during the terms of office of Haygood and Curry but from 1882–83 to 1932–33, a period of fifty years. It also shows the total grant for each year, the grants for colleges and universities, and the grants for Hampton and Tuskegee Institutes.

In 1903 Dr. Wallace Buttrick, a native of the state of New York, became general agent of the Slater Fund and served in that capacity for four years, discharging at the same time his duties as secretary and general manager of the General Education Board.[20] No striking change of policy relative to aid granted to colleges occurred during his administration. Appropriations for this purpose increased from $22,000 in 1903–04 to $27,600 in 1907–08.

[14] John F. Slater Fund, *Proceedings of the Trustees*, 1892, p. 16.   [15] *Ibid.*, 1902–03, p. 14.
[16] Butler, *op. cit.*, Table III, p. 111.   [17] *Ibid.*, Table IX, p. 161.
[18] Computed from the annual reports for the appropriate years. See Butler, *op. cit.*, pp. 111 and 161.   [19] *Ibid.*, Tables III and IX.
[20] See the tribute to Dr. Buttrick in The General Education Board, *Annual Report*, 1925–26, pp. ix–xii.

TABLE XII

TOTAL YEARLY APPROPRIATIONS MADE BY THE JOHN F. SLATER FUND AND AMOUNTS GIVEN TO COLLEGES AND UNIVERSITIES AND TO TUSKEGEE AND HAMPTON INSTITUTES, 1882–1932 *

Year	Total Appropriations	Appropriation for Colleges and Universities	Appropriation for Hampton and Tuskegee Institutes
1882–83	$16,250.00	$11,000.00	$2,100.00
1883–84	17,106.66	9,266.66	1,000.00
1884–85	36,764.10	23,614.10	3,000.00
1885–86	30,000.00	17,300.00	3,900.00
1886–87	40,000.00	23,375.00	4,000.00
1887–88	45,000.00	26,510.00	4,000.00
1888–89	44,310.00	28,660.00	3,500.00
1889–90	42,910.00	27,660.00	3,500.00
1890–91	49,650.00	33,100.00	4,000.00
1891–92	45,216.66	29,600.00	3,700.00
1892–93	37,100.00	27,500.00	7,100.00
1893–94	40,000.00	27,500.00	9,000.00
1894–95	42,400.00	27,500.00	11,400.00
1895–96	38,560.53	22,000.00	11,400.00
1896–97	41,900.00	24,500.00	13,900.00
1897–98	42,500.00	19,000.00	20,000.00
1898–99	45,000.00	19,000.00	20,000.00
1899–1900	43,331.00	18,998.00	20,000.00
1900–01	51,800.00	19,800.00	96,000.00
1901–02	53,400.00	19,600.00	27,000.00
1902–03	53,800.00	20,500.00	27,000.00
1903–04	59,200.00	22,000.00	26,000.00
1904–05	54,050.00	22,150.00	20,000.00
1905–06	54,600.00	20,150.00	21,000.00
1906–07	62,740.00	27,000.00	20,000.00
1907–08	65,290.00	27,600.00	20,000.00
1908–09	65,990.00	29,600.00	20,000.00
1909–10	72,950.00	30,600.00	20,000.00
1910–11	68,975.00	28,500.00	20,000.00
1911–12	69,045.00	27,250.00	18,000.00
1912–13	70,545.00	28,850.00	18,000.00
1913–14	66,220.00	27,050.00	18,000.00
1914–15	66,670.00	23,700.00	18,000.00
1915–16	68,275.00	19,475.00	14,000.00
1916–17	69,385.00	18,400.00	14,000.00
1917–18	76,615.00	17,500.00	12,000.00
1918–19	89,802.00	17,050.00	12,000.00
1919–20	108,758.10	18,200.00	12,000.00
1920–21	116,430.03	18,500.00	10,000.00
1921–22	113,040.30	17,400.00	10,000.00
1922–23	115,105.83	15,200.00	10,000.00
1923–24	117,077.48	16,200.00	10,000.00
1924–25	117,585.00	20,200.00	6,000.00
1925–26	136,525.00	12,250.00	10,000.00
1926–27	145,899.78	22,050.00	10,000.00
1927–28	141,661.39	22,050.00	10,000.00
1928–29	195,162.29	42,075.00	....
1929–30	178,423.91	45,450.00	....
1930–31	209,950.00	52,842.00	....
1931–32	169,675.00	51,195.00	....
Total	$3,802,645.06	$1,216,845.76	$604,500.00

*Adapted from Butler, *op. cit.*, Table XLV.

Dr. Buttrick was succeeded by Dr. James H. Dillard, who directed the affairs of the Slater Fund as general agent from 1910 [21] to 1917, and as president from 1917 to 1931, when he retired. His administration was highly successful and won for him enduring fame in the field of educational philanthropy. At the time of his election he was president of the Jeanes Fund, which position he retained, serving as the directing head of both boards until his retirement. Dr. Dillard believed firmly in the value of the Negro colleges, and under his administration the appropriations for these schools were continued, although they fell from $30,600 in 1909–10 to $12,250 in 1925–26.[22] Meanwhile, stress was being placed upon the development of public institutions, especially the county-training schools, which Dr. Dillard did much to develop and in which he took great pride. Beginning with an appropriation of $2,000 in 1911–12,[23] the amount granted to these schools rose rapidly until by 1929–30 they received $130,525,[24] or approximately 73 per cent of the entire sum disbursed during that year. Appropriations to Hampton and Tuskegee were discontinued after 1927–28.[25] The next year the amount granted to colleges rose to $42,075 and to $45,450 in 1929–30, the last year of Dr. Dillard's administration. For 1930–31 the appropriations for colleges amounted to $52,842 and for 1931–32, to $51,195, which is about 31 per cent of the total amount disbursed. [27]

The successor of Dr. Dillard is Dr. Arthur D. Wright, who was elected to the presidency of the Slater Fund in June 1931.[26] Dr. Wright, also born and reared in the South, had just completed a year's work as executive agent of the Southern Association of Colleges and Secondary Schools in the examination and rating of Negro colleges, having been granted leave of absence from a professorship in education at Dartmouth College for that purpose.

Since its foundation the Slater Fund has granted more than $1,200,000 to institutions classed as colleges and universities. If to this we add the $604,500 [28] received by Hampton and Tuskegee Institutes, which are included in that classification in this study, the amount reaches nearly $2,000,000. While this total, distributed over a period of fifty years and among forty-eight institu-

[21] John F. Slater Fund, *Proceedings*, April 29, 1910.   [22] See Table XII.   [23] *Ibid.*
[24] John F. Slater Fund, *Annual Report*, 1930, p. 27.   [25] Butler, *op. cit.*, Table XLV.
[26] John F. Slater Fund, *Proceedings and Reports*, 1931, p. 7.   [27] *Ibid.*, p. 12.
[28] Butler, *op. cit.*, Table XLV.

tions,[29] seems meager, as applied through the years it has been of incalculable benefit to the schools aided. Since no Slater Fund appropriations are made for grounds or buildings all this money has presumably been spent directly for the improvement of teaching by increasing salaries or by enabling teachers to receive better preparation.

THE GENERAL EDUCATION BOARD

From the standpoint of resources, the General Education Board, established January 12, 1903, by Mr. John D. Rockefeller, is the most important of the philanthropic foundations that has given aid to the Negro college. Its object as stated in the act of incorporation is as follows:

That the object of the said corporation shall be the promotion of education within the United States of America, without distinction of race, sex, or creed.

That for the promotion of such object the said corporation shall have power to build, improve, enlarge, or equip, or to aid others to build, improve, enlarge, or equip, buildings for elementary or primary schools, industrial schools, technical schools, normal schools, training schools for teachers, or schools of any grade, or for higher institutions of learning, or, in connection therewith, libraries, workshops, gardens, kitchens, or other educational accessories; to establish, maintain, or endow, elementary or primary schools, industrial schools, technical schools, normal schools, training schools for teachers, or schools of any grade, or higher institutions of learning; to employ or aid others to employ teachers, and lecturers; to aid, coöperate with, or endow associations or other corporations engaged in educational work within the United States of America, or to donate to any such association or corporation any property or moneys which shall at any time be held by the said corporation hereby constituted; to collect educational statistics and information, and to publish and distribute documents and reports containing the same, and in general to do and perform all things necessary or convenient for the promotion of the object of the corporation.[30]

By this broad definition of objectives and powers the trustees are permitted to use the funds entrusted to them in any project of an educational nature. Under this permission the schools for Negroes received from 1902 to 1914, the period covered in the first compiled report published by the board, the sum of $699,-781.13 out of a total expenditure of $15,894,364.89.[31]

The policy of the board in educational matters has been to investigate thoroughly any situation that appeared critical and

---

[29] Butler, *op. cit.*, p. 472.
[30] *The General Education Board, An Account of Its Activities, 1902-1914*, p. 212.
[31] *Ibid.*, p. 17.

then, by offering financial assistance conditioned upon vigorous self-help, to remove the difficulty and at the same time so stimulate a feeling of responsibility on the part of those aided as to make them more self-reliant and possibly self-supporting.[32] This policy has proved highly successful in aiding in the improvement of public school systems and has brought to other institutions a supporting constituency which otherwise might not have become interested.

Examples of the application of this policy to Negro colleges have been referred to in several of the preceding chapters of this study. As further illustrations of this policy the following quotation is taken from one of the annual reports of the board, showing its interest in stimulating more generous appropriation by the states for the publicly supported Negro colleges:

To supply Negro schools of all grades with well-trained teachers continues to be a major problem, and during the year 1928–1929, as in the past, the Board made appropriations to a number of state-supported institutions with a view especially to increasing their capacity for training teachers. Among the larger appropriations may be mentioned the following: To the Prairie View State Normal and Industrial College, $75,000 toward $305,500 for permanent improvements; to the State Agricultural and Mechanical Institute, Normal, Alabama, $100,000 toward $300,000 for permanent improvements; to the State Normal School at Fayetteville, North Carolina, $35,000 toward $70,000 for the construction and equipment of a practice school; to the North Carolina College for Negroes, Durham, $45,000 for furniture and equipment for a classroom and administration building; and to the state department of education in Alabama, for the Snow Hill Normal and Industrial Institute, $25,000 toward the cost of an academic building. In addition the Board appropriated $30,000, available over a period of five years, to the state department of education of Arkansas for an experiment in teacher-training in connection with a new and well-equipped Negro high school and junior college in Little Rock.[33]

In a later chapter of this study the merger of New Orleans University and Straight College, both located at New Orleans, is discussed. In the same chapter mention is also made of the merger of Atlanta University, Morehouse College, and Spelman College, in the city of Atlanta. The influence of the General Education Board was potent in both movements. It has seemed to many persons deeply interested in the higher education of the Negro that educational statesmanship dictates, at the present time, the development of several Negro universities at strategic points in

---

[32] *The General Education Board, An Account of Its Activities, 1902–1914,* pp. 13, 14.
[33] The General Education Board, *Annual Report,* 1928–29, pp. 78, 79.

the South.   Because of a combination of circumstances it seems
that Washington, D. C., Atlanta, Georgia, Nashville, Tennessee,
and New Orleans, Louisiana, are looked upon as the natural
places for the four university centers.   They are well distributed
with reference to the Negro population, and in each city there is
already located the nucleus for such an institution.   The following extracts from a single report of the board indicate what may
be interpreted as a sympathetic attitude toward this view.   The
first refers to Fisk University, which has always maintained the
highest standards and was the first Negro college in the Southern
area to receive the "A" rating by the regional association and the
only one to receive that rating during the first year of examination :

> Fisk University, at Nashville, Tennessee, has long occupied a prominent
> place in higher education for Negroes, and during the past few years has made
> substantial progress.   In common with most other colleges for Negroes, it finds
> that one of its most pressing needs is better library facilities.   For this purpose
> the Board authorized an appropriation of $400,000 toward $800,000 for the
> construction, equipment, and endowment for maintenance of a library build-
> ing.   The Board also made an appropriation of $125,000, available over five
> years, toward the salaries of members of the teaching staff in the college depart-
> ment, and an appropriation of $35,000, available over a period of three years,
> for equipment, books, and for other expenses in connection with an experiment
> in the training of teachers.[34]

The next refers to the Meharry Medical College, also located at
Nashville, which is one of the only two medical schools for Negroes
in the United States.

> In the chapter on Medical Education it is stated that the Board is withdraw-
> ing from the general field of medical education.   Coöperation in the promotion
> of medical education for Negroes, however, will be continued as part of the
> Board's program.   As the economic status of the race improves, opportunity
> for service in the professional fields becomes more and more attractive, and it is
> of the utmost importance that those who enter this service be well trained.   In
> 1928–1929 the Board made appropriations to two Negro institutions for medi-
> cal work: to Meharry Medical College, Nashville, Tennessee, $34,000 available
> over a four-year period, to furnish opportunity for additional training for
> members of the faculty, and a further sum of $75,000, available over three
> years, for current expenses, this being in addition to $45,000 previously voted;
> to Howard University, $85,000, chiefly to furnish additional training for mem-
> bers of the medical school faculty.[35]

By such aid, judiciously distributed, a broad coöperative policy
may be induced among those promoting higher education for

[34] The General Education Board, *Annual Report*, 1928–29, p. 80.   [35] *Ibid.*, p. 81.

Negroes, which, without such an outside stimulus, would probably be impossible at the present or in the immediate future.

In addition to direct financial aid to the Negro college, the board contributes to the improvement of the faculties of these schools by scholarship grants to teachers for advanced study. The importance of such aid is fully realized when one considers the poverty of the Negro student while in college and the low compensation which he receives when he enters the teaching profession. Such grants as those made by the General Education Board and the Julius Rosenwald Fund are practically the only sources of aid available to the hard-pressed but aspiring Negro college teacher.

TABLE XIII

DISBURSEMENTS OF GENERAL EDUCATION BOARD, 1927–1932

	1927–1928 *	1928–1929 †	1929–1930 ‡	1930–1931 §	1931–1932 **
Total for Whites........	$12,779,850	$20,869,006	$9,958,761	$3,647,621	$8,452,385
Total for Negroes.......	4,375,958	2,231,400	6,085,043	5,139,485	1,782,596
Colleges and Schools.....	3,244,000	1,756,000	3,286,193	4,691,085	1,170,796
Fellowships and Scholarships...............	30,000	40,000	50,000	55,000	55,000
John F. Slater Fund.....	313,750		15,000		35,000
Medical Education......	272,058	194,000	2,442,000	157,000	250,000
Education in Southern States...............	100,000	100,000	100,000		
Negro Rural School Fund.	318,900	119,400			
Rural School Agents.....	97,250		104,350	136,400	136,800
Division of Negro Education..................		22,000	30,000		
Anna T. Jeanes Foundation..................			22,500		
Association of Colleges and Secondary Schools of Southern States......			35,000		
Miscellaneous..........				100,000	35,000
Social Sciences.........					30,000

* The General Education Board, *Annual Report*, 1927–28, p. 37.
† *Ibid.*, 1928–29, p. 94.　　§ *Ibid.*, 1930–31, pp. 38, 39.
‡ *Ibid.*, 1929–30, p. 56.　　** *Ibid.*, 1931–32, pp. 56, 57.

Table XIII gives suggestive figures relative to the disbursements of the General Education Board for the five-year period 1927–28 to 1931–32.

From the date of the foundation of the board to June 1932 it granted for educational purposes the following sums:[36]

Total for Whites..........................$193,233,422.79
Total for Negroes.......................... 32,593,712.77
Total for Negro Colleges and Schools....... 23,193,329.93

THE JULIUS ROSENWALD FUND

Mr. Julius Rosenwald of Chicago established the fund bearing his name on January 1, 1928 as a result of his interest in the Negro, developed through his contacts with the Young Men's Christian Association and his activity in promoting rural schools for Negroes in the South.[37]   The market value of the fund, including the original grant and later additions, amounts to approximately $22,000,000.   The income of the fund and the principal (which is to be exhausted within twenty years after the donor's death) are to be used entirely upon Negro education.   The chief activities of the fund have been in the field of rural education.   These have consisted largely in the construction of school buildings, with the coöperation of the local communities.   Nearly six thousand schools of this kind have been built since the inception of the idea by Mr. Rosenwald, largely at the suggestion of Booker T. Washington.

The interest of the fund in the higher education of Negroes is seen in the assistance given to certain selected schools and in the financing of promising Negro students engaged in advanced study. For the year ending June 30, 1929, the sum of $84,725 was given to Negro schools and colleges for buildings and equipment, current expenses, and libraries.[38]   For the year ending 1930 the sum of $394,607 was granted for private colleges and professional schools, and $86,720 for fellowships.[39]   For the year ending June 30, 1931 the sum of $100,000 was appropriated for state colleges, $505,005 for private colleges and professional schools, and $136,692 for fellowships.   The largest contributions for private colleges and professional schools went to Howard University, Washington, D. C.; Fisk University, and Meharry Medical College, Nashville, Tennessee; Atlanta University, and Spelman College, Atlanta, Georgia; and Dillard University, New Orleans, Louisiana.[40]

[36] The General Education Board, *Annual Report*, 1928–29, pp. 52–55.
[37] Embree, Edwin R., *Julius Rosenwald Fund—A Survey* (1928), pp. 5, 6, and 7.
[38] Julius Rosenwald Fund, *Annual Report*, 1929, p. 35.
[39] *Ibid.*, 1930, p. 31.   [40] *Ibid.*, 1931, p. 36.

The value of the grants of the fund for the assistance of varied phases of Negro education below the collegiate level naturally contributes to the development of the Negro college by strengthening the foundations upon which it rests. The direct contributions to the Negro colleges have the same effect as those made by the General Education Board, discussed above. In the first place, they provide for a much-needed expansion of plant facility and stimulate self-help by being made conditional. In the second place, the contributions strengthen library facilities by supplying books, and thus strengthen the Negro colleges in one of their very weakest points. In the third place, the appropriation of funds to finance the members of faculties of Negro colleges who wish to do advanced study is not only beneficial to the individuals aided but heightens the academic tone of the institutions thus aided.

THE PHELPS-STOKES FUND

The Phelps-Stokes Fund was established April 28, 1910, and incorporated by the State of New York, May 10, 1911, in accordance with the will of Mrs. Caroline Phelps-Stokes of New York City. The board of trustees, soon after its organization, approved the report of its Committee on Plan and Scope, as follows:

1. That in providing for the establishment of the Phelps-Stokes Fund the testatrix showed a special, although by no means exclusive, interest in Negro education.
2. That it is wise for this board to dispense its philanthropy as far as possible through existing institutions of proven experience and of assured stability.
3. That the coöperation of the best white citizens of the South is of prime importance in solving the problem of Negro education.
4. That the board will be justified in meeting occasionally the whole or a part of the expense of securing investigations and reports on educational institutions or problems, when these are thought to be of great significance.[41]

The chief activities of the fund, therefore, while directed toward the improvement of Negro education, are not directly stressed in the work of Negro colleges except as an object of study. Out of a total expenditure of $570,100 by the fund since its establishment for educational activities for Negroes in the United States, $190,585 has been for Negro schools, colleges, and universities. Of this amount $49,984 has been for surveys of Negro education, $25,168 for Negro educational organizations, and $97,803 for organizations for the improvement of race relations. In addition to

[41] *The Twenty Year Report of the Phelps-Stokes Fund, 1911–1931*, pp. 9, 10.

this financial aid the board has coöperated heartily with educational institutions in meeting financial and other perplexing problems.

As a source and a disseminator of information, the Phelps-Stokes Fund has probably performed its greatest service to the Negro college. The study of Negro education made in 1914–15 is invaluable as a source of information concerning the condition of the Negro schools on all levels at that period. The contribution of $5,000 made by the fund in order to insure the Survey of Negro Colleges and Universities by the U. S. Bureau of Education in 1928 was also a contribution for the collection of factual information whose value can hardly be overestimated.[42]

[42] *The Twenty Year Report of the Phelps-Stokes Fund, 1911–1931*, pp. 14, 15.

PART IV
PROGRESS FROM 1922 TO 1932

CHAPTER XIV

THE SURVEY OF 1928

REFERENCE has been made to the effect of the survey of Negro education made in 1916–17 and the report of the findings. Because of the participation of the United States in the World War, during the greater part of 1917, 1918, and 1919 little attention was paid to problems of educational reform. At the same time, however, improvements and readjustments in the Negro colleges were going forward. About 1920 this group of schools began to be keenly interested in the problems of standardization. The general cause of this interest was the natural and laudable ambition of the colleges to have their work approved by one of the generally recognized accrediting agencies. The immediate cause, however, was the difficulty experienced by the graduates of a majority of these colleges in gaining admission to schools of medicine. This difficulty grew out of the practice of the American Medical Association in issuing its lists of approved colleges on the basis of the ratings given by the regional collegiate associations. Since the Negro colleges in the Southern area were not considered at all by the appropriate regional association prior to 1930, the American Medical Association, in rating the Negro colleges, took as its source of information the report of the 1916 Survey of Negro Education as the most reliable and authentic body of data available.

Considerable dissatisfaction was naturally expressed year after year by the Negro colleges at the practice of the American Medical Association in depending, for so important a matter, upon data which were constantly growing older and hence less reliable. So important had this question become by 1925, nine years after the survey had been concluded, that the Association of Colleges for Negro Youth, at the meeting held at Shaw University, Raleigh, North Carolina, April 10 and 11, 1925, appointed a committee "For working out a basis for rating our colleges."

The first act of the committee was to request the Phelps-Stokes

Fund to repeat its survey, at least as it related to higher education. This the trustees of that fund declined to do, but they offered the sum of $5,000 toward defraying the expenses of such a resurvey. The committee next appealed indirectly to the Association of Colleges and Secondary Schools of the Southern States, but found that events had not proceeded far enough to enable that body to examine and rate the Negro colleges in its area.   The next point of attack was the Federal Bureau of Education, which in 1926 finally undertook the task of surveying the Negro colleges, only, however, on the invitation of the individual colleges and with the financial coöperation of the Phelps-Stokes Fund.

In his letter to the Secretary of the Interior transmitting the report of the survey, the Commissioner of Education, Dr. John T. Tigert, said:

Sir: It is generally acknowledged that a report on negro education in the United States published by the Bureau of Education in 1917 has contributed greatly to the tremendous reconstruction of schools for negroes which has taken place during the past 10 years.

In view of the progress made since the appearance of that report, State departments of education, nationally known educators, both white and colored, the officials of universities in the North and in the South, and the representatives of church and other educational boards and foundations have for a long time urged upon my consideration the need for a resurvey of negro colleges and universities.

In recognition of this need and in response to the desire for another survey so generally expressed, I arranged for the study which is embodied in the report transmitted herewith.

The State departments of education in 19 States, 79 negro colleges and universities, the Association of Colleges for Negro Youth, the Phelps-Stokes Fund, and the educational boards and foundations of the seven church bodies coöperated in arranging for the study and in furnishing information.

The survey was made under the immediate direction of Dr. Arthur J. Klein, chief of the division of higher education, by a committee consisting of Dr. William B. Bizzell, president of the University of Oklahoma; Dr. C. C. Mc-Cracken, Ohio State University; Dean George B. Woods, American University; and from the staff of the Bureau of Education, John H. McNeely, assistant to the director, Dr. Walton C. John, and M. M. Proffitt.

The conclusions and recommendations contained in the report represent the consensus of opinion of the entire committee and have my approval.[1]

The survey covered a period of two years and the report was issued by the Bureau of Education as Bulletin 1928, No. 7, under the title, *Survey of Negro Colleges and Universities.*   It contains,

[1] *U. S. Bureau of Ed. Bul.*, 1928, No. 7, p. vi.

within about 964 pages, a mass of detailed information brought
up to 1928, concerning the seventy-nine colleges surveyed.
Only those schools were examined that made the request and
pledged the nominal fee required to pay part of the costs. The
expense of making the survey and issuing the report was approximately $23,000.[2]

This survey paved the way for a reopening of the question of
rating, since the Bureau of Education could act only as a fact-
finding body and not as a rating agency. As a temporary expedient the American Medical Association appointed a committee
on education for the purpose of revising the list of Negro colleges
capable of giving acceptable pre-medical work. The Bulletin of
the American Medical Association, revised June 1, 1930, contained the list thus created, with an introductory statement as
follows:

Until such time as provision for the approval of colleges for Negro students
can be made by all the associations of colleges and secondary schools, the following list of Negro colleges deemed worthy of approval has been prepared
under the auspices of the Council on Medical Education and Hospitals.

The approval is based, in the judgment of the committee, on the ability of the
Negro colleges to offer two years of acceptable premedical college work.

This list is based on a survey of all Negro colleges made in 1927 by a special
committee under the direction of Dr. Arthur J. Klein, chief of the Division of
Higher Education of the United States Bureau of Education. The publication of this list is made possible through the kindly coöperation of a special
committee consisting of Dr. G. B. Woods, Dean, American University, Washington, D. C. (chairman); Dr. C. C. McCracken, Ohio State University,
Columbus, and Dr. Louis R. Wilson, University of North Carolina, Chapel Hill.

A reinvestigation will be made each year of such colleges as will pay the cost,
so that due recognition can be given for such improvements as may have been
made. (Then follows a list of 31 colleges.)[3]

The third step in the program of examining and accrediting
Negro colleges was taken when the Southern Association of Colleges and Secondary Schools, as a result of a number of conferences, decided to assume the responsibility of examining and
rating the Negro colleges in its area and appointed from its membership a "Committee on Approval of Negro Schools" whose
duty it was to act for the association in this matter. With a
grant made for the purpose by the General Education Board, the

[2] Association of Negro Colleges, *Minutes*, 1929, p. 8.

[3] *The Bulletin* (Organ of the National Association of Teachers in Colored Schools, Charleston,
W. Va.), Vol. II, No. 4, Jan. 1931, pp. 7–8.

examination of Negro colleges in the Southern area began in September 1930 [4] under the direction of Dr. Arthur H. Wright, who was chosen as executive agent of the committee and placed in charge of the actual work of making the investigations of the colleges. He rigidly applied the standards of the association and at the end of the year rated only one school as fully accredited, but submitted also a "B" class of colleges whose work was of acceptable quality but which failed to meet fully the standards as specified by the association. In 1930, as related in the preceding chapter, Dr. Wright was elected president of the Jeanes and Slater Funds and was succeeded in the task of examining and rating Negro colleges by Mr. Fred McCuistion. As a result of the stimulus given by this activity the number of fully accredited colleges had increased to six by June 1933, while twenty-two were rated "B" and four were approved as junior colleges.[5]

The survey of 1928, therefore, not only supplied a valuable body of factual material relative to the Negro college but may justly be looked upon as a significant step toward the rating of the Negro colleges assumed by the recognized accrediting agency which covers the area in which 90 per cent of the institutions making up this group are located.

The report of the 1928 survey shows that during the decade following the survey of 1916, the Negro college had made remarkable progress along all lines. Indeed, it can be fairly said that, with a few exceptions, it was during this decade that this group of schools began creating for themselves a college atmosphere, so overwhelming had been the elementary and secondary emphasis before that time. But the entire American college world had also been making rapid strides during that decade.

While the report generously praises the Negro colleges for their great advancement under serious handicaps, yet it reveals, in general, a serious deficiency in support, in library facilities, in scientific equipment, in the preparation of teachers, and in administration, when these features were measured in terms of American collegiate standards.[6]

The statistical tables, summarizing the report, when condensed give the following approximate figures.

[4] Association of Colleges for Negro Youth, *Minutes*, 1930, p. 5.
[5] McCuistion, Fred, *Higher Education of Negroes*, p. 36.
[6] *U. S. Bur. of Ed. Bul.*, 1928, No. 7, pp. 945–56.

TABLE XIV

Summary Facts from the Survey of Negro Colleges for the Year
1926–27

	Number or Amount
Number of College students..........................	12,000
Average per school...............................	152
Volumes in libraries..............................	418,000
Average per school...............................	5,200
Total average annual expenditure on library..........	$107,410
Average per school...............................	$1,342
Total endowment.................................	$20,713,796
Endowment of Hampton and Tuskegee combined.....	$14,135,768
Endowment for the remaining 77 schools............	$6,577,928
Average endowment for the 77 schools..............	$85,426
Total income.....................................	$8,516,291
Average per school...............................	$108,000

CHAPTER XV

PRESENT STATUS AND TRENDS

THE *Report of the Survey of Negro Colleges*, issued by the United States Bureau of Education in 1928, came at a time when the country as a whole was in the midst of taking stock of its institutions of higher learning. The minds of those in charge of colleges and universities were keenly alert to the findings of the experimenters, the surveyors, and the philosophers working in that field, in order to adjust the institutions which had been intrusted to their care to the standards set up according to the latest findings. As has been pointed out this survey showed that the Negro colleges as a whole fell far short of the standards which had been established for colleges by the national and regional accrediting agencies of the country. There naturally followed a period of substantial improvement, made possible by larger appropriations of state funds, by the continued support of the church boards and the general public, and by an increased interest on the part of the great philanthropic foundations. Table XV lists all the schools for Negroes reporting students of college grade for the year 1931–32.

The data used for discussion in this chapter are taken or derived for the most part from information collected by Mr. Fred McCuistion, executive agent of the Southern Association of Colleges and Secondary Schools, as a basis for rating the Negro college in the Southern area, and by Dean T. E. McKinney, editor of *The Quarterly Review of Higher Education Among Negroes*.[1]

NUMBER OF COLLEGES

The number of colleges listed in the table is 109, distributed among nineteen states and the District of Columbia. If we are to assume that the Negro colleges are to be supported on approximately their present total combined income, it would seem a wise

---

[1] McCuistion, Fred, *Higher Education of Negroes*; McKinney, T. E., *The Quarterly Review of Higher Education Among Negroes*, July 1933, pp. 34–36; 39–41.

TABLE XV

INSTITUTIONS FOR NEGROES ENROLLING STUDENTS OF COLLEGE GRADE, AR-
RANGED BY STATES SHOWING LOCATION, YEAR FOUNDED, SUPPORT AND CONTROL,
YEARS OF COLLEGE WORK OFFERED, AND ENROLLMENT AS OF APRIL 1932

Institution	Location	Support and Control	Year Founded	Years of College Work Offered	Students Enrolled in College
ALABAMA					
Miles Memorial College...	Birmingham	C. M. E. Church	1902	4	91
Selma University........	Selma	Negro Baptist	1878	4	26
State A. & M. Institute...	Normal	Public	1875	2	82
State Teachers College...	Montgomery	Public	1874	4	338
Talladega College........	Talladega	A. M. A.*	1867	4	221
Tuskegee N. & I.........	Tuskegee	Independent	1881	4	576
ARKANSAS					
Arkansas Baptist College.	Little Rock	Negro Baptist	1885	4	51
Arkansas State College...	Pine Bluff	Public	1875	4	134
Dunbar Junior College...	Little Rock	Public	1929	2	128
Philander Smith College..	Little Rock	M. E. Church †	1877	4	111
Shorter College.........	No. Little Rock	A. M. E. Church‡	1886	4	25
DELAWARE					
State College for Colored Youth..............	Dover	Public	1891	2	52
DISTRICT OF COLUMBIA					
Howard University......	Washington	Independent	1867	4	1573
Miner Teachers College...	Washington	Public	1929	4	408
FLORIDA					
Bethune-Cookman College	Daytona Beach	M. E. Church	1904	2	67
Edward Waters College...	Jacksonville	A. M. E. Church	1883	2	49
Florida A. & M. College...	Tallahassee	Public	1887	4	472
Florida N. & I. College...	St. Augustine	Public	1892	2	77
GEORGIA					
Atlanta University.......	Atlanta	Independent	1860	4	69
Clark University........	Atlanta	M. E. Church	1870	4	344
Central City College.....	Macon	Negro Baptist	1899	2	12
Fort Valley, N. & I.......	Fort Valley	Independent	1893	2	47
Georgia N. & A. College..	Albany	Public	1905	2	48
Georgia State Industrial College..............	Industrial	Public	1890	4	137
Morehouse College.......	Atlanta	A. B. H. M. S.§	1867	4	281
Morris Brown University..	Atlanta	A. M. E. Church	1885	4	264
Paine College..........	Augusta	C. M. E. Church**	1882	4	154
Spelman College........	Atlanta	Independent	1881	4	211
State T. & A. College....	Forsyth	Public	....	2	63
KANSAS					
Western University......	Kansas City	A. M. E.	1877	2	37
KENTUCKY					
Kentucky State Industrial College..............	Frankfort	Public	1896	4	272
Lincoln Institute........	Lincoln Ridge	Independent	1912	2	37
Louisville Municipal College.................	Louisville	Public	1931	4	185
West Kentucky Industrial College..............	Paducah	Public	1910	2	103

* A. M. A.—American Missionary Association.   † M. E.—Methodist Episcopal.   ‡ A. M. E.
—African Methodist Episcopal.   § A. B. H. M. S.—American Baptist Home Mission Society.
** C. M. E.—Colored Methodist Episcopal.

TABLE XV (*Continued*)

Institution	Location	Support and Control	Year Founded	Years of College Work Offered	Students Enrolled in College
LOUISIANA					
Coleman College........	Gibsland	Negro Baptist	1890	2	10
Leland University.......	Baker	A. B. H. M. S.	1870	4	98
Louisiana N. & I. College..	Grambling	Independent	1905	2	57
New Orleans University..	New Orleans	M. E. Church	1869	4	473
Southern University and A. & M. College......	Scotlandville	Public	1914	4	297
Straight College.........	New Orleans	A. M. A.	1868	4	125
Xavier University.......	New Orleans	Catholic	1915	4	192
MARYLAND					
Coppin Normal School...	Baltimore	Public	1902	2	107
Maryland Normal School.	Bowie	Public	1911	2	111
Morgan College.........	Baltimore	Independent	1876	4	521
Princess Anne Academy..	Princess Anne	Public	1886	2	17
MISSISSIPPI					
Alcorn A. & M. College...	Alcorn	Public	1871	4	168
Jackson College.........	Jackson	A. B. H. M. S.	1877	4	56
Mississippi Industrial.....	Holly Springs	C. M. E.	1906	4	21
Natchez College.........	Natchez	Negro Baptist	1885	4	28
Rust College............	Holly Springs	M. E. Church	1886	4	84
Southern Christian Institute................	Edwards	Disciples of Christ	1881	2	19
Tougaloo College........	Tougaloo	A. M. A.	1869	4	96
MISSOURI					
Lincoln University.......	Jefferson City	Public	1866	4	196
Stowe Teachers College...	St. Louis	Public	1890	4	599
NORTH CAROLINA					
A. & T. College.........	Greensboro	Public	1891	4	279
Barber-Scotia College....	Concord	Presbyterian	1870	2	73
Bennett College for Women	Greensboro	M. E. Church	1926	4	157
Bricks Junior College	Bricks	A. M. A.	1895	2	94
Johnson C. Smith University.................	Charlotte	Presbyterian	1867	4	245
Kittrell College..........	Kittrell	A. M. E. Church	1885	2	58
Livingstone College......	Salisbury	A. M. E. Zion	1882	4	215
North Carolina College for Negroes..............	Durham	Public	1925	4	284
St. Augustine's College...	Raleigh	Episcopal	1867	4	179
Shaw University.........	Raleigh	Independent	1865	4	262
State Normal School.....	Fayetteville	Public	1877	2	284
State Normal School.....	Elizabeth City	Public	1889	2	181
Winston-Salem State Teachers College......	Winston-Salem	Public	1925	4	251
OHIO					
Wilberforce University...	Wilberforce	A. M. E. Church	1856	4	553
OKLAHOMA					
Colored A. & N. University	Langston	Public	1897	4	533
PENNSYLVANIA					
Cheyney Training School.	Cheyney	Public	1913	3	183
Lincoln University.......	Chester Co.	Independent	1854	4	318
SOUTH CAROLINA					
Allen University.........	Columbia	A. M. E. Church	1870	4	263
Benedict College........	Columbia	A. B. H. M. S.	1870	4	242

TABLE XV (*Continued*)

Institution	Location	Support and Control	Year Founded	Years of College Work Offered	Students Enrolled in College
Bettis College...........	Trenton	Negro Baptist	1881	2	32
Brewer Junior College....	Greenwood	A. M. A.	1872	2	8
Claflin University........	Orangeburg	M. E. Church	1869	4	122
Friendship College.......	Rock Hill	Negro Baptist	....	2	28
Morris College..........	Sumter	Negro Baptist	1905	2	120
State A. & M. College....	Orangeburg	Public	1895	4	322
Voorhees N. & I.........	Denmark	Independent	1879	2	26
TENNESSEE					
A. & I. State College.....	Nashville	Public	1912	4	681
Fisk University.........	Nashville	Independent	1865	4	447
Knoxville College........	Knoxville	Presbyterian	1872	4	300
Lane College.............	Jackson	C. M. E. Church	1878	4	263
LeMoyne College........	Memphis	A. M. A.	1870	4	220
Morristown N. & I. College	Morristown	M. E. Church	1881	2	37
Roger Williams..........	Nashville	Negro Baptist	1867	4	30
Swift Memorial College...	Rogersville	Presbyterian	1883	2	28
TEXAS					
Bishop College..........	Marshall	A. B. H. M. S.	1881	4	388
Butler College..........	Tyler	Negro Baptist	1905	2	71
Guadalupe College.......	Seguin	Negro Baptist	1887	2	32
Houston Colored Junior College...............	Houston	Public	1927	2	322
Jarvis Christian College ..	Hawkins	Disciples of Christ	1909	2	38
Mary Allen Seminary	Crockett	Presbyterian	1886	2	125
Paul Quinn College......	Waco	A. M. E. Church	1881	2	90
Prairie View State College	Prairie View	Public	1886	4	661
St. Phillip's Junior College	San Antonio	Episcopal	1898	2	64
Samuel Houston College..	Austin	M. E. Church	1900	4	217
Texas College..........	Tyler	C. M. E. Church	1894	4	264
Tillotson College........	Austin	A. M. A.	1877	4	155
Wiley College..........	Marshall	M. E. Church	1873	4	336
VIRGINIA					
Hampton N. & I. Institute	Hampton	Independent	1868	4	889
St. Paul N. & I. School....	Lawrenceville	Episcopal	1888	2	81
Virginia College & Seminary...............	Lynchburg	Negro Baptist	1888	4	...
Virginia State College....	Petersburg	Public	1883	4	568
Virginia Union University.	Richmond	A. B. H. M. S.	1865	4	333
WEST VIRGINIA					
Bluefield State Teachers College...............	Bluefield	Public	1921	4	274
Storer College..........	Harper's Ferry	Independent	1867	2	51
West Virginia State College	Institute	Public	1891	4	621

procedure, educationally, to reduce this number very drastically, rather than to continue to dissipate the limited resources available among such a large number of schools, many of which cannot possibly offer a standard grade of college work with the income now available or that can reasonably be expected for many years. Eleven of the 109 colleges enroll 500 or more students; twenty-five from 250 to 500; twenty-nine from 100 to 250; and forty-four less than 100. The number of students accounted for in the table is 22,917. This number could be accommodated by fifty colleges enrolling an average of less than 500 students with all the advantages that would naturally result from such an adjustment in the form of increased educational efficiency.

STUDENT ENROLLMENT

On the other hand, on the basis of the Negro population and in view of the rate of college attendance among white people, the number of Negro colleges is by no means excessive. In the sixteen Southern states and the District of Columbia there was, in 1930, a total Negro population of 9,552,815 while the number of resident Negroes attending college was 18,550. These figures give a ratio of 515 residents in these states to each student attending college. In the same area there are approximately 100 white residents to each college student. If the Negro is expected to attain the American standards in culture, character, and efficiency he must attend college in at least the same ratio to the population as do the white students. At the present time Negro college students, in the area in question, are only one-fifth as numerous in relation to the Negro population as are white students in relation to the white population. The number of Negro college students, therefore, would have to be increased fivefold in order to reach parity in relative numbers with the white college students. This means that the 18,550 students in the Southern area would have to be increased to 92,750, a situation which would require nearly two hundred colleges, each accommodating about five hundred students. Table XVI presents the pertinent facts relative to college attendance and population for the area under consideration.

As one would expect, there has been a definite shift in the enrollment in Negro colleges from elementary and secondary levels to work of college grade. Table XVII makes this clear. It shows that although the total number of students of all grades enrolled in Negro colleges was about the same in 1931–32 as in 1921–22, the period of eleven years had witnessed a reversal in the distribution of students enrolled at the three levels. In 1921–22 only 5,231 students or 15 per cent of the total enrollment were of college grade. In 1931–32 the enrollment of college

TABLE XVI

NEGRO POPULATION AND COLLEGE ATTENDANCE BY STATES, 1930 *

State	Total Negro Population	Number of Residents Attending College	Number of Residents in Each State to Each College Student
West Virginia............	114,893	732	157
District of Columbia......	132,068	725	183
Kentucky...............	226,040	796	284
Texas..................	854,964	2,791	309
Tennessee..............	477,646	1,453	329
Oklahoma..............	172,198	521	330
North Carolina..........	918,647	2,595	354
Maryland..............	276,379	740	373
Virginia................	650,165	1,465	444
Florida................	431,828	659	670
Missouri...............	223,840	326	687
South Carolina..........	793,681	1,089	729
Georgia................	1,071,125	1,376	778
Alabama...............	944,834	1,189	794
Louisiana..............	776,326	894	868
Arkansas..............	478,463	465	1,029
Mississippi.............	1,009,718	734	1,366
Total................	9,552,815	18,550	Av. 515

* McCuistion, *op. cit.*, p. 17.

students had risen to 22,609 or 85 per cent of the whole. This means, first, that the schools are rapidly evolving from elementary and secondary schools as the public school systems take over their proper function; second, that the cost of operating the institutions should be much higher than it was when college students

TABLE XVII

ENROLLMENT IN NEGRO COLLEGES, 1921–22 to 1931–32 *

Year	Number of Institutions	Enrollment			
		College	High School	Elementary	Total
1921–22........	70	5,231	15,361	13,692	34,284
1923–24........	82	7,641	18,706	11,938	38,285
1926–27........	99	13,197	18,387	10,325	41,909
1931–32........	106	22,609	8,859	4,321	35,789

* McCuistion, *op. cit.*, p. 15.

were greatly in the minority; and third, that not until after 1927 did the institutions of higher learning for Negroes expend their major energies on work above the high school level.

THE MOVEMENT TOWARD CONSOLIDATION

Even if the accommodations could be supplied at once for 90,000 Negro college students, the students would not be available in the immediate future. The Negro secondary schools will be unable to prepare such a large number of college students and the Negro parents will be unable to finance their college education for at least a generation or more. Meanwhile it is becoming increasingly evident that steps must be taken to readjust the facilities offered by the Negro colleges to the demand of the present and the immediate future through coöperative action in the form of mergers, affiliations, coöperative agreements or the actual closing of individual institutions. Significant beginnings have been made in this direction, notably at Atlanta where, in 1928, there were five Negro colleges, and at New Orleans where there were three. Except for the sake of tradition or as a matter of denominational pride, there seems little reason at present to maintain two Negro colleges in the same city anywhere in the country, unless their combined enrollment of college students exceeds 750.

The arrangements made at Atlanta and New Orleans, largely on the advice and with the assistance of the larger educational foundations, are examples of what can be done in this direction.

DILLARD UNIVERSITY

New Orleans is so situated that a Negro population of nearly 5,000,000 lives within a radius of five hundred miles of it. It is also a thriving commercial and educational center. The Negro colleges located there in 1930 were Straight University, a school under the American Missionary Association, founded in 1869; New Orleans University, a school of the Methodist Episcopal Church founded in 1873; and Xavier College, a Roman Catholic institution opened in 1915. The origins, histories, and objectives of New Orleans and Straight were practically the same. Both schools were looking forward to and planning for a program of expansion, and both appealed to certain of the philanthropic foundations for substantial assistance. As a result of these negotiations, the boards of both schools were invited to consider the possibility of launching upon a much more significant project than either could hope to accomplish alone by merging to form a new school of true university proportions. The suggestion was favorably received by the two church boards concerned, and the local boards and faculties took favorable action. On February 2, 1929 a meeting was attended by representatives of the church boards, the college presidents, and representatives of the Julius Rosenwald Fund and of the General Education Board. On the next day a special committee of the New Orleans Chamber of Commerce met with the committee already mentioned for the purpose of offering their assistance in carrying out the plans then in the process of formulation and in procuring a suitable site for the proposed university. Within a year from the date of this meeting all difficulties had been composed and Dillard University had officially become a fact. The following statement by President O. E. Kriege of New Orleans University, written in 1930, gives the important facts concerning the agreement:

The Trustee Board is composed of seventeen members of whom the Board of Education of the M. E. Church selects six, the American Missionary Association six and these twelve select the five trustees at large. The trustees are as follows:

For the M. E. Church, Dr. M. J. Holmes and Dr. Thomas F. Holgate of Chicago, Mr. Frank Jensen of Dallas, Texas, and Bishop R. E. Jones and Dr. Thaddeus Taylor of New Orleans.

For the Congregational Church Dr. Fred L. Brownlee, Mr. Charles B. Austin, Dr. George E. Haynes, Mrs. Lucius R. Eastman and Mr. W. A. Daniel of New York.

Trustees at large are Alvin P. Howard, Edward B. Stern, Warren Kearney and Monte M. Lemann.

The temporary chairman of the new Board is Mr. Stern, the secretary is Mr. Austin. This is an unusually strong Board of Trustees, the equal of any in the land and it has taken up the work for Dillard University in a spirit that bids fair to make of it one of the outstanding Negro universities in America.

Dillard University is to begin with an expenditure of $2,000,000 for site, buildings and equipment of which sum the two church boards contribute $1,000,000 in cash, the two philanthropic boards, $750,000 and the citizens of New Orleans $250,000. The first unit to be built will be the new Flint-Goodridge Hospital which has been affiliated with New Orleans University from the beginning. The site at Louisiana and Howard Avenues, a most advantageous one, has already been secured. The recent campaign for $250,000 in the city of New Orleans was one of the most heartening experiences in interracial amity and understanding ever witnessed in the South. Leading men of both races worked and contributed in splendid fashion and at the end of the brief period of the campaign over $300,000 had been subscribed. Another beautiful experience was the undivided moral and financial support given to the hospital campaign by the colored population of the city, for it meant the merger of an independent hospital project with the larger program.   The new Flint-Goodridge hospital will mean much for improved health conditions for the Negro population of New Orleans.   It will be the first unit of Dillard University and construction will begin at an early date.   Probably no greater thing has ever been undertaken by and for the Negro race in any city than is being undertaken here.   Everyone interested in educational matters and interracial affairs is watching the progress of events in New Orleans with keen interest.

It will be at least two years before a new campus can have been secured and a new group of buildings erected and made ready for occupancy.   Meanwhile both New Orleans University and Straight University will "carry on" in their present plants.   Buildings, equipment, faculties and curricula will be kept at par and students at either school will find a fine loyalty of alma mater and a joyful anticipation of the enlarged educational facilities soon to open for them in Dillard University.[2]

THE ATLANTA-MOREHOUSE-SPELMAN AFFILIATION

For many years Atlanta, Georgia, second only to New Orleans in size among Southern cities, was the seat of five Negro colleges. These were Atlanta University, an independent coeducational college founded in 1869; Morehouse College, a school for men founded in 1867 and developed by the American Baptist Home Mission Society; Spelman College, an institution for women founded in 1881 and controlled by an independent board of trustees; Clark University, founded in 1870 and developed as one of the principal institutions of higher learning of the chain of schools under the Methodist Episcopal Church; and Morris Brown University, founded in 1885 and developed under the auspices of the African Methodist Episcopal Church.   All these schools were serving the same purpose, while none had found any distinctive function or activity that could not be performed by any one of the remainder, unless we divide the functions of Morehouse and Spelman on the basis of sex.

For several years prior to 1929 there had been talk of the possibilities of closer coöperation among these schools, and advanced students from Spelman for several years before that date had taken courses at Morehouse by agreement between the two schools, whose grounds are virtually contiguous.   On April 1, 1929 an agreement was reached between Atlanta, Morehouse, and Spelman for the affiliation of the three schools under an agreement by which Atlanta shall carry on the professional and graduate

2 *The Bulletin*, p. 26.

work of a university organization while Morehouse and Spelman shall take care of the college work. Spelman and Morehouse each retained its board of trustees and its president. Atlanta University, however, underwent a reorganization in its government by which its board of trustees is composed of three members of the board of trustees of Morehouse, three of the board of Spelman, and other members elected at large. As a result of the affiliation the educational work of the group has been strengthened by consolidations, by the enrichment and extension of courses, and by making graduate work available through the offerings of Atlanta University.[3] The following statement from the report of the General Education Board for 1930–31 indicates the extent of its endorsement of the affiliation.

It is recognized that if the Negro race is to develop its own leaders in the professions and in business, opportunity must be given for university study under favorable conditions. One favorable point for the development of Negro education is Atlanta, Georgia, which has several colleges for Negroes. The affiliation of three of them—Spelman College (for women), Morehouse College (for men), and Atlanta University—has provided a nucleus for the development of a university centre. As one result of this step Atlanta University has been enabled to discontinue undergraduate work in the arts and sciences, and to begin a program of graduate and professional instruction. The new plans are taking form as rapidly as is practicable under circumstances requiring that the trustees of Atlanta University raise substantial sums for buildings, equipment, and endowment. The problem of the University is of a twofold character: first, to provide needed buildings and to capitalize the present scope of its work, now largely financed through annual gifts, for which a sum of $3,000,000 is needed; second, to secure endowment funds for a reasonable expansion by the end of a six-year period, for which purpose the University estimates that capital of $3,400,000 will be required, including an amount for strengthening undergraduate work in Morehouse College. To accomplish these purposes the University has undertaken a campaign for funds. Toward $3,000,000 the General Education Board made a conditional pledge of $1,500,000, which, at five per cent, will capitalize its present annual grants. Upon successful completion of the first portion of the plan within a specified time, the Board has agreed to give a dollar for every dollar up to $1,700,000 collected by the University from other sources before July 1, 1936.

In addition the Board voted annual grants of $75,000 for each of the two years to assist Atlanta University in meeting the costs of current operation.

Library for Negro Institutions of Higher Education in Atlanta. For some time it has been recognized that one of the chief needs of the Negro institutions of higher education in Atlanta is for adequate library facilities. In the opinion of the Board this need could be most effectively met by the erection of a central

---

[3] *Spelman Messenger*, October 1929.

library building in proximity to the three affiliated and contiguous institutions—Atlanta University, Morehouse College, and Spelman College—with the provision that it shall also serve other Negro colleges in Atlanta that may enter into coöperative relations with the university centre. Such a building is now in course of construction. The library will be maintained and administered by Atlanta University, to which the General Education Board made an appropriation of $450,000 for the purchase of the site and the construction and equipment of the building.[4]

These outstanding examples of the possibilities of coördination and combination in the two largest cities of the South are, in all probability, symbolic of what will necessarily take place elsewhere in the near future. A combination of circumstances would seem to make this inevitable. The first is that a constantly increasing percentage of the students attending this group of schools each year enroll at the college level, thus greatly increasing the cost of instruction. At the same time the denominational boards which have supported these schools for so long are finding the burden harder to bear each year, with increasing costs without corresponding growth in income. A third factor in the situation is the inability of the Negro student to keep financial pace with increased charges which might be levied against him were the race in a more favored economic condition. Hence it has been impossible for the colleges to match the increased costs with greatly increased income from student fees.[5]

As a result of the simultaneous operation of these three factors, the schools are compelled to look more and more to the philanthropic foundations for aid in meeting both capital and current expenses. These foundations are thus placed in a position where they can affect action most decisively by offering or withholding aid where appealed to. The boards charged with the management of these huge funds are in honor bound to spend them to the best advantage, as they see it. At the present time they seem to favor the policy of aiding schools which show vitality and promise and offering to aid less promising schools provided they make obviously justifiable combinations. Table XVIII shows those cities where two or more Negro colleges are located, with the total enrollment of college students in each as reported in 1931–32. (See also Table XVII.)

[4] The General Education Board, *Annual Report*, 1930–31, pp. 16–18.
[5] Thompson, Charles H., "The Socio-Economic Status of Negro College Students," *Journal of Negro Education*, Vol. 2, pp. 26–37, January 1933.

TABLE XVIII

NUMBER OF COLLEGES AND STUDENTS IN CITIES CONTAINING
MORE THAN ONE NEGRO COLLEGE

City	Number of Colleges	Number of College Students
Little Rock, Ark.	3	290
Washington, D. C.	2	1981
Atlanta, Ga.	5	1169
New Orleans, La.	3	790
Baltimore, Md.	2	628
Holly Springs, Miss.	2	105
Greensboro, N. C.	2	436
Raleigh, N. C.	2	441
Columbia, S. C.	2	505
Orangeburg, S. C.	2	444
Nashville, Tenn.	3	1158
Marshall, Tex.	2	724
Austin, Tex.	2	372

Even though the institutions may not be located in the same city, there are many cases in which competing colleges attempt to serve an area which could be adequately served by one. The action at Atlanta and New Orleans and the arrangements for exchange of teachers between adjacent colleges, as now practiced in several places, indicate the beginning of a definite movement toward consolidation.

THE INCREASING IMPORTANCE OF PUBLICLY SUPPORTED COLLEGES

As indicated in Chapter XI of this study, the state-supported colleges play an increasingly important part in the field of the higher education of Negroes. Before 1920 the number of college students in the public colleges for Negroes was negligible. By 1932, however, in fifteen Southern states the enrollment of Negro college students was so distributed between public and private institutions that 49.7 per cent were in public colleges and 50.3 per cent in private colleges, indicating approximate equality in enrollments.[6]

The income of the public colleges has also increased rapidly during the same period. In 1926 thirty public colleges reported a total income of $3,029,398 as compared with seventy private colleges with a total income of $3,778,506. By 1931 thirty-two

[6] McCuistion, *op. cit.*, p. 18.

public colleges received a total of $4,688,261 as compared with $4,502,802 received by sixty private colleges.[7] This gives an average income for 1931 of $142,060 for the public colleges as opposed to $68,080 for the private colleges.

ACCREDITATION

In Chapter XIV of this study the successful efforts of the Negro colleges in the Southern area to be studied and rated were described. The Southern Association of Colleges and Secondary Schools, which accepted the responsibility in 1930, has applied to the Negro colleges the standards used for the white colleges. Colleges rated "A" meet these requirements in full. Those rated "B" do not meet in full one or more of them. However, the general quality of the work of colleges rated "B" is considered by the association such as to warrant admission of their graduates to any academic or professional work requiring an approved Bachelor's degree. In 1930 one college was rated "A" and six were rated "B." These numbers have been increased so that at the present time (December 1933) the list stands as shown in Table XIX. Enrollment figures are taken directly from Table XV and are for April 1932.

The Negro colleges fully accredited by other regional associations, with enrollment as of 1932, are given in Table XX.

According to Tables XV, XIX, and XX only 47 of the 109 colleges for Negroes are approved by any national or regional accrediting association. This means that much remains to be done in the way of increasing the financial resources of the Negro colleges for the improvement of faculties, plants, and equipment in order that they may possess the means of offering standard college work. An encouraging feature of the situation, however, is that while less than 47 per cent of the schools are approved, yet the students are so distributed among them that over two-thirds are enrolled in approved colleges. Seventeen of the four-year colleges with a combined enrollment of 8,161 college students, are fully accredited by national or regional bodies. In addition to these, twenty-three four-year colleges with a combined enrollment of 6,607, are given Class "B" rating by the Southern Association. Thus we have a total of 14,768 college students attending forty four-year approved colleges. There are also seven approved

7 McCuistion, *op. cit.*, p. 20.

TABLE XXI

NEGRO COLLEGES ACCREDITED BY THE SOUTHERN ASSOCIATION OF COLLEGES
AND SECONDARY SCHOOLS, 1933, WITH ENROLLMENT FOR 1932 *

Type of College	Number of Students
Standard Four-Year Colleges—Class "A"	
ALABAMA	
Talladega College	221
GEORGIA	
Atlanta University	69
Morehouse College	281
Spelman College	211
NORTH CAROLINA	
Johnson C. Smith University	245
TENNESSEE	
Fisk University	447
TEXAS	
Wiley College	313
VIRGINIA	
Hampton Institute	889
Virginia State College	568
Total Class "A"	3,244
Standard Four-Year Colleges—Class "B"	
FLORIDA	
Florida A. & M. College	472
GEORGIA	
Clark University	344
Morris Brown College	264
Paine College	154
KENTUCKY	
Kentucky State Industrial College	272
Louisville Municipal College	185
LOUISIANA	
Xavier University	192
Southern University	297
MISSISSIPPI	
Tougaloo College	96
NORTH CAROLINA	
Bennett College	157
Livingstone College	215
North Carolina College for Negroes	284
North Carolina A. & T. College	279
St. Augustine's College	179
Shaw University	262
SOUTH CAROLINA	
State A. & M. College	322
TENNESSEE	
Knoxville College	300
LeMoyne College	220
TEXAS	
Bishop College	388
Prairie View State N. & I. College	661
Tillotson College	155
VIRGINIA	
Virginia Union University	333
Total Class "B"	6,031
Standard Four-Year Teachers College—Class "B"	
ALABAMA	
Tuskegee Normal and Industrial Institute	576
TOTAL, FOUR-YEAR COLLEGES	9,851
Standard Two-Year Junior College—Class "A"	
TEXAS	
Mary Allen Seminary	125
Standard Two-Year Junior College—Class "B"	
ALABAMA	
State A. & M. College	82
FLORIDA	
Bethune-Cookman College	67
N. & I. Institute	77
GEORGIA	
Fort Valley N. & I. School	47
NORTH CAROLINA	
Barber-Scotia Junior College	73
TEXAS	
Houston Municipal Junior College	322
Total Class "B"	668
TOTAL, TWO-YEAR COLLEGES	793

* *The Quarterly Review of Higher Education Among Negroes*, Vol. 2, No. 1, p. 53, January 1934;
McCuistion, *op. cit.*, pp. 9, 10.

TABLE XX

Negro Colleges Accredited by Rating Bodies Other than the Southern Association of Colleges and Secondary Schools, 1932

Organization	Number of Students
The Middle States Association of Colleges and Secondary Schools	
Howard University, Washington, D. C.	1,573
Lincoln University, Lincoln University, Pa.	318
Morgan College, Baltimore, Md.	521
	2,412
The North Central Association of Colleges and Secondary Schools	
West Virginia State College, Institute, W. Va.	621
The American Association of Teachers Colleges	
Miner Teachers College, Washington, D. C.	408
Tennessee A. & I. College, Nashville, Tenn.	681
Lincoln University, Jefferson City, Mo.	196
Stowe Teachers College, St. Louis, Mo.	599
Total	1,884
Group Total	4,917

TABLE XXI—Summary of Tables XIX and XX

Type of College	Number of Colleges	Number of College Students Enrolled
Four-Year Colleges Fully Accredited by		
Southern Association of Colleges and Secondary Schools	9	3,244
Middle States Association of Colleges and Secondary Schools	3	2,412
North Central Association of Colleges and Secondary Schools	1	621
American Association of Teachers Colleges	4	1,884
	17	8,161
Two-Year Colleges Fully Accredited by		
Southern Association of Colleges and Secondary Schools	1	125
Total Enrollment in Fully Accredited Colleges	18	8,286
Colleges Rated as Class "B" by the Southern Association of Colleges and Secondary Schools		
Four-Year Colleges	22	6,031
Four-Year Teachers' College	1	576
Two-Year Colleges	6	668
Total Enrollment in Class "B" Colleges	29	7,275
Grand Total	47	15,561

junior colleges with a combined enrollment of 793. Taken together, then, these groups show a total of forty-seven approved colleges with a total enrollment of 15,561. This enrollment is approximately 68 per cent of the total enrollment of college students in the 109 colleges under consideration.

Considering the age of this group of schools and the circumstances under which they have developed, the showing made by them under the rigid test of rating by unsentimental regional and national accrediting bodies is altogether creditable. It means that today Negro students in the South have available nearly fifty colleges whose Bachelor's degrees merit recognition in the academic world. This is in sharp contrast to the conditions revealed by the Phelps-Stokes study in 1916 and indicates remarkable improvement over the conditions revealed by the survey conducted by the United States Bureau of Education in 1926 and 1927. This gratifying improvement is due, to some extent at least, to the progress made by the country in general along educational lines during the period in question. The main credit is due, however, to the earnest desire of those interested in and responsible for the development of these schools to bring them into line with accepted standards.

It is an open question, of course, whether all the institutions now included under the designation "Negro Colleges" should strive to meet the standards set up for approved rating. Some doubtless should change their objectives and their names and become junior colleges, academies, normal schools, or trade schools. For it must be remembered that even those colleges that have received formal approval have merely taken the first step toward winning a whole-hearted acceptance into the sisterhood of American institutions of higher learning. During the few years which the Negro college has existed students, faculty, and administrators have been largely engaged in a desperate struggle for mere survival. For a long time work of sub-collegiate grade not only consumed the funds and dominated the activities of these schools but also too often determined the intellectual tone of the whole institution. During the past forty years, even though the emphasis has been shifted upward when judged by enrollment figures, yet, because of the generally inferior quality of the secondary schools for colored people and the poor socio-economic condition of the Negroes as a group, these colleges have had to deal with relatively inferior raw material.   Meanwhile the Negro college teacher, who had usually been compelled to terminate his own education too soon, was struggling to give to this raw material in four years a training that would place him on cultural parity with graduates of the most favored colleges and universities of the North and, at the same time, was attempting to continue his own progress toward the higher degrees.   Only recently have a few doctors of philosophy begun to join the faculties of the schools of this group, although the number is rapidly increasing.   It will take large expenditures for equipment, much time for the development of faculties, and a careful sifting of incoming students to enable even the best of the Negro colleges to turn out a regular product on a par with what the best American colleges as a whole can produce.[8]

Those Negro colleges, therefore, that plan to maintain that status must never cease to strive for approval by the standards set up for higher education in America at any given period.   For it is by the American standard that the Negro is measured in life. In some quarters the standardization movement in the American scheme of education is condemned as having been overdone, and there is doubtless much validity in the criticisms offered.   Until the existing standards are abandoned or modified, however, the Negro college must insist upon being measured by those set up for the colleges of the nation and must constantly strive to meet them.   So long as racial segregation exists in the United States the Negro college will be necessary as a means of introducing Negro youth to the larger life.   In view of this fact the American people will hardly be content to permit this group of schools to be operated at a lower level of efficiency than that required by the standards set for American colleges as a whole.

CONTROL

It has been pointed out that the private colleges for Negroes depend largely upon philanthropy for their support.   The funds from this source naturally come from America's accumulated wealth, which is almost entirely in the hands of the white race. Even the colleges owned and controlled by the Negro churches are finding it increasingly necessary to seek aid from wealthy in-

---

[8] Thompson, Charles H., "The Problem of Negro Higher Education," *Journal of Negro Education*, Vol. 2, No. 3, July 1933, pp. 257–71.

dividuals and foundations. The public institutions are supported primarily from the public treasuries to which all citizens contribute either directly or indirectly. Appropriations from this source, however, for educational as well as other purposes, are determined by the racial group in charge of the machinery of government. Since control usually follows support, it is evident that the ultimate control of the Negro colleges will be mainly in the hands of the white people of this country for many years to come. Therefore, the future of these schools depends largely upon the wisdom and benevolence of those who hold the purse strings. Even if the Negro race should miraculously find the resources to finance their schools, it is very unlikely that they could muster the managerial ability to promote successfully such a large and important enterprise without long and careful tutelage at the hands of those who have had centuries of experience in learning how such things should be done.

This does not mean, of course, that the Negro is to take no part in the control of his colleges. It means, on the contrary, that he should take a larger part than he has formerly. It has been the policy of the majority of the bodies controlling the private Negro colleges to change the faculties of their several schools from white to Negro as rapidly as the supply of competent Negro teachers would permit. In nearly every case, as soon as the complexion of the faculty has been completely changed, a Negro has been appointed to the presidency and has thus been given the opportunity to develop his powers of leadership and gain practice in the management of large affairs. In addition to serving as administrative officers and faculties, the Negro race is frequently represented on the trustee boards of private, independent colleges and even on the denominational boards controlling a number of schools. Except on the boards of the Negro denominations, the membership of these bodies is predominantly composed of white persons. However, the presence of Negroes on the denominational boards and on the boards of trustees of individual schools is recognition of the need and the value of their counsel and, at the same time, constitutes an important step in the training of members of the race in the technique of management at the highest level.

In the colleges under public control both presidents and faculties have, from the beginning, been chosen from the Negro race.

The board of control of the latter group, however, in nearly every case, is composed entirely of white men. In such cases, while the Negro as faculty member and president of these schools has entire control at the lower level, he is deprived of any participation in actual control at the higher level since Negroes as a rule are not represented on the board that does the actual voting. There is reason to believe that a changing attitude in the South on the question of the participation of Negroes in the determination of policies concerning those things that are of intimate interest to them will correct this situation to the advantage of all parties concerned.

CHAPTER XVI

SUMMARY AND RECOMMENDATIONS

SUMMARY

As stated at the beginning of this study, its purpose has been to determine the circumstances surrounding the establishment and development of the Negro college and the nature of the agencies responsible for the creation and promotion of this group of schools; and to interpret the events, the social forces, and the attitudes of individuals and organizations that have affected these schools and have, therefore, determined the character of the opportunities for higher education available for Negro youth today in segregated institutions of higher learning. In summary, the findings of this study are as follows.

Chronological Periods

The history of the Negro college falls into four fairly well defined periods.

1. The first period includes the years from 1860 to 1885. During this time the Union army, Northern benevolent societies and denominational bodies, the Negro church, and the Freedmen's Bureau were busily engaged in applying emergency measures in an attempt to bring order out of confusion and to extend to the Negroes not only material aid but the beginnings of educational opportunity. From these initial efforts there emerged a class of schools which were designated as colleges and universities, but which naturally were compelled for some years to spend their major energies in work at the elementary level.

2. The second period begins with 1886 and extends to 1916. After about 1885, although very inadequately equipped and supported, a number of these schools were fairly well organized, and enrolled a few students in work above what was considered the secondary level at that time. This work followed in general the pattern of the classical academies and colleges in which the white teachers from the North had been trained, who, in the main,

constituted the faculties of the Negro schools. The schools supported by Negro church denominations, of course, maintained Negro faculties from the first.

3. The third period in the evolution of the Negro colleges dates from 1917, when an epoch-making survey of Negro education, made by the Phelps-Stokes Fund, was completed and published by the United States Bureau of Education, and extends to 1928. This survey caused an awakening which focused attention in a comprehensive way upon the condition of the Negro college and produced a critical attitude which led to rapid improvement through more adequate support from the responsible bodies. During this period several of the great philanthropic foundations, such as the General Education Board and the Julius Rosenwald Fund, began to give serious attention to plans for the systematic and rational improvement of Negro education all along the line. The state governments of the South were also impressed by the findings of the survey and gave more serious attention to the development of the land-grant colleges.

4. The fourth period in the development of this group of schools dates from 1928 because in that year the publication of the Survey of Negro Colleges by the United States Bureau of Education definitely marked the beginning of a new era. This survey not only supplied a valuable body of factual material relative to the Negro college but may justly be looked upon as a significant step toward the rating of the Negro colleges assumed by the recognized accrediting agency which covers the area of the Southern states, where most of the institutions making up this group are located. At the present time, therefore, the Negro colleges are making serious effort to satisfy the requirements of standardization, with all that such activity implies.

Responsible Agencies

The study reveals four groups of agencies which have been primarily responsible for the development of the Negro colleges.

1. The first of these was the Federal Government which, through the Union army, first gave emergency relief to the thousands of Negro refugees who fled to its camps when the South was invaded during the Civil War. These emergency measures continued until the establishment of the Freedmen's Bureau, which not only aided materially in starting the freedmen toward

economic stability but was largely instrumental in the promotion of educational institutions, some of which have since grown into schools of collegiate grade.

2. The second agency is the Christian Church which, through the operation of the several denominational boards, has been responsible for the establishment and maintenance of the majority of the most influential colleges for Negroes.

3. The third agency consists of the governments of the seventeen states which have established and supported the land-grant colleges for Negroes. During the past twenty years these schools have been taking a position of constantly increasing importance in the higher education of the Negro. This is due to the fact that the resources of the religious denominations available for the support of the Negro colleges have been barely ample to keep pace with the increased budgetary requirements of the schools under their direction, while the state governments, with the taxing power at their command, have found it possible, in a comparatively short time, so to improve the land-grant colleges in equipment and personnel as to bring them into serious rivalry with the best of the colleges supported by the denominational boards.

4. The fourth agency is organized philanthropy as represented by the great educational foundations, such as the John F. Slater Fund, the Julius Rosenwald Fund, and the General Education Board, which, since 1882, have become a constantly increasing factor in the support of the Negro college.

Enrollment

In 1932 the number of institutions for Negroes offering work of college grade was 109, distributed among nineteen states and the District of Columbia and enrolling approximately 23,000 college students. Eleven of these schools enrolled 500 or more such students; twenty-five from 250 to 499; twenty-nine from 100 to 249; and forty-four less than 100. The preponderance of very small colleges is thus made evident.

In the decade from 1922 to 1932 the percentage of college students in the entire enrollment of the Negro colleges rose from 15 to 85, indicating a rapid decrease in the proportion of students of elementary and secondary grades attending these schools. This rapid shift in emphasis toward the collegiate level indicates also a rapid increase in the cost of operation.

Accreditation

Forty-seven of the 109 colleges for Negroes are approved by national or regional accrediting associations. It was found that 15,561 college students, or about 68 per cent of the 23,000 enrolled in these schools, are receiving instruction in these accredited colleges, while only 32 per cent attend colleges not yet accredited.

Consolidation

Because of the rapidly rising cost of college education, it is becoming increasingly evident that every reasonable economy must be practiced in the operation of these institutions of higher learning. The colleges for Negroes are not too numerous to accommodate the number of students who should be in college if we estimated the enrollment at the same ratio to the total Negro population that the white college enrollment bears to the total white population in the Southern area. They are too numerous, however, on the basis of the actual enrollment at the present time or the probable enrollment in the immediate future. To meet this situation, a definite movement toward consolidation has been set up in the interest of increased efficiency. This movement is illustrated by the Atlanta-Morehouse-Spelman affiliation at Atlanta, Georgia, and the merger of Straight and New Orleans Universities to form Dillard University at New Orleans.

RECOMMENDATIONS

This study has been made as an historical investigation, for the purpose of recording what has happened in the past rather than to project the future. The findings, however, exhibit conditions which seem to justify further comment, followed by forecast and recommendation. For, in spite of the gratifying progress that has been made, the operation of the colleges of this group, taken as a whole, is faulty in several important respects which seriously affect their efficiency. Some of the most obvious of these defects may be corrected within a reasonable time if they are squarely faced and if the necessary remedies are fearlessly applied. Some of the most obvious of these follow.

1. In certain areas, there is intensive and undesirable competition among colleges for students where the supply of opportunity

for college education exceeds the demand. Such a practice is not only economically unsound but frequently leads to a lowering of admission standards in order to maintain enrollment figures. The reason for such situations is that the provision of collegiate facilities is the result of chance rather than of a study of the actual requirements of the situation.

2. Another serious defect is the lack of definite and clear-cut objectives on the part of the several colleges. There is a fairly unanimous agreement among these institutions that they must meet the requirements of some accrediting body. The answer to the question "To what end?" is not always so certain. It is impossible, of course, for all these schools to offer all desirable forms of educational opportunity. This is a difficult contract even for the wealthiest of our great metropolitan universities. It is obviously out of the question, therefore, for the struggling Negro colleges to attempt to do so. A few may become university centers, but the majority must confine themselves for many years to limited and well-defined objectives.

3. The most glaring fault of a number of these schools is the effort to operate a four-year college on an entirely inadequate income. As a result of such attempts, equipment is stinted, faculties are either poor or poorly paid, and administrative officers are so busily engaged in trying to secure support that the educational interests of the institutions are neglected. As a result of such unfavorable conditions the best students frequently go elsewhere so that the work suffers still further in quality. In a number of such cases a good four-year college is being successfully operated either in the same city or only a few miles away.

4. A fourth difficulty faced by the Negro college is the economic condition of the parents, who often find it difficult, if not actually impossible, to offer to sons and daughters of unquestioned ability the opportunity to procure a college education. As a result, many able students never reach college, while many who do manage to enroll are so handicapped by the necessity of earning a living while attending school that the quality of their work suffers severely. This condition is all too prevalent among Negro youth. In sharp contrast to the white colleges, the Negro colleges, themselves poverty-stricken, have little in the way of scholarships to offer the worthy student who is in need of financial assistance.

In order to correct these basic deficiencies from which many minor difficulties spring, it is recommended that a carefully organized continuing survey of the field of higher education among Negroes as a whole be instituted for the purpose of planning for the development of this group of schools for a period of from twenty-five to fifty years. Such a survey would gather and present such data as would aid in determining the following facts:

1. The number of students to be served annually.
2. The extent and character of the several kinds of service needed.
3. The number and kinds of schools needed to perform the several classes of service.
4. The cost of operating these schools for a high quality of service and at a high rate of efficiency.
5. The probable ability of students to pay the cost of the service rendered.
6. The best locations for the several kinds of schools required.
7. The necessary adaptations required to fit the present group of Negro colleges to the needs indicated by the survey.

In order to promote such a survey and to apply its findings to the situation at hand, it is suggested that a permanent commission on higher education among Negroes be organized, its membership consisting of representatives of the state and Federal Governments and of all the boards, foundations, denominations, educational associations, and other bodies interested in the work included in this field. On the basis of the findings of the survey, it would be the duty of this commission to bring about coöperative action among the colleges in making such adjustments as would best serve the purposes of a coördinated program. Following agreements to coöperate in such a program, plans could be made and put into operation for building up adequate endowments in order to insure a stable income for each institution in carrying forward the program assigned to it.

In the opinion of the writer, the time is ripe for the inauguration of some coöperative movement, as here described, looking toward a more effective plan of organizing and administering the group of Negro colleges in a systematic way. It is believed that those primarily responsible for the operation of these schools are ready for such a movement.

BIBLIOGRAPHY

GENERAL HISTORICAL WORKS

CHADWICK, FRENCH E. *Causes of the Civil War.* The American Nation Series, Vol. 19. New York, Harper & Brothers, 1906.

CHANNING, EDWARD. *A History of the United States,* Vol. VI. New York, The Macmillan Company, 1927.

DUNNING, WILLIAM A. *Reconstruction, Political and Economic.* The American Nation Series, Vol. 22. New York, Harper & Brothers, 1906.

HART, ALBERT BUSHNELL. *Slavery and Abolition.* The American Nation Series, Vol. 16. New York, Harper & Brothers, 1906.

HASMER, JAMES K. *The Appeal to Arms.* The American Nation Series, Vol. 20. New York, Harper & Brothers, 1906.

KNIGHT, EDGAR W. *Education in the United States.* Boston, Ginn and Company, 1929.

——. *Public Education in the South.* Boston, Ginn and Company, 1922.

——. *The Influence of Reconstruction on Education in the South.* New York, Teachers College, Columbia University, 1913.

MCMASTER, JOHN B. *A History of the People of the United States from the Revolution to the Civil War.* New York, D. Appleton and Company, 1910.

MCPHERSON, EDWARD. *Political History of the United States during the Period of Reconstruction.* Washington, 1880.

——. *Political History of the United States during the Great Rebellion.* Washington, 1864.

MOORE, FRANK. *Rebellion Record.* 12 vols. New York, 1864.

NICOLAY, JOHN G. AND HAY, JOHN. *Abraham Lincoln: A History.* 10 vols. New York, The Century Co., 1917.

RHODES, JAMES FORD. *History of the United States, 1850–1877.* New York, The Macmillan Company, 1904.

SMITH, THEODORE C. *Parties and Slavery.* The American Nation Series, Vol. 18. New York, Harper & Brothers, 1906.

War of Rebellion Official Records of Union and Confederate Armies. Washington, Government Printing Office, 1880–1899.

CHURCH HISTORIES AND RELATED WORKS

ANDERSON, MATTHEW. *Presbyterianism in Its Relation to the Negro.* Philadelphia, McGill, White & Company, 1897.

BRAGG, GEORGE F. *History of the Afro-American Group of the Episcopal Church.* Baltimore, Church Advocate Press, 1922.

DuBois, W. E. B. *The Negro Church.* Atlanta, The Atlanta University Press, 1903.

GILLARD, JOHN T. *The Catholic Church and the American Negro.* Baltimore, St. Joseph's Society Press, 1929.

HOOD, J. W. *One Hundred Years of the African Methodist Episcopal Zion Church.* New York, The A. M. E. Zion Book Concern, 1895.

JORDAN, LEWIS G. *Negro Baptist History, 1875–1930.* Nashville, The Secondary School Publishing Board, National Baptist Convention, 1931.

MAYS, B. E. AND NICHOLSON, J. W. *The Negro's Church.* New York, Institute of Social and Religious Research, 1933.

MOORE, J. J. *History of the African Methodist Episcopal Zion Church.* York, Pa., 1884.

PAYNE, DANIEL A. *History of the African Methodist Episcopal Church.* Nashville, A. M. E. Sunday-School Union, 1891.

———. *Recollections of Seventy Years.* Nashville, A. M. E. Sunday-School Union, 1888.

SIMPSON, MATTHEW. *A Hundred Years of Methodism.* New York, Methodist Book Concern, 1885.

TANNER, BENJAMIN T. *An Apology for African Methodism.* Baltimore, 1867.

WOODSON, CARTER G. *The History of the Negro Church.* Washington, The Associated Publishers, 1921.

REPORTS OF RELIGIOUS AND PHILANTHROPIC BOARDS

AMERICAN BAPTIST HOME MISSION SOCIETY. *Annual Report,* 1843–1932, New York.

AMERICAN MISSIONARY ASSOCIATION. *Annual Report,* 1847–1932, New York.

Duke Endowment Yearbook, No. 1. Charlotte, N. C., The Duke Endowment, 1928.

FREEDMEN'S AID SOCIETY OF THE METHODIST EPISCOPAL CHURCH. *Annual Reports.* Chicago.
  1867–1888: Freedmen's Aid Society of the Methodist Episcopal Church.
  1888–1908: Freedmen's Aid and Southern Education Society of the M. E. Church.
  1908–1920: Freedmen's Aid Society of the M. E. Church.
  1920–1924: Board of Education for Negroes of the M. E. Church.
  1924–   : Board of Education of the M. E. Church.

General Education Board, An Account of its Activities 1902–1914. New York, General Education Board, 1914.

GENERAL EDUCATION BOARD. *Annual Report,* 1915–1932. New York, General Education Board.

JOHN F. SLATER FUND. *Proceedings and Report,* 1883–1932. Washington, John F. Slater Fund.

JULIUS ROSENWALD FUND. *Annual Report*, 1929–1932. Chicago, Julius Rosenwald Fund.

————. *A Review to June 30, 1928.* Chicago, 1928.

PHELPS-STOKES FUND. *The Twenty-Year Report of the Phelps-Stokes Fund, 1911–1931.* New York, Phelps-Stokes Fund, 1932.

"Race Problems of the South." *Proceedings of the First Annual Conference at Montgomery*, 1900. Richmond, 1900.

PUBLIC DOCUMENTS

ALVORD, J. W. *Letters from the South Relating to the Condition of the Freedmen.* (Addressed to General O. O. Howard.) Washington, Government Printing Office, 1870.

————. *Semi-Annual Report on Schools for Freedmen*, Jan. 1866 to July 1870. Washington, Government Printing Office.

CALIVER, AMBROSE. *A Background Study of Negro College Students.* Washington, Government Printing Office, 1933.

Court of Inquiry in Case of Brigadier-General Oliver O. Howard, Proceedings, Findings, and Opinions of. Washington, Government Printing Office, 1874.

CURRY, J. L. M. "The Slater Fund and the Education of the Negro." In *Report of the United States Commissioner of Education for 1895.* Vol. 5, Pt. 2, pp. 1367–1424. Washington, Government Printing Office, 1896.

HOUSE MISCELLANEOUS DOCUMENTS. Forty-second Congress, 2nd Session, *The Ku Klux Investigation.* Washington, Government Printing Office.

HOWARD, OLIVER O. *Report of the Commissioner of the Bureau of Refugees, Freedmen, and Abandoned Lands, 1866–1871.* Washington, Government Printing Office.

JONES, THOMAS JESSE. *Negro Education, A Study of the Private and Higher Schools for Colored People in the United States.* U. S. Bureau of Education Bulletin, 1916, Nos. 38 and 39. Washington, Government Printing Office, 1917.

MAYO, A. D. "The Work of Certain Northern Churches in the Education of the Freedmen, 1861–1900." In *Report of the United States Commissioner of Education for 1902.* Washington, Government Printing Office, 1903.

MILLER, KELLY. "The Education of the Negro." In *Report of the United States Commissioner of Education for 1901*, Vol. 1. Washington, Government Printing Office.

NORTH CAROLINA. *Study of Institutions of Higher Learning for Negroes.* Raleigh, Department of Public Instruction, 1931.

Senate Documents, 39th Congress, First Session, No. 27. Washington, Government Printing Office.

Statutes at Large of the United States, Vols. 12, 13, 14, 15, 18, 26, 44, 45, 46. Washington, Government Printing Office.

TEXAS. *Negro Education in Texas.* Bulletin S. Austin, State Department of Education. 1931.

U. S. BUREAU OF EDUCATION. *Federal Legislation and Administration Pertaining to Land-Grant Colleges.* Bulletin, 1924, No. 30. Washington, Government Printing Office. 1924.

————. *Survey of Negro Colleges and Universities.* Bulletin, 1928, No. 7. Washington, Government Printing Office, 1929.

U. S. OFFICE OF EDUCATION. *Survey of Land-Grant Colleges and Universities.* Part X, Negro Land-Grant Colleges. Bulletin 1930, No. 9. Washington, Government Printing Office.

Congressional Globe, 37th, 38th, 39th, 40th, 41st, 42nd Congresses. Washington, John C. Rives.

House Executive Documents. Washington, Government Printing Office.
  38th Congress, 1st Session, Vol. 5, No. 1.
  39th Congress, 1st Session, Vol. 1, No. 2.
  39th Congress, 1st Session, No. 11.
  39th Congress, 1st Session, No. 70.
  39th Congress, 1st Session, No. 118.
  39th Congress, 2nd Session, Vol. 3, No. 1.
  40th Congress, 2nd Session, No. 1.
  41st Congress, 2nd Session, No. 121.
  41st Congress, 2nd Session, No. 142.
  41st Congress, 3rd Session, No. 2.

MISCELLANEOUS BOOKS AND PAMPHLETS

ADAMS, MYRON W. *A History of Atlanta University.* Atlanta, Atlanta University Press, 1930.

BEARD, AUGUSTUS F. *A Crusade of Brotherhood.* New York, The Pilgrim Press, 1909.

BRAWLEY, BENJAMIN. *A Short History of the American Negro.* New York, The Macmillan Company, 1931.

————. *A Social History of the Negro.* New York, The Macmillan Company, 1921.

————. *History of Morehouse College.* Atlanta, Morehouse College, 1917.

BRUCE, R. C. "Tuskegee Institute." In *From Servitude to Service,* Chap. III. Boston, American Unitarian Association, 1905.

BUMSTEAD, HORACE. *Secondary and Higher Education in the South for Whites and Negroes.* Publication of the National Association for the Advancement of Colored People, No. 2, 1910.

DAVIS, JACKSON. "Recent Developments in Negro Schools and Colleges." Commencement Address, Atlanta University, June 1, 1927.

DUBOIS, W. E. B. "Atlanta University." In *From Servitude to Service,* Chap. V. Boston, American Unitarian Association, 1905.

———— (Ed.). Atlanta University Publications, Nos. 1 to 10. Atlanta, Atlanta University Press, 1896–1908.

———. *The College Bred Negro.* Atlanta, Atlanta University Publication, 1906.

———. "The Talented Tenth." In *The Negro Problem.* New York, James Pott & Co., 1903.

DYSON, WALTER. *The Founding of Howard University.* Washington, Howard University Press, 1921.

———. *A History of the Federal Appropriation for Howard University, 1867–1926.* Washington, Howard University Press, 1927.

EATON, JOHN, JR. *Colored Schools in Mississippi, Arkansas, and Tennessee, April, 1865.* Memphis, 1865.

———. *Grant, Lincoln and the Freedmen.* New York, Longmans, Green and Co., 1907.

———. *Report of General Superintendent of Freedmen, Tennessee and Arkansas, 1864.* Memphis, 1864.

EMBREE, EDWIN R. *Brown America: The Story of a New Race.* New York, The Viking Press, 1931.

FRISSELL, H. B. "Hampton Institute." In *From Servitude to Service*, Chap. IV. Boston, American Unitarian Association, 1905.

FROST, W. G. "Berea College." In *From Servitude to Service*, Chap. II. Boston, American Unitarian Association, 1905.

HENNINGS, LLOYD. *The American Missionary Association, a Christian Anti-Slavery Society.* Oberlin, Ohio, Oberlin College, 1933.

JOHNSON, CHARLES S. *The Negro in American Civilization.* New York, Henry Holt & Company, Inc., 1930.

McCUISTION, FRED. *Higher Education of Negroes.* Nashville, Southern Association of Colleges and Secondary Schools, 1933.

———. *The South's Negro Teaching Force.* Nashville, Julius Rosenwald Fund, 1931.

McKENZIE, FAYETTE A. *Ideals of Fisk.* Nashville, 1915.

MERRILL, J. G. "Fisk University." In *From Servitude to Service*, Chap. VI. Boston, American Unitarian Association, 1905.

MILLER, KELLY. "Howard University." In *From Servitude to Service*, Chap. I. Boston, American Unitarian Association, 1905.

PEIRCE, PAUL S. *The Freedmen's Bureau.* Bulletin of the State University of Iowa, New Series, No. 74. Iowa City, 1904.

REUTER, E. B. *The American Race Problem.* New York, Thomas Y. Crowell Company, 1927.

STOWELL, JAY S. *Methodist Adventures in Negro Education.* New York, The Methodist Book Concern, 1922.

THIRKIELD, WILBUR PATTERSON. *The Training of Physicians and Ministers for the Negro Race.* Washington, Howard University Press, 1909.

THOMAS, WILLIAM HANNIBAL. *The American Negro.* New York, The Macmillan Company, 1901.

WESLEY, CHARLES H. *Negro Labor in the United States.* New York, Vanguard Press, 1927.

WHITE, CHARLES L. *A Century of Faith.* Philadelphia, The Judson Press, 1932.

WILKINSON, R. S. *The Negro Colleges of South Carolina.* Orangeburg, State Agricultural and Mechanical College, 1928.

WILLIAMS, G. W. *History of the Negro Race in America.* New York, 1883.

WOODSON, CARTER G. *The Education of the Negro Prior to 1861.* New York, G. P. Putnam's Sons, 1915.

————. *The Mis-Education of the Negro.* Washington, The Associated Publishers, 1932.

————. *The Negro in Our History.* Washington, The Associated Publishers, 1932.

WOODY, FRANCIS B. AND SIMPKINS, ROBERT H. *South Carolina During Reconstruction.* Chapel Hill, The University of North Carolina Press, 1932.

THESES AND DISSERTATIONS

BAILY, FLAVIUS J. *The Policies of the American Missionary Association in Relation to Negro Education.* Unpublished Master's thesis, Howard University, Washington, 1933.

BORDERS, T. K. *The Status of Teachers in the Approved Four-Year Negro High Schools of Tennessee, 1931–32.* Unpublished Master's thesis, University of Michigan, Ann Arbor, 1932.

BUTLER, JOHN H. *An Historical Account of the John F. Slater Fund and the Anna T. Jeanes Foundation.* Unpublished Doctor's dissertation, University of Southern California, Los Angeles, 1932.

CALIVER, AMBROSE. *A Personnel Study of Negro College Students.* Doctor's dissertation, Teachers College, Columbia University, New York, 1931.

CLEMENT, RUFUS. *The Educational Work of the African Methodist Episcopal Zion Church.* Unpublished Master's thesis, Northwestern University, Evanston, 1922.

DABNEY, LUCY L. G. *The Present Status of the Problem of Racial Differences Between American Negroes and American Whites.* Unpublished Master's thesis. Howard University, Washington, 1931.

DANIEL, W. A. *Education of Negro Ministers.* Doctor's dissertation at University of Chicago. New York, Doran & Co., 1925.

DAVIS, T. EDWARD. *A Study of Fisk Freshmen, 1928–1930.* Unpublished Master's thesis, Fisk University, Nashville, 1932.

GALLOWAY, GLADYS G. *The Education of the Negro during Reconstruction.* Unpublished Master's thesis, Howard University, Washington, 1930.

GALLOWAY, OSCAR F. *Higher Education for Negroes in Kentucky.* Unpublished Doctor's dissertation, University of Kentucky, Lexington, 1932.

HOLT, FAYE E. *Efforts of the South to Free Itself from Slavery.* Unpublished Master's thesis, State University of Iowa, Iowa City, 1932.

HORNE, FRANK S. *The Present Status of Negro Education in Certain of the Southern States, Particularly Georgia.* Unpublished Master's thesis, University of Southern California, Los Angeles, 1932.

HUGGINS, WILLIS N. *The Contribution of the Catholic Church to the Progress of the Negro in the United States.* Unpublished Doctor's dissertation, Fordham University, New York, 1932.

JENKINS, MARTIN D. *Personnel Work in Twenty-two Negro Institutions of Higher Learning.* Unpublished Master's thesis, Northwestern University, Evanston, 1933.

JOHNSON, GLADYS. *A Study of the Music Schools and Departments of the A and B Class Colleges for the Negro.* Master's thesis, Northwestern University, Evanston, 1928.

LEAVELL, ULLIN W. *Philanthropy in Negro Education.* Doctor's dissertation, The George Peabody College for Teachers, Nashville, 1930.

NICHOLSON, JOSEPH W. *Occupational Study of the Christian Ministry Among Negroes.* Doctor's dissertation, Northwestern University, Evanston, 1932.

OAK, VISHU. *Commercial Education in Negro Colleges.* Unpublished Master's thesis, State University of Iowa, Iowa City, 1932.

SUMNER, FRANCEES. *The Mental Health of White and Negro College Students.* Unpublished Master's thesis, Howard University, Washington, 1932.

TALBERT, CHARLES A. *The Methodist Episcopal Church and the Negro during the Reconstruction Period* (1865–1885). Unpublished Master's thesis, Northwestern University, Evanston, 1932.

TURNER, WILLIE L. *Federal Aid to Negro Education.* Unpublished Master's thesis, Howard University, Washington, 1930.

WILLIAMS, JUANITA L. *Legislation in Relation to Negro Land-Grant Colleges.* Unpublished Master's thesis, Howard University, Washington, 1933.

MAGAZINE ARTICLES

ALDERMAN, E. A. "Higher Education in the South." *Educational Review,* 11: 29, 1896.

ATKINSON, R. W. "Interracial Conference of Florida Colleges and Universities." *Southern Workman,* 60: 229–31, May 1931.

"Atlanta University Library." *School and Society,* 34: 87–8, July 18, 1931.

BINNION, R. B. "Solving the Negro Problem Through Education." *Current History,* 30: 231–36, May 1929.

BOND, HORACE MANN. "Human Nature and Its Study in Negro Colleges." *Opportunity,* 6: 38–39, February 1928.

CALIVER, AMBROSE. "Negro College Students and the Need of Personnel Work." *Journal of Negro Education,* 2: 359–78, July 1933.

———. "Some Tendencies in Higher Education and Their Application to the Negro College." *Opportunity,* 6: 6–9, January 1928.

"Careers of Negro College Graduates." *Outlook,* 65: 710, July 1900.

Colson, Edna M. "The Negro Teachers' College and Normal School." *Journal of Negro Education*, 2: 284–98, July 1933.

DAVIS, EDWARD P. "The Negro Liberal Arts College." *Journal of Negro Education*, 2: 299–311, July 1933.

DAVIS, JACKSON. "New Head of Jeanes and Slater Funds." *Southern Workman*, 60: 404–06, October 1931.

————. "The Outlook for the Professional and Higher Education of Negroes." *Journal of Negro Education*, 2: 403–10, July 1933.

DAVIS, JOHN W. "The Negro Land-Grant College." *Journal of Negro Education*, 2: 312–28, July 1933.

DILLARD, JAMES H. "The Negro Goes to College." *World's Work*, 55: 337–40, January 1928.

DuBois, W. E. B. "Education and Work." *Journal of Negro Education*, 1: 60–74, April 1932.

————. "Negroes in College." *The Nation*, 122: 228–30, March 1926.

————. "The Negro College." *Crisis*, 40: 175, August 1933.

"Enrollment in Negro Universities and Colleges." *School and Society*, 28: 401–02, September 29, 1928.

FAVROT, LEO M. "Schools for Negro Children: Past Practices and Present Hopes." *Nation's Schools*, 10: 59–65, October 1932.

FRAZIER, E. FRANKLIN. "Graduate Education in Negro Colleges and Universities." *Journal of Negro Education*, 2: 329–41, July 1933.

"Higher Education for the Negro." *The Nation*, 74: 381, May 15, 1902.

HILL, LESLIE PINCKNEY. "The State Teachers College at Cheyney and Its Relation to Segregation in the North." *Journal of Negro Education*, 1: 408–13, October 1932.

HOLMES, D. O. W. "The Present Status of College Education Among Negroes." *Bulletin* (official organ of the National Association of Teachers in Colored Schools), 11: 5, January 1931.

————. "Fifty Years of Howard University." *Journal of Negro History*, 3: 3, 128–38 and 368–80, July and October 1918.

————. "The Negro College Faces the Depression." *Journal of Negro Education*, 2: 16–25, January 1933.

HURT, HUBER W. "The Land-Grant Colleges." *Southern Workman*, 53: 147, April 1924.

ILES, R. E. "Standardizing the Negro College." *Peabody Journal of Education*, 6: 96–101, September 1928.

JOHNSTON, J. HUGO. "Graduates of Northern High Schools as Students at a Southern Negro College." *Journal of Negro Education*, 2: 484–86, October 1933.

JONES, LANCE G. E. "An Englishman Sees Hampton." *Southern Workman*, 58: 370–73, August 1929.

KLINEBURG, OTTO. "The Question of Negro Intelligence." *Opportunity*, 9: 366–67, December 1931.

KNOX, ELLIS O. "The Negro as a Subject of University Research." *Journal of Negro Education*, 2: 165–74, April 1933.

LANE, DAVID A., JR. "The Junior College Movement Among Negroes." *Journal of Negro Education*, 2: 272–83, July 1933.

LEAVELL, ULLIN W. "Trends of Philanthropy in Negro Education: A Survey." *Journal of Negro Education*, 2: 38–52, January 1933.

McCRORY, HENRY L. "A Brief History of Johnson C. Smith University." *The Quarterly Review of Higher Education Among Negroes*, 1: 2, April 1933.

McKINNEY, T. E. "A Summary of Findings and Policies Bearing on Problems of Administration in Institutions of Higher Learning." *The Quarterly Review of Higher Education Among Negroes*, 1: 1, January 1933.

MARONEY, T. B. "Catholic Educational Effort for the Negroes." *Educational Review*, 18: 511–23.

MAYS, B. E. "The Education of Negro Ministers." *Journal of Negro Education*, 2: 342–51, July 1933.

McCUISTON, FRED. "The Present Status of Higher Education of Negroes." *Journal of Negro Education*, 2: 379–96, July 1933.

McNEELY, J. H. "Higher Education of Negroes Is Making Marked Progress." *School Life*, 14: 37, October 1928.

"Meharry Medical College." *Opportunity*, April 1924.

MILLER, KELLY. "Function of the Negro College." *The Dial*, 32: 267–70, April 16, 1902.

———. "Practical Value of the Higher Education of the Negro." *Educational Review*, 36: 234–40, December 1915.

———. "The Higher Education of the Negro Is at the Crossroads." *Educational Review*, 72: 272–78, December 1926.

———. "The Past, Present and Future of the Negro College." *Journal of Negro Education*, 2: 411–22, July 1933.

MOTON, R. R. "Negro Higher and Professional Education in 1943." *Journal of Negro Education*, 2: 397–402, July 1933.

"Municipal College for Negroes." *School and Society*, 32: 692, November 22, 1930.

"New Buildings at Atlanta University." *School and Society*, 34: 693, November 21, 1931.

NEWBOLD, N. C. "Unfinished Tasks and New Opportunities in Education in North Carolina." *North Carolina Teachers' Record* (official publication of the North Carolina Negro Teachers' Association), 2: 66, 67–75, 76, November 4, 1931.

———. "Has North Carolina Made Any Progress in Negro Education?" *North Carolina Teachers' Record*, 2: 3–4, January 1931.

"Our Negro Colleges." *Opportunity*, 1: 12–18, April 1923.

POSEY, THOMAS E. "The Socio-Economic Background of Freshmen at West Virginia State College." *Journal of Negro Education*, 2: 466–76, October 1933.

RIVERS, W. NAPOLEON, JR. "A Study of the Modern Foreign Languages in Thirty Negro Colleges." *Journal of Negro Education*, 2: 487–93, October 1933.

SCARBOROUGH, WILLIAM SANDERS. "The Negro and Higher Learning." *Forum*, 26: 349–55, May 1902.

SCOTT, EMMETT J. "Howard, The National University of the Negro Race." *School Life*, 9: 243–44, June 1924.

SHANNON, IRWIN V. "The Teaching of Negro Life and History in Relation to Some Views of Educators on Race Adjustment." *Journal of Negro Education*, 2: 53–64, January 1933.

SIMS, DAVID H. "Religious Education in Negro Colleges and Universities." *Journal of Negro History*, 5: 166–207, April 1920.

SLOWE, LUCY D. "Higher Education of Negro Women." *Journal of Negro Education*, 2: 352–58, July 1933.

SUMNER, F. C. "Morale and the Negro College." *Educational Review*, 73: 168–72, March 1927.

————. "Mental Health Statistics of Negro College Freshmen." *School and Society*, 33: 874–76, April 25, 1931.

The Crisis. Annual Education Numbers for Reviews of Higher Education Among Negroes.

THOMPSON, CHARLES H. "The Problem of Negro Higher Education." *Journal of Negro Education*, 2: 257–71, July 1933.

————. "The Socio-Economic Status of Negro College Students." *Journal of Negro Education*, 2: 26–37, January 1933.

"University Education for Negroes." *The Independent*, 68: 613–18, March 24, 1910.

"Value of Higher Education to the Negroes." *The Independent*, 52: 677, May 15, 1900.

VILLARD, OSWALD G. "Higher Education of Negroes." *The Nation*, 74: 381, 1902.

Washington, Booker T. "Observations on Negro Colleges." *World's Work*, 21: 14230–38, April 1911.

————. "University Education for Negroes." *The Independent*, 68: 613–18, March 24, 1910.

BIOGRAPHIES

ALDERMAN, EDWIN A. *J. L. M. Curry; A Biography.* New York, The Macmillan Company, 1911.

FEE, JOHN G. *Autobiography.* Chicago, National Christian Association, 1891.

HOWARD, OLIVER O. *Autobiography.* New York, The Baker & Taylor Co., 1907.

TALBOT, E. A. *Samuel Chapman Armstrong.* New York, Doubleday, Page and Co., 1904.

BIBLIOGRAPHIES

CALIVER, AMBROSE. *Bibliography on the Education of the Negro.* Bulletin No. 17. Washington, Office of Education, 1931.

DuBois, W. E. B. *Bibliography of the Negro American.* Atlanta, Atlanta University Press, 1905.

The Quarterly Review of Higher Education Among Negroes. Book Reviews on higher education among Negroes in each number; published quarterly since January 1933. Charlotte, Johnson C. Smith University.

The Journal of Negro Education. Bibliographies and book reviews on Negro education in each number; published quarterly since April 1932. Washington, Howard University.

U. S. OFFICE OF EDUCATION. *Bibliography of Research Studies in Education, 1930–31.* Bulletin No. 16, 1932. Section on Negroes, pp. 375–80. Washington, Government Printing Office, 1932.

WORK, MONROE N. *Bibliography of the Negro.* New York, The H. W. Wilson Company, 1928.